90 0881717 5

D1756629

Un

Su

MULTIFACETED IDENTITY OF INTERETHNIC YOUNG PEOPLE

Studies in Migration and Diaspora

Series Editor:
Anne J. Kershen, Queen Mary College, University of London, UK

Studies in Migration and Diaspora is a series designed to showcase the interdisciplinary and multidisciplinary nature of research in this important field. Volumes in the series cover local, national and global issues and engage with both historical and contemporary events. The books will appeal to scholars, students and all those engaged in the study of migration and diaspora. Amongst the topics covered are minority ethnic relations, transnational movements and the cultural, social and political implications of moving from 'over there', to 'over here'.

Also in the series:

The Invisible Empire
White Discourse, Tolerance and Belonging
Georgie Wemyss
ISBN 978-0-7546-7347-7

Lifestyle Migration
Expectations, Aspirations and Experiences
Edited by Michaela Benson and Karen O'Reilly
ISBN 978-0-7546-7567-9

International Migration and Rural Areas
Cross-National Comparative Perspectives
Edited by Birgit Jentsch and Myriam Simard
ISBN 978-0-7546-7484-9

Accession and Migration
Changing Policy, Society, and Culture in an Enlarged Europe
Edited by John Eade and Yordanka Valkanova
ISBN 978-0-7546-7503-7

Migrant Women Transforming Citizenship
Life-stories From Britain and Germany
Umut Erel
ISBN 978-0-7546-7494-8

Multifaceted Identity of Interethnic Young People
Chameleon Identities

SULTANA CHOUDHRY
London Metropolitan University, UK

ASHGATE

Published by
Ashgate Publishing Limited
Wey Court East
Union Road
Farnham
Surrey, GU9 7PT
England

Ashgate Publishing Company
Suite 420
101 Cherry Street
Burlington
VT 05401-4405
USA

www.ashgate.com

British Library Cataloguing in Publication Data
Choudhry, Sultana.
   Multifaceted identity of interethnic young people :
   chameleon identities. -- (Studies in migration and
   diaspora)
   1. Racially mixed children--Psychology. 2. Ethnicity in
   children. 3. Identity (Psychology) in children. 4. Identity
   (Psychology) in adolescence. 5. Identity (Psychology)--
   Religious aspects. 6. Interracial marriage. 7. Racially
   mixed children--Research.
   I. Title II. Series
   305.8'0083-dc22

Library of Congress Cataloging-in-Publication Data
Choudhry, Sultana.
   Multifaceted identity of interethnic young people : Chameleon identities / by Sultana
Choudhry.
       p. cm. -- (Studies in migration and diaspora)
   Includes bibliographical references and index.
   ISBN 978-0-7546-7860-1 (hbk.) -- ISBN 978-0-7546-9691-9 (ebook)
   1. Ethnicity in children. 2. Ethnicity. 3. Racially mixed children--Race identity. 4. Racially
mixed people--Race identity. I. Title.
   GN495.6.C52 2010
   155.8'405--dc22
                                                                        2009045840

ISBN 9780754678601 (hbk)
ISBN 9780754696919 (ebk)

Mixed Sources
Product group from well-managed
forests and other controlled sources
www.fsc.org Cert no. SGS-COC-2482
© 1996 Forest Stewardship Council
FSC

Printed and bound in Great Britain by
TJ International Ltd, Padstow, Cornwall

Contents

List of Figures

List of Tables

Series Editor's Preface
A Multi-Faceted Identity of Mixed
Race Children: A Masala Mosaic

Human identity is neither static nor singular: it is multiple and constantly evolving. Identity construction begins in childhood, often in the first stages of primary school. The tools that enable us to construct who we are – how we know ourselves and how we are known by others – are selected from both our past and our present. To greater and lesser extents we are influenced by colour, language, place, race and religion, the balance determined by parenthood and community. We identify ourselves by difference, by recognising what we are by what we are not. For the non-white child one of the prime indicators of self-identity is colour; for others it might be religion and/or language. For the progeny of ethnic minorities the process of identity construction will be most strongly influenced by their minority status and 'separateness'; parental and familial background and primary education providing the foundations. However, for the children of interethnic partnerships the construction and maintenance of identity is far more complex and, at times, when external influences conflict, confusing. Although an increasingly significant constituent of contemporary migration and diasporic life, as the author of this pioneering volume points out, in the sphere of social studies the recognition of otherness and the corresponding construction of self-identity by interethnic children is one that has been, at best, under-researched.

In this fascinating and original study Sultana Choudhry highlights the intricacies of identity formation for the 'mixed race' or 'interethnic' child. While she acknowledges that there has been some work carried out into the progeny of interethnic relationships, she emphasises that these have focused on black (as in African-American or African-Caribbean) and white unions, rarely if at all on Asian and White or Asian and Black. This book sets out to redress the balance. From the author's in-depth interviewing of both parents and children, the stages, confusions and pressures of interethnic identity formulation are identified. There is no doubt that for the offspring of an Asian/White relationship the overriding determinants of identity are religion, colour and language. In the case of the former, whilst for some it is Islam which is the most powerful in the construction of self-identity for others the 'chameleon' role comes into play. As one interviewee explains: '(W)hen I am with Muslim friends I tell them I'm Muslim ... but when I am with white friends I take on my mum's side of things more, you know Christian'. However, it is colour which presents the instant source of identification for the onlooker. Those that can identify both with the mainstream and with a minority ethnic group appear to take most advantage of, what the author terms, situational or 'chameleon' identity. To paraphrase the words of one interviewee: 'When I am with whites I identify as white, but when I am with my Asian friends I talk and act like an Asian'.

A reading of this book encourages the reader to explore identity formation in a new context, one which incorporates the psychological and physical issues interethnics confront. To this end, insights into the chameleon persona have been facilitated by an individual who, at the present time, is the most well-known 'chameleon' of all – Barack Obama. The author has no doubt that the incumbent President of the United States has carefully weighed up the pros and cons of situational identity and has, as Choudhry concludes, come down on the side of that which has provided him with accession to the most coveted political position in the modern world. At last chameleons have a role model par excellence.

Anne J Kershen
Queen Mary University of London
2010

Acknowledgements

I am grateful to all the people who participated in the research and to Neil Jordan, from Ashgate. My special thanks to James, Zac and Haris.

PART 1
Placing Identity Theory and Research in Context

Chapter 1

Introduction

The increase in the number of 'mixed race' or interethnic[1] individuals is one of the most striking demographic changes in Britain over the last decade. They are the fastest growing group in the UK and America. In the UK, the interethnic are now the sixth largest group and form 1.4 per cent of the population (ONS, 2004) and that is widely believed to be an underestimate. Over 80 per cent of these were born in Britain (Parker and Song, 2001). Whilst black and white interethnic individuals have been studied, previous research has not sought to explore how being of interethnic might impact upon children who have one white and one South Asian origin parents. This subject area has suffered from academic neglect and for this reason alone this book is long overdue. Whilst focused on the Asian and white interethnic children and adolescents and their families the book draws on other interethnic groups such as white and Asian, Chinese and white; and non-interethnic individuals. Important questions at the heart of interethnic identity will be addressed.

Historically social psychologists did not view identity formation as a matter of individual choice or negotiation. However, in today's society human beings are confronted with high levels of choice in their lives, including in personal issues. Within this context, this book offers an insight into the processes of forming an identity – with a specific focus on individuals of an interethnic background. It provides an understanding into the processes of identity adoption in society's high level of emphasis on choice. The ideas of Mead, Goffman, Moscovici, Tajfel and Turner have been particularly influential in shaping this book. The model of identity used is a socio-psychological one that seeks to understand the psychological and socio-cultural processes of identity.

The findings of this book are based on a PhD thesis. Research for this was approached in three stages. First, semi-structured interviews were conducted with three groups: interethnic (Asian/white adolescents), non-interethnic (Asian and white adolescents) and their parents. Factors such as language, culture and physical appearance were central themes that emerged from the analysis. The aim of the second study was to further investigate and develop findings from the first. This follow-up study was based on 16 interethnic participants. They completed retrospective diaries on their experiences of being of interethnic; these were followed up with semi-structured interviews. Analysis revealed a number of interpretative repertoires used in the process of negotiating ethnic identity. The

---

1 For reasons discussed later the term 'interethnic' will be used through out this book rather than 'mixed race' as commonly used.

third study involved a questionnaire administered to 87 participants of different interethnic background. Many of the findings from the two qualitative studies were supported by the data from this questionnaire, for example, ideas concerning choice and perceptions of being interethnic.

In taking this multi-method approach this book makes three important contributions. First, it researches and discusses the experiences and ethnic identity construction of south Asian and white interethnic adolescents; a group previously neglected in social sciences literature. Second, it documents the importance that interethnic participants, not just of South Asian and white background, place on exercising choice and autonomy over presentation of ethnic identity. It was found that interethnic individuals feel they have a greater ability to adopt a situational/chameleon identity than other individuals because of their dual ethnic backgrounds.

Excluding the USA, 'The most recent data gave Britain the highest rate of interracial relationships in the world, with a rate ten times that of the European average' (Parker and Song, 2001, p. 2). Fifty per cent of Caribbean men and 30 per cent of women are married or cohabiting with a white partner (Parker and Song, 2001). The increase in such relationships means more interethnic children. The aim of this book is to bring about a greater understanding of the ways these children construct their ethnic identity, with a particular focus on those of Asian and white interethnic. It examines the ways in which individuals, largely of interethnic background, negotiate and assert their ethnic identity with reference to the wider society. There is a potential tension between an individual's ideas and assertion of ethnic identity and the wider society's collective attributions. It is important to understand how individuals negotiate this tension, in doing so they perceive themselves as active agents who shape their ethnic identities. However, the extent to which people really are active agents of their own identity and the amount of choice they have given the constraints and boundaries they faced is debatable.

Increase in Interethnic

According to the Labour Force Survey (ONS, 2004), ethnic minority groups make up 7.6 per cent (4.5 million) of the total population in Great Britain. Out of the 7.6 per cent over half were of South Asian origin. Indians form the largest ethnic minority group, followed by Pakistanis and Black Caribbeans and Africans.

In Britain black mixed groups have increased by 50 per cent and South Asians by over 27 per cent (ONS, 2004). In the United States there are two million interethnic individuals, one in 20 children born are of interethnic (Interracial Voice, 2002). However, actual numbers are probably higher because the 'one drop rule' (Interracial Voice, 2002) has led many black and white interethnic people to label themselves as 'black'.

The increasing number of interethnic children has become the subject of extensive research. But much of the research is now dated and tends to focus on African Caribbean and white relationships and their children (Dover, 1937, Collins, 1957, Patterson, 1963, Benson, 1981, Wilson, 1987, Alibhai-Brown and Montague, 1992, Tizard and Phoenix, 1993). This is even though statistics show that in Britain there are more interethnic people of Asian-White heritage than African Caribbean white (Phoenix and Own, 1996).

In the USA the focus is also on black and white parentage although Japanese Americans have more relationships with white people (Root, 1992). This concentration on black and white interethnic is despite the fact that the South Asian community is a significant and sizable minority with distinct customs and traditions that may impact on interethnic children's identity. For example, the choice between two distinct religions, languages and communities may impact on the children's identity development. Social scientists have recognised that aspects of the African-Caribbean culture have been infused into some working class Asian youth culture (Back, 1996, Kundnani, 2001). But it is nevertheless acknowledged that Asian culture itself is still distinct to the black and white cultures (Anwar, 1998, Modood et al., 1997, Samad, 1997, Kundnani, 2001, Alexander, 2000).

The Theoretical Position

Identity has been the subject of much research and theorising. However, over the years it has moved away from a notion of a fixed identity to a more postmodernist discourse. The concept of identity deployed here is based upon the belief that a range of personal and social factors influences identities. It is accepted that identities are never unified, and are constantly in the process of flux and transformation. Identity changes over time, but more crucially from moment to moment, from people to people.

The book makes three main theoretical contributions: a) that identity is not a fixed entity but is fluid and multifaceted and; b) that people of an interethnic background do not necessarily experience identity conflict as proposed by some social scientists and in fact c) are more successful than others because of the ways in which they utilise their interethnic backgrounds.

The first theory that identity is not fixed but is fluid is illustrated by proposition of the situational/chameleon like identity that has emerged from three research studies. The fluid identity is discussed in reference to sociologists such as Hall (1992, 1996) and psychological literature such as Goffman (1959, 1964). Furthermore, in the USA and UK there is a growing body of biographical literature on the experience of interethnic individuals. A key theme in this literature is the issue of choice and the right to choose ethnic identities and affiliations. Recent studies in the USA have touched on the possibility of interethnic individuals possessing multiple identities (Root, 1992, 1996, Zack, 1995).

Secondly, it is argued that being of an interethnic background does not mean identity conflict as proposed by theorists such as Park (1928, 1964) who originated the concept of the 'marginal man'. On the contrary, and thirdly, it is suggested that being of an interethnic background is an asset, in some situations. A fluid, chameleon like identity permits individuals to adopt a particular identity/ personality to suit the situation they find themselves in and to negotiate challenges such as racism with a greater degree of success than other ethnic minorities. Use of this chameleon identity can also facilitate high achievement within a cross-cultural groups of people as illustrated by Obama, Tiger Woods, Keanu Reeves, Mariah Carey etc and South Asian and white interethnic successful figures such as Freddie Mercury, Engelbert Humperdinck and Melanie Sykes who are/were all of an Asian and white background.

This book attempts to describe and understand the factors and experiences of those participants who willingly and kindly gave up their time to participate in this research and spoke openly about their feelings and experiences. The aim of the research projects was not to generalise about the ethnic identity construction processes of interethnic children and adolescents. Apart from the quantitative study, the book will not specifically explore gender differences for two main reasons. First, it was not an issue that generally emerged in the accounts of the participants and, therefore, to discuss gender differences as a separate category would not have been a correct portrayal of the accounts. Second, the aims of the qualitative studies were not specifically to make gender comparisons but to get an insight into the participants' experience of being interethnic as they portrayed it. Nevertheless, gender differences in expressions of ethnic identity are important. Such differences will be highlighted and discussed as they arise.

Terms Used in this Book

The terms 'Asian' and 'South Asian' are used to refer to people whose origin is from the Indian subcontinent such as India, Pakistan and Bangladesh. There were some differences that exist within these categories linked to religion and culture. For example there were marked differences between Pakistanis/Bangladeshis, who are largely Muslims and Indians who tend to be Hindus. These differences are discussed in the book as they emerged.

Terminology regarding the 'interethnic' or 'mixed race' remains a sensitive and fluid topic. The participants in this study used a variety of terminology to describe themselves, including mixed race, half-caste and half white and half Asian. Whilst some psychologists such as Weinreich (2003) use the term 'hybrid'; this is seen by others as being pejorative. What is acceptable differs depending on groups and over time. 'Mixed parentage' has now achieved some currency (in place of 'mixed race') largely as a result of the ongoing discourse surrounding 'race' and is the term currently most accepted in academic circles (Own, 2001, Tizard and Phoenix, 2001). But this term is by no means perfect. Participants in the research presented here expressed distaste for names that incorporated the word mixed: 'it implies that we're *mixed* up.' Also it is a term that is ambiguous and can mean a 'mixed' background of religion, culture, social etc. As all of these terms seemed inappropriate the term 'interethnic' was used because it was felt to be the least 'offensive' and more precise i.e. encompasses ethnic and racial backgrounds.

Research Beyond the Black and White Model

In Britain social science researchers such as Benson (1981), Wilson (1987) and Tizard and Phoenix (1993, 2001) have helped to ensure that the interethnic is now an important group to research. However, their samples were confined to those who are black and white interethnic. There is now a new body of literature, which criticises the lack of research/writing about other forms of interethnic families and individuals. For example, Mahtani and Moreno (2001, in Parker and Song, 2001) recently wrote about the lack of research regarding their experiences as Chinese and Mexican-American and South Asian and Iranian. They related that their experiences were different to 'black and white' interethnic people and needed to be a focus of research. This book is a first step, in Britain, towards studying a group other than the traditional 'black and white'. It is hoped there will be more research in future encompassing other ancestries.

Chapter 2
Social Science Theories and Research on Identity

This chapter will outline theories and research on interethnic relationships and identity. The literature on the self and identity is so vast, it would be impossible to cover them comprehensively; therefore only directly relevant literature sources will be discussed. It begins by taking a look at social psychological theories of the self and identity, followed by ethnic identity and interethnic identity. The second section examines social science theories and research on identity in general and explores research on ethnicity and identity, interethnic identity and family and peer influence on identity. The chapter ends by taking a look at the debate on terminology.

The Social Psychology of the Self and Identity

Social psychological research on the self is largely driven by the pioneering works of James (1890), Mead (1934) and Cooley (1962). James and Mead's distinctions between the 'I' and the 'Me' have resulted in much discussion and writings on the constructs of self, reflexivity and self concept. Cooley's 'looking glass self' has been the source of writings on self esteem; reflect appraisal and their influence on strategies of self presentation (Baumeister, 1986). The issues addressed in the psychological literature on the self include: What is the relationship between the self 'as the knower' and the self as 'known'? (Gergen, 1986) Can the self be understood in terms of cognitive processes? Others have explored how personal self conceptions are constructed in terms of collective conceptions of identity; Phinney (1990) for example looked at ethnic identity from this viewpoint. From a social psychology perspective researchers have addressed questions about the historical and cultural origins of the self and the ways it is constructed has changed as a result of cultural values and social structures (Baumeister, 1986).

In 1890 James wrote "a man has as many social selves as there are individuals who recognise him" (1890, p. 281). He argued that an individual shows a different side of himself depending on the people and groups he is with. According to him a personal identity is based on the present and the past "a present self and a self of yesterday" (p. 315). That is, our sense of identity is based on our history, past memories and present experiences and feelings. The self, he argued, was made up of four components; the material self, the spiritual self, the social self and the ego.

He also stressed the importance of similarities and differences and a distinction from the 'Other' when constructing our personal identity.

The work of pioneers such as Williams James, Charles Horton Cooley and George Herbert Mead (1934) laid the groundwork for a concept of the social self and 'symbolic interactionism'. Cooley (1962) draws heavily on William James and talks about the 'empirical self'. Cooly's 'looking glass self' holds that we tend to see ourselves as others see us, although the evaluation of others is selective. The empirical self is 'interactional' and is particularly important in early socialisation of children where the self adjusts to others and norms are internalised. James and Cooley's works have spawned much writing about the self. All of these have resulted in a significant amount of social psychological literature that addresses the personal self and the social self and interactional and structural level of analysis. Gergen (1986, 1989) for example focuses on ideas of the 'self as knower' and the 'self as known', Baumeister (1986) on reflexive cognition, self-esteem.

Key theories by Mead, Goffman, Erikson, Tajfel and Turner, Moscovici and others provided important contribution to our understanding of identity and its processes.

Mead

Mead tells us that the self is social in almost every respect; we continuously create and recreate it based on the social context and relationship. His work is underpinned by the fundamental question 'how do we know who we are?' He observed that we do not experience ourselves as 'objects', our self is bound up with the experiences of other objects, however it is only when the self becomes an object of experience that it can enter into the experience of the self. It is this recognition that can help us to identify 'the essential psychological problem of selfhood or self-consciousness" (Mead and Strauss, 1964, p. 202). Mead believed that communication enables the ability to create shared meanings, allows us to see us as others do and to act with foresight. It is then that the individual can 'become an object to himself'.

An individual's knowledge of the self depends on their childhood socialisation and the three concepts he called: the 'I', the 'generalised other' and the 'me'. The 'I' is the impulsive part of the individual and is the basis of actions before socialisation. However, the understanding of others and the views and attitudes in a social group mean that individuals will engage in more reflective interactions. Once this has been achieved he or she will be in the 'game stage' and will have an understanding of the generalised other. Over time, the individual will develop a sense of me, essential to self-consciousness, and this represents the understanding of actions as a result of the development of the 'I' and the generalised other.

Mead (1934) argued that there are two stages in the development of the self. First, the self is constructed by an organisation of the attitudes of others towards him or herself and the specific social context. Second, is the social attitudes of the 'generalised other', the social group that the individual belongs in. These two stages will be explored throughout this book. The self reaches its full development by 'becoming a reflection of the systematic pattern of social or group behaviour' (p. 235). The self can be both 'subject' and object'. That is the self can take a rational objective attitude toward itself and it is only through this that it can act intelligently and have *self consciousness* as opposed to simple consciousness. For Mead, the individual can only become an object into himself or herself through social interactions and relations and by processing these experiences and attitudes into social meaning – thereby formulating the self.

An important process of developing a psychological self is the ability to accurately perceive what others think of us. This ability is more evident in mature adolescents. Therefore, parents and peers, for example, play a significant role in self evaluation. Negative feedback can lead to low self-esteem; however, an individual may engage in *perceptual distortion* and deliberately misinterpret a negative experience to maintain positive self esteem (Liebert and Spiegler, 1990). Mead emphasised the importance of social processes and implicitly referred to a situational identity:

> We carry on a whole series of different relationships to different people. We are one thing to one man and another thing to another. There are parts of the self which exist only for the self in relationship to itself. We divide our selves up in all sorts of different selves with reference to our acquaintances ... A multiple personality is in a certain sense normal (Mead, 1934, p. 219).

We therefore present different selves to different people and the identity we present is influenced by the social context. The development of language is a crucial aspect of this. Speech 'can react upon the speaking individual as it reacts upon the other ... the individual can hear what he says and in hearing what he says is tending to respond as the other person responds' (1934, p. 69). Therefore an individual can adopt the attitude *of* the other as well as adopting an attitude *about* the other. In language reflexivity emerges and it is by reflexivity that the individual is able to evaluate himself by understanding the attitude of other people toward himself and adjust accordingly (Mead 1934).

To summarise, Mead describes identity processes with three levels as illustrated by his book *Mind, Self and Society* (1934). The personality (mind), interaction (self) and social structure (society) provide a framework for the understanding of identity. This framework will underpin much of this book, explicitly and implicitly.

Goffman

Paralleling Mead's three levels of identity analysis Goffman developed the concept of identity much further, particularly in *Stigma: Notes on the Management of Spoiled Identities* (1968). In this work he discussed ego identity, personality identity and society identity in terms of stigma management. But Goffman is best known for his focus on impression management techniques (*The Presentation of the Self in Everyday Life*, 1959).

Goffman eloquently illustrated how individuals manage the presentation of their self, the activities they engage in and the props they use for their 'performance'. And, importantly for this book, the different identities that are presented based on the individual's social context. Goffman's theory will be referred to specifically in chapter seven to illustrate the ways that individuals presented a situational 'chameleon' like identity. Goffman's ideas on 'Stigma' (1963) and the management of a discredited self are also important and will be referred to in the findings chapters.

Combining sociology, social anthropology and social psychology Goffman focuses on the routines and rituals of everyday interaction. Identity is an important theme running through his work. Individuals present an image of themselves, of self, for acceptance by others. Goffman suggests that the art of impression management of the self consist of a number of elements: The interactional tools with which particular identities are portrayed to others. These include dramatic style and ability, idealisation (identification with collectively defined roles) expressive control, misrepresentation and mystification. Many of these techniques are gained from early socialisation and are routinely used in verbal and non verbal communication. Underpinning all of these are the concepts of the self-image (private) and public image.

Goffman recognises that identity can be 'spoiled'. In 'Stigma' (1963) he is concerned with how individuals manage their 'virtual social identity' (their appearance to others during interaction) and their 'actual social identity'. Individuals with a 'stigmatised' discredited identity want to be 'normal'. There is shame attached to a stigmatised identity and the individual attempts to 'manage' this identity being found out by others – as also illustrated in this book.

He also distinguishes between 'social identity' and 'personal identity'. Personal identity consists of individual sets of factors, organised as history or biography. It is not a reflexive self, 'Social and personal identity are part, first of all, of other person's concerns and definitions regarding the individual whose identity is in question' (1968, p. 129). To illustrate his theories Goffman uses examples such as having a colostomy, being a criminal to being an ethnic minority – all of which have little in common to illustrate 'stigmatised' identities. Goffman's theories offer useful explanations on the discrepancies between a private self and a public image.

Erikson

Erikson's (1963) psychological studies, based on the psychodynamic approach, of identity development in adolescents are another important contribution to the understanding of identity. For Erikson, identity formation "arises from the selective repudiation and mutual assimilation of childhood identification" (p. 158). Erikson appreciated the psychosocial nature of identity, in that he recognised the community as being an important realm in shaping an individual's identity. He suggested that the self is largely derived from identification and identity formation in childhood and during adolescence. Individuals at different times identify with different parts of people by which they are most affected.

In his opinion adolescents almost invariably experience identity problems. The turmoil of achieving an integrated identity leads them to experience identity crisis. However, during the adolescent phase they are able to resolve any crisis by transcending from previous identifications and coming up with a new self. Erikson believed that this final identity is one that is fixed and is a sum of all identifications, "the final identity, then, is fixed, at the end of the adolescence, is superordinated to any single identification with individuals of the past: it includes all significant identifications" (Erikson, 1968, p. 161).

Identity stability lies in the interplay between the social and the psychic. A person needs a viable social identity to nurture an ego identity. Once a sense of ego identity is developed people are protected from social conflicts. According to Erikson people of all cultures can develop a sense of ego identity based on role validation and community integration. A person's relationship with others is important to maintain the stability of personal and social identity. Community relations are also important as illustrated in this book – when these relations are stable an individual's personal and social identity is safeguarded. Unstable community relations can create difficulties for the individual.

Erikson's influence on the study of identity is widely recognised. He developed a multi-dimensional framework of identity: the psychological, social and personal dimensions of identity. However, what is not so widely recognised is that he also identified the importance of choice to individuals:

> The process of American identity formation seems to support an individual's ego identity as long as he can preserve a certain element of deliberate tentativeness of autonomous choice. (Erikson, 1963, p. 286).

For Erikson, it is important for the individual to be convinced that he or she has a certain amount of choice with regard to their identity.

Tajfel and Turner

Tajfel (1974, 1978, 1982) social identity theory and Turners (1978) self categorisation theory attempted to address cognitive processes underpinning personal and social self and collectively based group identities. They are both important areas of work in the field of social psychology. The originator of social identity theory Tajfel, (1974, 1978a) constructed his theory around three concepts: social categorisation, social identity and social comparison. 'Personal identity' (the unique self) is from 'social identity' which is the internalisation of collective identifications. Social identity is sometimes more influential on individual behaviour. Group membership is important to individuals, as it confers social identity. Group membership tells us who we are and how we are valued, they exaggerate similarities and differences between the in-group and the out-group. It is important to be favoured and valued and Tajfel proposed that a group strives to enhance self-esteem. If group distinctiveness or value is challenged it can lead to prejudice and conflict.

This theory holds that an important motive behind inter-group attitudes and behaviour is the creation and maintenance of a positive identity. It follows then that threats to identity can lead to hostility towards the out-group. Individuals and groups with unsatisfactory identification attempt to acquire positive identification via competition, mobility or assimilation.

Social identity theory is valuable in explaining certain inter group prejudices; however some of its central ideas can be questioned (Abrams and Hogg, 1990). There are complex factors of choice that it does not explain, for example, what determines the choice of out-groups to compare with, apart from the belief that the in-group can be made to look good. Other authors have argued that the hypothesis that self-esteem as a determining factor in-group biases cannot be unambiguously sustained (Chin and McClintock, 1993). A second problem is that the assumption that there should be positive correlation between the strength of group identification and levels of in-group bias was proven to be unstable (Hinkle and Brown, 1990). More significantly, the social identity theory does not address how separate group identities are integrated into an overall sense of identity. In contemporary society, an individual's whole sense of identity can be impacted by a range of different groups. How does an interethnic individual with a potential range of group identities construct his or her identity? Research shows that it is difficult to apply the social identity theory where two groups were so different to each other as to have few points to compare (Brown, 1995).

Further, the social identity theory (Tajfel, 1978, 1982, Turner, 1978) asserts that when people are assigned to a group, they automatically think of that group. An in-group for them is better than an out-group because they are motivated to achieve and maintain a positive self-image. If in-group preferences raise the value of social identity then it could be argued that there is little chance of a multicultural and harmonious society.

Nevertheless this theory contributes much to the understanding of group relationships. It illustrates the importance of group identification as a generic process and the powerful influence it has on human behaviour. The theory also recognises the power of collective identification and the interplay between group differences and similarities. And also points to power and inequality and the influence that this has on human behaviour.

Moscovici

The concept of social representation, introduced by Moscovici (1973, 1976), assumes that knowledge of the world is not an individual property but is organised as collective structures, which illustrate the understanding of a community. It is through our 'representations', that we make sense of our world. According to Moscovici representations can be considered as social because it is through social processes that they emerge. The representations are always concerned with aspects of the social world that we live in, have a symbolic value and located within a social system:

> Social representations are systems of values, ideas and practices with a twofold function: first to establish an order that will enable individuals to orientate themselves in their material and social world and to master it: and secondly to enable communication to take place among the members of a community by providing them with a code for social exchange and a code for naming and classifying unambiguously the various aspects of their world and their individual and group history (Moscovici, 1973: xiii).

He argues that 'the purpose of all representations is to make something unfamiliar familiar' (Moscovici, 1984, p. 24). This is achieved through anchoring and objectification. Anchoring – a process of classification and naming – is a means of representing something unfamiliar to make it familiar. It can lead to emphasising some aspects and ignoring or omitting others, for example to maintain an existing belief or identity. Objectification is the way in which representations are projected into the world to constitute a reality of the world. Every representation, Moscovici believes, is made up of a complex cluster of meanings which include values and attitudes. We are influenced by many of these images, so what we know is made up of 'a complex of images' that we turn into a 'complex of ideas' (1984, p. 38).

Moscovici's theory of social representation is a significant contribution to psychology and social psychology and demonstrates the move beyond the limitations of individual cognitive perspectives. It is focused on the way the world is seen via shared representations in a particular community or culture. And is an approach that can be applied to explore identity, as Jovchelovitch (1996) wrote "there is no possibility of identity without the work of representation" (p. 126).

Other Important Contributors

Blos (1962), Kohlberg (1969 in Kroger, 1995), Loevinger (1976) and Kegan (1982) are other psychoanalyst theorists who wrote about adolescent identity. Blos saw adolescence as a time when the old self, adopted in early life, is relinquished for a new self, allowing them to undergo a second individuation process. This involved regressive thoughts and actions which then led to a heightened sense of being different from others who were recognised as being 'agents' in their own right rather than as merely affecting their responses.

Kohlberg concentrated on identity as linked to the functions of the ego. Although he did not write directly about identity formation, his developmental model focused particularly on moral reasoning. He also illustrated the importance of the adolescence phase in identity formation. Loevinger suggested that during adolescence self interest as the primary motivator (in childhood) shifts to self awareness and an appreciation of the social context. This self has the ability for greater social interactions and conformity than the earlier childhood one.

Kegan (1982) views identity development as a lifelong process. He argued that at various stages of life the self is structured and then reformed and engaged in a subject-object cycle. The young child's identity is embedded in its own needs and self interests (subject), however late adolescence leads to reflectiveness, rethinking of interests – achieving a balance between pure self interest and a growing awareness of other people (object). Kegan's theory is drawn from Kohlbergian and Piagetian theorists. Piagetian theory suggests that human beings are actors that perform 'roles' defined by an institution. Socialisation is the process whereby the objective social reality becomes subjective (Piaget, 1951). The actions of others become internalised as the social world they are familiar with.

All of the above psychological theories outlined illustrated the importance of the internal organisation of identity development. In addition, traditional psychological approaches of identity such as 'role theory' focused attention on how individuals fit into socially prescribed roles, for example, fatherhood etc (Micheal, 1996). Also, theories such as 'trait theory' and 'psychoanalysis' have generally been based on the belief that individuals have a definable, and somewhat pre-determined identities. They have been criticised for: 1) paying little attention to the discourses at play in the construction and adoption of an identity; 2) not recognising the kinds of performances through which actors went beyond roles or created new ones; and 3) not adequately addressing the complexity of issues surrounding multiple roles/identities, and the notion that identities can be fluid and multifaceted. Traditional theories have, nevertheless, facilitated recognition of the social dimensions of identity development and construction of self in social life.

Postmodernist and Social Constructionist Theories of Identity

Many of the intellectual ideas of social constructivism are drawn from postmodernism. Postmodernists would disagree with traditional psychological theories discussed above. They reject the idea of structuralism as an ultimate truth and the idea of the world as a series of hidden structures. Technology, media and mass communication mean that there are different kinds of knowledge, which we can dip in and out of. For postmodernists the self in modern society is influenced by external factors; modern institutions, for example, create tension between self and society leading to identity confusion, alienation, fragmentation and loss of sense of authentic self. The distinction between the real and presented self (Goffman) is blurred as "Fashion and personal appearance increase in importance as central meanings of creating the self and influencing the definition of the situation" (Gecas and Burke, 1995, p. 57). Therefore, the traditional distinction between 'false self' and 'real self' is lost as post-modern society means that a number of identities can be selected and discarded by an individual.

The emergence of social constructivism in psychology is usually dated from Gergen's (1986) *Social Psychology as History* where he argues that all knowledge is historically and culturally specific. He suggested that psychological enquiries should move beyond the individual and extend to social, political and economic realms. Gergen has contributed extensively to social psychology since the 1970's. In 1994 he moved towards a postmodernist perspective of the self, paralleling sociological approaches. He identified periods into which the western view of the self can be broken down; the romantic, modern and post-modern. In the romantic period the self was seen as an inner core that was passionate and volatile. Individuals had deeply committed relationship and life purposes. This changed in the modernist period as a result of new technologies and the self came to be perceived as being governed by reason while volatility was viewed as a mental problem. The most common type of individual in this period would be a person who valued a stable family life, education and moral training.

However, according to Gergen we are now into the period of the postmodernist self where the reasoned self has transformed into the relational self. Gergen (1987) points out that in the last decades there has been a shift in social psychology from a search for objective self knowledge to self knowledge as being socially constructed. He believes that psychological principles themselves are a product of social interaction and there is thus no independent self. The self is a product of a relationship between the individual and his or her social environment. Further, the self is an agent and a process. Gergen's interpretation of the self as being an agent implies that individuals have choice over the presentation of their self.

Gergen believed that 'social saturation' and the sheer numbers of relationships and technologies mean that everyday life is about trying to get the best out of a situation. Face to face encounters are being replaced by interaction through technologies like the Internet. Consequently the self now changes according to the situation, from moment to moment. The self now exists only in relation to external images. Gergen theorised that the post modernist self manifests itself in three stages. The strategic manipulator – becoming alienated from his or her beliefs, social institutions and with superficial interactions (for example via the Internet) life becomes about trying to get social gains and managing false impressions. The next stage consists of a pastiche personality:

> The pastiche personality is a social chameleon, constantly borrowing bits and
> pieces of identity from whatever sources are available and constructing them as
> useful or desirable in a given situation (p. 150).

Gergen used the example of fashion and the ways that identities are constructed through fashion and contrived appearance to illustrate the pastiche personality. He wrote that 'The boundary between the real and the presented self – between substance and style – is erased. The real self is played in relation to others. Though his work contributes to the understanding of psychological effects of external factors such as media and technology on identity he provided little evidence in his argument that 'inner resources' are no longer important and that people are helpless when faced with external influence. Postmodernist views differ. Some are more extreme than this, for example those of Derrida and Foucault, define the self as multiple, not fixed and always under construction.

Berger and Luckmann's (1966) ideas on identity formation provide a major sociological contribution to social constructivism. They argued that human beings create and maintain all social phenomena through social practices. And put forward the argument that identity formation occurs through primary and secondary socialisation. Primary socialisation starts at birth when the parents' view of the world is seen as the reality and the child internalises their attitudes. Language is viewed as the mechanism for being socialised and children learn the language of their parents. Children cannot choose an alternative reality to the one that they have internalised from their parents because for them that is *the* world. Secondary socialisation is the 'internalisation of institutional or institution based knowledge' (Berger and Luckmann, 1985, p. 138). Secondary socialisation is essential for fully participating in society. It is influenced by peers, teachers, environmental factors etc. Unlike primary socialisation, secondary socialisation is taught rather than being internalised as the *world*. Successful socialisation occurs when both internal identity and reality complement the external world.

This theory of socialisation offers a valuable explanation of the relationship between an individual's identity and the ways in which wider society and the social structure affects their identity. Berger and Luckmann's discussion on identity conflict also offers an insight into the internal conflicts that individuals can experience. However, they place a strong emphasise on language and socialisation, without addressing what happens to the child before he or she is able to speak and pick up on the parents' language. Also, what kind of conflict can interethnic children experience? Can they experience identity conflict with two inherited cultures? Even so, Berger and Luckmann's (1966) work was a powerful influencing force on the social constructivism theory.

Another influencing factor to social constructivism was the intellectual ideology of postmodernism, which rejected the idea of grand theories and structuralism. After the 1960's social psychologists were increasingly challenging the positivist ideology of an objective and definable world. Social constructionists take the view that people construct or represent their social world through means/resources that are available to them. The difference between traditional social psychology and social constructionist is succinctly captured by Burr (1995) who wrote:

> While most traditional psychology and sociology have put forward explanations in terms of static entities, such as personality traits, models of memory and so on, the explanations offered by social constructionists are more often in terms of the dynamics of social interaction. The emphasis is thus more on processes than structures (p. 8).

Today, the influence of social constructionist has become widespread and it has many contributors. Sarbin (1986) has suggested that people's identification of themselves is socially constructed. Others have concentrated on the constructive power of language and its functions (Foucault, 1972, Parker and Burman 1993, Holloway, 1989, Billig, 1987, Potter and Wetherell, 1997). According to Gergen, "our vocabulary of self shifts as pragmatic exigencies dictates" (Gergen, 1989, p. 71). He argues that vision of the world and knowledge of it consists of activities rather than the 'I'. Shotter (1989) also criticises psychological research which assumes that "one's self (one's I, ego or whatever it may be called) exists somewhere 'inside' one … which guarantees one's personal identity" (p. 137). He argues for a social construction discourse approach and a focus on the 'you' rather than the 'I'.

Social constructivism challenges ideas that identity is given naturally and that it is produced purely by acts of individual will. Social constructionist arguments also challenge 'essentialist' notions that individual persons can have singular, integral harmonious and unproblematic identities. Harré (1987) for example, suggested that an individual's understanding of themselves is based on the beliefs about being a person. This is indicated in the language that they use. Individuals present a self in the best possible light relative to their situation. Sarbin (1986) believed that individuals select, consciously and/or unconsciously, a story or narrative depending on a theme (or an identity) that they wish to portray. For example, they 'craft' their story depending on whether they wish to portray themselves as a hero or a non-hero. Gergen and Gergen (1986) have developed this idea further to say that individuals have a plot to the ways that their identities are shaped. For example, there are narrative phases of 'tragedy', or 'romance'.

Potter and Wetherell's (1987) work on discourse analysis is also underpinned by social constructionist theory, and suggests that attitudes are not coherent or stable, that they are socially constructed and perform certain functions. This theory asserts that individual's narratives, with regard to their identity, will be flexible and inconsistent. All of these social constructionist approaches agree that individuals construct their identities and that it is based on social interactions. The uses and effects of language are of importance to social constructionists; that is, how individuals use language to construct their accounts. The discourse analysis approach will feature in the book and is elaborated in chapter seven.

As with most theories, social constructionist has come under some criticism. One critique is that it blurs the difference between explanation, description, theory and evidence and does not discover theories or mechanisms but merely retells social phenomena in a more prosaic way (Turner, 1998, Manning, 1998). Another critique is that the reflexive nature of social constructionist means that findings can undergo an endless cycle of reflexivity and deconstruction by anyone (Micheal, 1996, Manning, 1998). Some researchers believe that the non-social needs to be included within the equation (Micheal, 1996). Finally, social constructionist does not generally offer practical techniques, though Potter and Wetherell (1987) have provided techniques of discourse analysis.

Conclusion

This chapter discussed the theoretical perspectives of Mead, Goffman, Social Identity Theory and Social Representation Theory. It also refers to a number of other key psychologists as well as citing sociologists who have written about ethnic identity. It sets out a social psychological framework of interethnic identity that is based on the notion of identity being influenced by the social context. However, it welcomes the view of identity being socially constructed and multiplicitous. This book embraces Goffman and Mead's argument that different identities can be presented to different people depending on the situation but also takes the view that agentic choice is limited – there are always some constraints with regard to the type of ethnic identity an individual can adopt. Identification processes over one's biographical development are largely made without awareness. Choices are made within the limitations of these biographical experiences and the social constraints of the particular historical era.

Chapter 3
The Science of Ethnic and
Interethnic Identity

The focus of this chapter will be on what the literature says about ethnic identity and interethnic identity. Hall (1996) argues that identity is constructed through recognition of common or shared characteristics with another person or group. The concept of identity is a strategic and positional one. He believes that, in modern times, identities are never fixed or unified but 'increasingly fragmented and fractured; never singular but multiply constructed across different, often intersecting and antagonistic, discourse, practices and positions. They are subject to a radical historicisation, and are constantly in the process of change and formation" (1996, p. 4). Identities are about using resources such as history, language and culture and about becoming, not being '"who were are, or where we came from" as much as what we might become and how we represent ourselves. Identities are therefore constituted within, not outside representation' (1996, p. 4).

Weinreich (2003) suggests that ethnicity is the individual's interpretation of 'past ancestry' and 'future aspirations in relation to ethnicity' (p. 28). He also argues that contextual elements are important, for example, the context and identification patterns with an individual's own group and another ethnic group. He distinguishes between ethnic identity and racial identity. According to him the two are quite different: 'The markers for ethnicity are cultural manifestations of ancestry and those for race is physical features from genetic inheritance' (2003, p. 30), although he acknowledges that confusion between the two may arise when the markers are indistinguishable from one another.

There is not a universally accepted definition of ethnicity. Bulmer (1986) for example defines it as 'a collectivity within a larger society real or putative common ancestry, memories or a shared past, and a cultural focus on one or more symbolic elements which define the group's identity, such as kinship, religion, language shared territory, nationality or physical appearance' (Bulmer, 1986, p. 54). Nagel (1994) asserts that ethnicity is 'the result of a dialectical process involving internal and external opinions and process, as well as the individual's self-identification and outsiders ethnic designations – i.e. what *you* think your ethnicity is, versus what *they* think your ethnicity is' (1994, p. 154).

According to some theorists ethnicity is not a fixed entity. It can fluctuate depending on time, situation and interests (Wallman, 1978, Nagel, 1994). Others have argued that ethnicity has become synonymous with community, culture and nationalism (Alexander, 2000, Baumann, 1996). Hall has proposed that the 'new' ethnicity is concerned with the constructed notions of identity and what he has termed as 'positioning'. He writes 'what is at issue here is the recognition of the extraordinary diversity of subjective positions, social experiences and cultural identities which compose the category "black" that is, the recognition that "black"is essentially a politically and culturally constructed category, which cannot be grounded in a set of transcultural or transcendental racial categories and which therefore has no guarantees in nature"' (Hall, 1992, p. 254).

Furthermore, the terms race and ethnicity are sometimes interchangeably used, although social scientist have distinguished between the two. For example race is based on biological membership and ethnicity is fluid and can change boundaries as it is socially constructed (Gilroy, 2000, Hall, 1992, Bulmer, 1986). Although others have also argued that ethnicity, like race, can have essentialist characteristics based on the belief that groups are endowed with a fixed set of cultural practices and values rather than those which continually change and are socially constructed (Gilroy, 2000). Individuals however, do not normally choose between race and ethnicity in their everyday interaction, as according to Bashi 'one does not choose between ethnic labels and race labels. Individuals have both ethnic and racial identities, at one and the same time' (1998, p. 962). Bulmer, Nagel and Hall's definitions of ethnicity will therefore be used throughout this book.

Two positions have emerged in the social sciences to explain ethnic identity: primordialism and situationism. Primordialism (essentialist) views ethnicity as being rooted in deep-seated alliances, part of the human herd instinct located in territory, place, kin or religion (as defined in Weinreich, 2003). Situationism (constructionist) sees ethnic identity as rational reaction to social processes and socially constructed. In this context, ethnicity can be manipulated according to the situation, although not created out of nothing (Lange and Westin, 1981). Lange and Westin argue that both primordialist and situationist positions are examples of an unnecessary polarisation of inherently complementary aspects of human life' (Lange and Westin, 1985, p. 22).

Some social scientists today argue that there is no biological or philosophical basis for race, however race cannot be ignored: 'our contemporary scepticism toward race ignores the compelling social reality that 'race', or racialised identities, have as much political, sociological and economic salience as they ever had (Alcoff, 1999, Brah et al., 1999). 'Race tends toward opening up, or shutting down job prospects, career possibilities, places to live, friends and lovers, reactions from police' (Alcoff, 1999, p. 31). Alcoff illustrates the powerful way in which individuals are judged on their physical appearance, the 'visibility of racial identities' by linking it to the interethnic (Alcoff, 1999, p. 31).

Psychologists have long been aware of the critical role that race and ethnicity plays in identity formation. In America ethnic identity became a subject of exploration from 1930 onwards as it was recognised that differences between people might be due more to social processes than to racial and biological differences. Black American psychologists, Clark and Clark (1947), conducted their famous study of racial identification with the use of black and white dolls. The Clarks' study showed that the majority of children preferred the white doll and had distaste for the brown doll. Their findings were illustrated as evidence that black children suffer from identity confusion and low self-esteem.

Since the Clark's study there have been major advances in the study of ethnic identity both from a psychological and sociological perspective. One such work is Back's (1996). He examined how black identities are constructed in the context of South London. Language and music were central to the ways that they expressed their identity. He discussed the ways that young black people switched between linguistic codes, in most cases between Creole and a regional English e.g. London, Birmingham accent. Black music and popular culture as well as black history and legacy of slavery were also very important to their identity and sense of 'root'. In discussing music and popular culture Back also briefly explores south Asian adolescents and music. It is commonly suggested that South Asian adolescents had turned to black popular music and culture. However, Back cites the examples of Apache Indian and Bally Sagoo both of whom used black *and* South Asian music. In fact Back himself acknowledged this and also points out 'Afro-Caribbean musicians are answering the call of the music of the South Asian Diaspora' (Back, 1996, p. 228). Ethnic identity construction is therefore complex – it is not just a case of one group borrowing from another group's culture to illustrate their identity. For example, in the case of South Asians turning to black popular culture or vice versa, it is much more complex than *either/or,* it is in fact multifaceted, negotiated, switched, mutually exchanged and complex.

Much theory is a product of its time. The themes of choice concerning ethnic identity reflect this. Ethnic minority groups are active in constructing and recreating the cultural practices and values associated with them (Sollors, 1989, Nagel, 1994). The literature on interethnic people in America has also highlighted the concept of choice and of choosing ethnic identity. There is therefore, now more interest in the ways that people shape, choose and assert their ethnic identities. Some social psychologists use the concept of 'social creativity strategies' whereby there is recognition that ethnic identities are bounded, although limited, by choices. According to Nagel, for example, since ethnicity changes according to the situation, the individual carries a portfolio of ethnic identities that are more or less salient in various situations and *vis-à-vis* various audiences. 'As audiences change, the socially-defined array of ethnic choices open to the individual changes' (1994, p. 154).

The criticism of old paradigms has led to the emergence of new ideas that emphasise situational and changeable aspects of identity formation. This is also reflected by Hall 'Cultural identity … is a matter of "becoming" as well as "being" … Far from being eternally fixed in some essentialised past subject to the continuous play of history, culture and power' (Hall, 1990, p. 225). Whilst there is an emphasis on choice and a dismissal of static and essentialist notions of identity, consideration has to also be given to the constraints faced by people. Hence, the emphasis that this book places on the ways that choice is influenced and negotiated by a range of factors in wider society.

Interethnic Identity

'Interethnic' people are defined in numerous different ways. Weinreich (2003) defines what he calls 'hybrid' identity as 'when one's origins are construed as dimensions derived from different ethnic or racial parental constituents, and continue to be construed as future aspirations expressing multiple distinctive origins' (2003, p. 32). Tizard and Phoenix (1993, 2000) view it from the stance of an individual who has parents of two different ethnic backgrounds. They use the term 'mixed parentage'. In their study when asked how the adolescents viewed themselves, 39 per cent said they viewed themselves as black, 10 per cent said they did so in certain situations and 49 per cent said they did not view themselves as black. Of the 49 per cent who said they did not call themselves black, viewed themselves as 'brown', half and half' 'mixed' or 'coloured'.

Back (1996) found that the interethnic participants used a variety of terminology such as 'mixed race', 'light skinned' 'coloured' and 'half caste'. There was however, at the time his study was conducted, a political and ideological move at the local level to redefine these groups as 'mixed race' rather than 'half caste'.

Identity Conflict

Most of the traditional research on the identity of interethnic children suggests that they are prone to identity conflict. In America the issue of interethnic identity was explored by Park (1928) and Stonequist (1937). Park introduced the concept of the 'marginal man'. He believed that the 'marginal man' was destined to live in two cultures and two social worlds and possibly to experience a divided sense of self (Park, 1928). According to Park's theory interethnic children face rejection from both their ethnic cultures because of their mixed ethnicity. This rejection may lead to marginalisation from society, which means that they display neurotic personality traits and negative identity.

Stonequist (1937) elaborated on the negative concepts of the marginal man. In adding a developmental dimension he analysed the psychological difficulties experienced by 'half-castes' (as they were called then in US society). According to him there are three main stages in the life cycle of interethnic people: the pre-marginal, the marginal and the adjustment stage. In the pre-marginal and marginal stage interethnic children identify with both the majority white group and the black group but are not accepted by either and this leads to identity crisis. The stage of adjustment is the final phase when there is either assimilation into the majority or minority group or accommodation between the two. The marginality theories are important because they point to the psychological conflicts that interethnic children can experience because of conflicts in the wider society. It is also important because of its impact on later research.

The description of interethnic people in America being marginalised had a wide influence in Britain. The literature that followed, in Britain, emphasised Park and

Stonequist's concept of the 'marginal man'. In 1954, Richmond studied 'colour prejudice' in Liverpool, in which he briefly mentioned the psychological problems experienced by 'mixed race children'. He assumed that interethnic children would experience such problems as a result of the discrimination they faced by the wider society. However, Hill (1965) who studied 36 interethnic couples in London, though still assuming that interethnic children would experience identity conflicts, attributed it to their white extended family rather than to white society at large. According to him, the white grandparents had shunned the interethnic family after the first grandchild was born, if not before, because they were unable to accept a mixed 'blood relative'. An earlier study by Collins (1957) made similar conclusions. He distinguished three types of ethnic identity for the interethnic people in his study: to be white, 'coloured' or to be 'marginal'. However, he felt that their identity types were constrained by the attitudes of the white community in the areas they lived. Little (1972) conducted a study in Cardiff and concluded that the interethnic adolescents in his study were 'typical marginal men' because they found the choice of identification with their white and black parents ambiguous and difficult.

Studies after the 1960's saw a shift in attitudes. Apart from Benson (1981) and Hitch (1988) who felt that being of interethnic was detrimental to the children, other literature began to steer clear of the difficulties of being interethnic. Durojaiye's (1970) research changed the emphasis from looking at the identity conflicts of interethnic children to exploring their friendship patterns. He found that interethnic children preferred the friendship of other interethnic children, rather than non-mixed black or white children. Kannan (1972, in Henriques, 1975) conducted a study of 100 interethnic families, including 20 African/Caribbean and white families being of interethnic. He found it to be a positive experience for the children. Similarly, Verma and Bagley's (Verma and Bagley, 1979) study of identity found that the children had very positive views of being interethnic.

Research on interethnic identity became the subject of debate in the 1970's and 1980's and 1990's, in Britain, as a result of the issue of trans-racial adoptions (Gill and Jackson, 1993, Gaber and Aldridge, 1994, Tizard and Phoenix, 1993). Prior to the 1970's, many black and 'mixed race' children were placed with white families based on the 'melting pot' assimilationist theory. It was felt to be a way towards achieving a multicultural Briton. However, in the mid 70's in USA and Britain the thinking changed. It was argued that black and interethnic children, once placed transracially, developed little sense of racial pride or identity. Transracial adoption left black children unable to identify with either black or white communities and unable to cope with racism that they may experience. For example, Bagley and Young (in Verma and Bagley, 1979), using the doll test, found that half of the British adopted interethnic children they surveyed said that they resembled the white doll. Similarly, Gill and Jackson (1983), in a study of transracially adopted children with one or more Asian parents, found that few agreed with the statement that they 'felt proud of being black'. The majority said that they were different from Asian children in Britain and did not feel close to them. However, Tizard and Phoenix,

1994 (in Gaber and Aldridge, 1994) took issue with the opposition to transracial adoption. According to them it is not necessary for black or interethnic children to be placed with families with a similar background to be 'psychologically healthy' and to have a high self-esteem.

Tizard and Phoenix's (1993, 2001) study of young people of interethnic also reflected that, contrary to popular belief, interethnic children had a high self-esteem and positive attitudes to their heritage. Using in-depth interviews, analysed quantitatively, they illustrated the many issues faced by adolescents from a black and white background. They interviewed adolescents from the age of 15-16, boys and girls from middle class and working class families as well as black, white and mixed-parentage adolescents, 60 from each group. And found that the majority of the interethnic adolescents, 86 per cent, were happy with their ethnic identity and did not want to change. Of the rest, three wanted to be white, one wanted to be black and four wanted to be either white or black.

Tizard and Phoenix's findings do not support the concept of the 'marginal man'. In their study, the majority of the mixed-parentage adolescents did not experience rejection and social isolation as predicted by the marginal theorists. Although most had experienced racism from black and white people, they also had both black and white friends. Their findings revealed a large number of interethnic adolescents to have a positive racial identity and concluded that being interethnic does not necessarily equate to having low-self esteem and negative ethnic identity.

Wilson (1987) was one of the first researchers, in Britain, to conduct empirical academic research on interethnic identity. She explored this from a sociological point of view and studied 51 children from the ages of 6 to 9. The children had one white and one African or Afro-Caribbean parent. She found that young children saw racial categorisation as a series of skin colour gradations, ranging from very dark to very light. Children's identity and attitudes greatly varied according to the areas. For children in 'white areas' racial categorisation was simply a matter of whether one was white or not. On the other hand, for the children in multi-racial areas knowledge of ethnic differences came earlier. As one 7 year old in the study said: 'Indians all have straight black hair, at least the ones that I know do' (Wilson, 1987, p. 179)

Wilson presented photographs of black, white and interethnic children. When asked which of the children they identified with over 80 per cent of participants picked a photograph of an interethnic child. When asked which of the children they would prefer to be half the children chose a child similar to themselves, and a third chose a lighter-skinned child.

She concluded that 14 per cent of the 'mixed race' children had a white identity, 8 per cent a black identity, 20 per cent were inconsistent and 59 per cent did not see themselves as black or white but as 'coloured', 'half and half', 'half-caste' or 'brown'. She argued that the majority of the children were secure with positive identities. This again casts doubt on the 'marginal' theories, that mixed-parentage children experience rejection from both black and white people.

Another piece of research to be published in the UK is Christian's exploration of black and white interethnic adults (2000). Christian writes that he was surprised to find that many of the participants were proud of their interethnic status and did not wish to change their physical appearance. 'This was something I was not readily expecting from the cohort of mixed origin respondents at the outset of this qualitative research. For example, I would have expected a greater number of the "older generation" to have experienced feelings of "wanting to be white"' (Christian, 2000, p. 84).

Influences on Interethnic Identity

Family and Peer

Many studies have put forward the importance of parental influence on a child's identity. Wilson (1987) found, for example, that the mother's view on racism related to the child's identity. That is, if the mother emphasised race the child had a strong black/mixed identity. She found that if the mothers denied the existence of racism or underplayed the amount of discrimination the child might suffer then the child reasons that he or she is not really black. They understand that they may have 'brown' skin but are not really part of the black community. Wilson also suggested that most of the women experienced some form of racial discrimination and were aware of race relations. This was reflected in their children's attitude, the majority of whom did not suffer from identity problems.

In addition, Tizard and Phoenix's (1993, 2001) study illustrated that the parent's attitude to race and racism affected the strategies they employed for helping their children to deal with racism. Interviews with 16 parents led them to conclude that half the parents tended to underestimate the amount of racism that their children experienced. The children, of those parents, Tizard and Phoenix predicted, may run the risk of dealing with racist incidents without support and internalising the incidents as their own personal deficiencies. However, they found two parents (out of 16) who had very politicised views of racism and overestimated the amount of racism their children experienced. These children were more likely to either think that their parents were paranoid or react against their views or were very sensitive to racist incidents. The rest of the parents saw racism as less politicised and as an undesirable form of prejudice caused by ignorance or psychological problems. Most of the families' key strategies for dealing with racism were by attempting to foster their children's self-esteem and provide them with a good education.

Katz (1996) researched interethnic families with infants and showed how parents prepare their children for the external society and the ways in which families deal with issues of identity. He based his research on 14 families and used a combination of ethnographical observations of infants, interviews and the biographical method. His biographical method was in the form of unstructured interviews and elicited the 'life history' of participants (Bertaux, 1981, Denzin,

1983) to see how this relates to their social and cultural context. Although Katz interviewed couples from an Asian and white background along with couples from a black and white background, he did not differentiate between the two, but classed them all under the banner of 'inter-racial families'. His research was framed within the theoretical approaches of psychoanalysts and developmental psychologists' theory of identity development and the belief that cognitive and emotional processes of identification are an internalisation of the mother's beliefs and attitudes. Katz's findings showed that parents influenced the child's identity:

> The children in the observations were shown to develop a sense of self largely
> as a response to parenting (Katz, 1996, p. 181).

Mothers particularly brought into the relationship beliefs and feelings from their past which influenced the way they treated their children. In most of the families issues of race, ethnicity and culture were a central part of the family. Although Katz stressed that peer relationships and environmental factors may later affect the children's identity, it should be noted that the children might encounter and negotiate these factors as well as influence from relatives and siblings at an early time in their lives. That is, it is not just the mother's influence that they would come under.

In the US, social scientists have also found that for children to negotiate a positive identity the role of the family is an important one. If the child does not receive a sense of integrated self, of racial consciousness, from the family he/she may not be adequately prepared to deal with racism in society and may subsequently have low self-esteem (Bradshaw 1992). However, for some interethnic individuals society may fail to confirm the sense of self-esteem and integration that the family had offered.

Class was found to be another fundamental factor in the interethnic children's ethnic identity development by Katz, (1996). In fact, he felt that class affected the family more than race and culture. For example, in the middle class families the children were brought up to have the freedom to choose their own identity. Children from working class families were not given the freedom of choice. Wilson (1987) also suggested middle class children to have more of a tendency to misidentify with the dolls than working class children. Tizard and Phoenix, however, did not find a strong link between class and identity in the interethnic adolescents they studied. They, contrary to Katz's findings, felt that the parents' attitudes to race and racism had more of an influence on the children's identity than social class.

The Media and Literature

The complex issues surrounding interethnic children need also to be examined in terms of how the media and literature represent them. Literary representations of interethnic people have appeared throughout American and British literature. There were also times, throughout history, when literature on interethnic relationships was banned. For example, in 1930, the state of Mississippi passed a legislation to punish anyone who was involved in publishing interethnic literature (Werbner, 1997). Historical literature indicates black people were to be admired for being sensuous and loved. For example, Ovid was in love with a black slave in Amores. Moses loved Tharbis, an Ethiopian. Later, Shakespeare addresses interethnic relationships in many of his plays, although his depiction of the interethnic was not necessarily positive. For example, in Titus Andronicus, the interethnic child of the queen is described as 'joyless, dismal, black and sorrowful issue' (Henriques, 1975).

Today the media are a major source of ideas about race and ethnicity. This industry sends a powerful message in the way it portrays interethnic people. Individuals of that background often receive increased attention to their physical appearance; this is expressed in labels such as exotic, beautiful or fascinating. Bradshaw (1992) has argued that the media have two representations of interethnic people: 'The Beauty' and 'The Beast'. The 'Beauty' emphasising physical looks and the 'Beast' focusing on the vulnerable fear of rejection. In *From Melodrama to the Movie*, Giles (1995) explores American film and television's representation of interethnic people. The mulatto figure is used in most films where miscegenation is addressed. Examining American films such as *No Place to be Somebody*, *Guess Who's Coming to Dinner* and Spike Lee's *Jungle Fever*, Giles asserts that the mulatto character is a scapegoat for the prejudice of the white audience. The actors who are cast to portray interethnic characters reflect the cultural stereotype of race. They are often played by white people or 'people who look white', for example, in the stage show *Miss Saigon* and in the film *Map of the Human Heart*.

The media, it is said, reproduces society's dominant racist discourse (Zack, 1998). Media figures, because of social and institutionalised racism, like Merle Oberon (the famous Indian and white Hollywood actress) and the deceased Freddie Mercury (Indian and white); often feel the need to hide their dual heritage. For many decades now concerns have been expressed about the role of the media in not reflecting a multi-cultural society and pandering to prejudices. The way forward is for the British media sector to re-consider the stereotypes it projects as well as its representation of blacks and Asians to reflect cultural shifts in Britain and also to play a proactive part in changing society's racial attitudes. In recent times, however, there have been increasingly positive representations of Asians and blacks in the media, for example, *Baby Father*; *East is East*, *Anita and Me*, *Buddha of Suburbia*, *White Teeth* and *Slumdog Millionaire*.

The Terminology Debate and the Categorisation of the Interethnic

There has been a further shift in the theorising of 'mixed race' identity. This has largely been driven by interethnic individuals themselves voicing their opinions and experiences. Contemporary authors are challenging the very use of the terms 'mixed race' and 'bi-racial' in the belief that the discourse of race is founded on discrimination' (Ifekwunigue, 1999, Werbner, 1997, Root, 1996, Zack, 1995, 1998, Parker and Song, 2001).

In the UK, Werbner (1997) points out the problems of discourses that celebrate 'hybridities' without examining its origins in racism. Similarly, Ifekwunigue (1999, 2004) believes that terms such as 'biracial' and 'mixed-race' stem from racist discourses or are too ambiguous. She prefers to use the term 'metissage' instead of 'mixed race'. However, this term is still grounded within 'race' and the notions of a 'superior race'. In America some have even declared a 'bill of rights' (Root, 1996) in which interethnic people have the right to assert an identity that they have chosen for themselves.

The growth of interethnic people has raised questions with regard to the adequacy of both the British and USA Census. As a result the USA Census (2000) and Britain attempted to address this. And it was only in the 2001 census that 'mixed-race' people were finally given an ethnic category of their own. Before 2001, such people, since they were not counted, were invisible in public sector policy making. The Census showed that the interethnic is now a larger ethnic group than black Caribbean or black African, and is only slightly smaller than the Pakistani-origin group. The Census also showed that more than 50 per cent of 'mixed-race' people are under the age of 16, making them the fastest growing ethnic minority group in Britain.

The Census information collected is important – this is the information that is generally used as the standard ethnic classification for all official statistics, ethnic monitoring etc. However, just applying a 'mixed race' category in the Census does not ensure accurate information about interethnic people in Britain. Some, in the USA, have opposed the use of a 'mixed' category arguing that it would encourage interethnic people to leave the black community which would result in a reduction of the black population and thus its political strength (Davis, 1991, Spencer, 1997). In Britain black political leaders such as Bernie Grant have argued along similar lines suggesting society sees interethnic people as black. However, Tizard and Phoenix's findings (1993, 2001) contradict this. They argue that because many of their participants looked different from non-interethnic black people they were perceived as being different to other black people by society (p. 163).

Parker and Song's book *Rethinking Mixed Race* (2001) highlights the difficulty of categorisation and finding a suitable lexicography to describe the interethnic. These authors, from a wide range of interethnic backgrounds, also argue that the British literature on 'mixed race' focuses on black and white interethnic almost exclusively. The book also explores the meaning of 'race' in the context of the interethnic. The process of terminological dispute is important to social construction and should be subject to ongoing debate as it is now. One theme of this debate is the role of choice as an important factor in the formation of identity. It seems that interethnic children may not only have more freedom in choosing a sense of identity than other children, but would like the freedom to choose terms other than 'bi-racial' and 'mixed race', assigned to them by others.

Interethnic Families and Society

There is a long history of interethnic relationships or 'miscegenation' between Asians and white. In the 1500s the Portuguese 'colonisation' of India led to Portuguese men marrying local Indian women. The Indians frowned upon such unions because the women converted to Christianity. Consequently, their children, known as 'Luso Indians', were also rejected by the Indians (Henriques, 1975). Later when the English went to India, like the Portuguese, they married native women. The founder of Calcutta, Job Charnock, married an Indian widow he saved from 'suttee'. William Palmer, from the East India Company, married an Indian Muslim from a royal ancestry, Bibi Faiz Baksh in the 1780s. Relationships and marriages between Europeans – Portuguese, Dutch, French and English – and Indian women, mainly Muslim, were therefore not uncommon.

In India, the Anglo-Indians identified with England and many joined the British army during the period that the English were in India. In Britain, Indian slaves were sold in the eighteenth century; later in that century Indians started arriving in Britain to study, visit or campaign against the British colonisation of India. Some of these men formed partnerships with English women. In contemporary Britain, Indians, including East African Asians, are the longest resident Asians in Britain, followed by Pakistanis. This may explain why more Indians have white partners, followed by Pakistanis and then Bangladeshis. During the early migration period there was an imbalance between the sexes, for example 5,380 Pakistani males for every 1,000 females (Anwar, 1998). This gender imbalance meant that Asian men entered into relationships with white women. However the emergence of second and third generation Asians born in Britain has seen an increase in the forming of mixed relationships. This and a consequence of Asian men in the 1960's marrying white women means there is today an increase in Asian and white interethnic individuals.

So why do people choose to form interethnic relationships in contemporary society? There are several theories put forward. Katz (1996) suggested that some people are less prejudiced than others and fall in love with partners of a different race. Being less prejudiced meant they were more open to falling in love with partners from outside their race. Another possibility that Katz has proposed is that the individuals believe in the myth of black women being highly sexed and black men having large penises. According to him, the choice of a partner is not a random one. Race is a significant factor in their choice and their inter-personal relationships reflect this. They can become 'racialised' and both partners in their relationships, consciously or unconsciously, play out the dynamics of race relations in society. Therefore, 'personal conflicts are related and unconscious prejudices picked up or a personal conflict may be projected in a racial way' (Katz, 1996, p. 27). For example 'that is typical of a black man' (Katz, 1996, p. 27). Katz cites quotes such as these as well as Benson's (1981) research to support his theory.

Benson (1981), in her study of 20 white and Afro-Caribbean couples in Brixton found that the reasons for entering into interethnic relationships varied.

For example, 1) individuals felt that they had very little in common with people from their culture 2) they were unable to find someone from their own culture or 3) entered into an interethnic relationship to make a political statement about being 'colourless'. Her study demonstrated the complexity of interethnic coupling. She believed that people who married black partners did not necessarily have positive attitudes towards black people in general and were not less prejudiced than others.

According to Benson, those who form interethnic unions are going against society's norms and therefore have negative experiences. Some of the couples experienced hostility from their friends, acquaintances, their families and their communities. Of the 20 couples, six found themselves without any kin either for support or to spend their leisure time with. Disapproval from the wider community included hostility from neighbours, friends and work colleagues. Benson's study found many negative aspects of interethnic relationships including, in her opinion, negative identity of the interethnic children. Although she does not fully explain the concept of negative identity, it appears that the children were seen as having a negative ethnic identity if they seemed to reject their black heritage or were unsure about their mixed heritage. This is based on the belief that black and white interethnic individuals should adopt the black identity because of the 'one drop' rule.

However, other studies have indicated that entering into an interethnic relationship can be very positive for both partners in the relationship. Alibhai-Brown and Montague (1992) interviewed couples that had formed mixed ethnic relationships, parents whose children had entered into mixed relationships and children of such relationships. In contrast to Benson's findings, the majority of the people in their study had benefited from an interethnic relationship and the children who were interethnic had positive attitudes and high self-esteem. Their research was not based on scientific research methods but on journalistic interviews. Alibhai Brown's book (2001) on mixed relationships and children examines children's identity in more depth than the 1992 book. Although taking a simplistic view to interethnic relationships and the identity of interethnic children, her book successfully sets out some of the current debates surrounding this field.

Attitudes to Interethnic Relationships and the Interethnic

Much has been written about attitudes to interethnic relationships and the children of such relationships. Even as late as the 1960's the banning of such relationships in America and the UK was being advocated, and there was much negative treatment of interethnic people (Henriques, 1975, Zack, 1998, Tizard and Phoenix, 1993, 2001). In Nazi Germany many interethnic people were sterilised or killed in concentration camps (Hoyles and Hoyles, 1999).

In the UK, according to Walvin (1973) there were many white women having relationships with black men in the eighteenth century. Although the upper-class relationships (generally women with their black servants) were seen as relatively harmless, the working class relationships were seen as problematic. The interethnic children resulting from such relationships were seen as a social problem and biologically inferior. This attitude remained as late as 1961 when Reverend Hill received hate mail and was attacked at his house for declaring on a radio programme that he would allow his daughter to marry a black man (Hill, 1965). He was told 'interbreeding is evil'. Later in the 1960's and 1970's interethnic children were viewed, by academics, as the key to racial harmony, the idea being that the assimilation of such children would mean there would mean the end of racial conflict (Henriques, 1975, Benson, 1981).

In contemporary society, within the South Asian community arranged marriage is still very popular, particularly amongst Asians parents, 88 per cent of whom (compared to 58 per cent of children) said that arranged marriages work best. Only 8 per cent of parents and 17 per cent of children disagreed with this (Anwar, 1998). According to Anwar, more and more young people disagree with arranged marriages and wish to choose their own partners.

In 1975, the reaction to the statement 'it is better to marry someone from your own group' was positive. Ninety per cent of the parents and 78 per cent of young people agreed with the statement (CRE, 1976). This attitude to marriage is changing, though very slowly. In 1983, the figure changed to 85 per cent of parents and 69 per cent of young people agreeing with the statement (Anwar, 1998). The parents who agreed with the statement felt that it was important for couples to have an understanding and experience of each other's cultures. Also marrying 'out' would strain relationships with families, relatives and the community.

The PSI survey in 1994 showed that 51 per cent of Pakistanis, 40 per cent of Bangladeshis and 39 per cent of Indians would mind very much 'if a close relative were to marry a white person' (Modood et al., 1997). In terms of white respondents' attitude, 52 per cent of them said that they would mind if a relative married an ethnic minority.

In 1998, 72 per cent of Pakistanis, 68 per cent of Indians (73 per cent of Sikhs out of the Indians) and 50 per cent of Bangladeshis thought that their ethnic groups would mind if a close relative married a white person. This indicating that there may be less support for such relationships than in the past. Only 33 per cent of Caribbeans thought mixed marriages would be viewed negatively (Modood et al., 1997). Three quarters of whites would mind if a close relative married a black or Asian person (Young, 1992, in Modood et al., 1997).

Research revealed more black people indicating they would marry someone of another ethnicity (71 per cent) and 46 per cent of Asians and whites (ICM, 2002). Black people were also less likely to oppose interethnic marriages. Four percent said that they would oppose it, compared to 7 per cent of whites and 13 per cent of Asians who agreed with the statement 'I'd oppose the marriage because different races don't mix'. Asians were also the most likely to agree with the statement 'I'd think they are turning against their own people and betraying their culture/ identity'. Nine percent of them agreed with this, compared to only 2 per cent of white and 1 per cent of black people.

More Asians also said that there would be discrimination against such relationships from wider society. Thirteen percent of them said that there would be no tolerance at all, compared to 6 per cent of whites and 5 per cent of blacks. This indicates that greater proportions of Asians thought there would be less tolerance to interethnic relationships. Overall, however, when comparing the statistics from 1975 to 2002, it appears that attitudes towards interethnic relationships are changing, though gradually. It is shifting towards a trend of greater support for such relationships.

Multiculturalism/Ideas of Assimilation and the Interethnics

The majority of social science research on interethnic relationships has traditionally relied on an assimilation framework (Henriques 1975, Benson, 1981). Social scientists describe the process of ethnic integration as 'assimilation' or 'acculturation' or even 'amalgamation'. Parkes introduced the assimilationist perspective in 1921 and described assimilation as:

> Assimilation is a process of interpretation and fusion in which persons and groups acquire the memories, sentiments, and attitudes of other persons or groups, and, by sharing their experience and history, are incorporated with them in a common cultural life (Parkes, 1921, in Gordon, 1964, p. 62).

Assimilation is, therefore, seen as a way of social groups integrating together. This, according to theorists, would help solve the problem of racial conflict. A prevalent ideology of assimilation is the 'melting pot' theory, which emerged in the 1960's. This theory assumes that individuals or subcultures will 'melt' together to form one group identity. Assimilation has been put forward as being the cure for racism, through minorities marrying people from the majority group. For example, according to Henriques interethnic marriage was the only certain way of resolving interethnic conflict:

> ... if the world is to solve the problem of inter-racial conflict the only sure foundation is inter-racial marriage (Henriques, 1975, p. 3).

Some parents of interethnic-parentage children also echoed the 'melting-pot' vision that interethnic families were the key to solving racial conflicts and achieving racial harmony (Benson, 1981, Wilson, 1987). However, it is unrealistic and simplistic to expect that interethnic relationships would lead to the ideal of a racially amalgamated society. There are other barriers to overcome. The dynamic of the assimilation process, generally, is that the minority group will undergo the process of acculturation. The process consists of people's acculturation being rewarded by being accepted by the majority group.

Another difficulty with the assimilation approach is that it is assumed that the minority group will assimilate into the majority group. As one of the original theorisers of assimilation, in the early 1940's argued:

> In essence, assimilation is the substitution of one nationality pattern for another. Ordinarily, the modifications must be made by the weaker or numerically inferior group (Henry Pratt Fairchild, 1944, in Gordon, 1964, p. 64).

In Fairchild's opinion, it is the minority groups that must integrate, that is adapt to the majority group culture. This preoccupation with the dynamics of incorporation of minority into the majority group may lead to the erasure of ethnic differences and cultures. Moreover, it is an approach that underestimates the dynamics of racism. Not only does the assimilation theory assume that the minority must adapt to the dominant group and lose their specific identity but it also assumes that the minorities will be accepted or 'accommodated' by the host society. Black and Asians have not been fully accepted into the British society. As a Policy Studies Institute poll (Modood et al., 1997) revealed only 16 per cent of white respondents replied positively to the statement 'White people have now accepted people of West Indian Origin'. When asked about Asians, the figure went down to 12 per cent. Hiro (1991) in examining assimilation used the examples of the Jewish community who began to arrive in Britain in 1875. He cited Krausz's work (1969, in Hiro, 1991) and argued that the Jewish community have not assimilated into the British society, 80 per cent were affiliated to synagogues and nearly two thirds felt more comfortable in a Jewish district:

> The results showed unmistakably that Jews in Edgware are on friendly terms mostly with other Jews and that their close friendships are almost exclusively from within the Jewish rank (Krausz, 1969, as cited in Hiro, 1991).

It should be noted that they might have formed close relationships with other Jews by choice rather than as a result of not being accepted by the wider society. Hiro (1991) makes the point that if assimilation has been unsuccessful with a minority group that is visually indistinguishable from the majority, and which arrived earlier than most other immigrants, there is very little chance of Asians and black, who have cultural and physical differences, to be assimilated.

The assimilation theory ignores the reality of the impact that race, religion and culture has on people's lives. It is difficult for ethnic minorities to strive for assimilation in a community that demands them to relinquish their heritage. That same community classifies them as different despite this. That is, even if minority individuals attempt to assimilate they are still often judged on their skin colour or race. Unfortunately currently the government, through many of its policies, seems to be advocating the assimilation of ethnic minority groups.

Research shows that individuals are more likely to interact with members of their own group and they share common knowledge and values that are negotiated amongst them (Farr and Moscovici, 1984). Group identity is, according to the social representation framework, about groups differing from one another. In this framework, it would be difficult for groups to completely assimilate. If they do, the minority group would be expected to assimilate with the host group. However, social representation theorists recognise that this may not be possible.

> Many have realised, however, that some minority group members either do not want to, or are not permitted to, assimilate into the so-called dominant culture (Bergman, 2000, p. 10).

Bergman argues that assimilation does not permit/encourage multiculturalism whereby groups are able to understand and respect each other's cultures. Nor does it permit individualism where interethnic individuals can withdraw from sharing representations of both cultures. For assimilation to work it needs to expand into an acculturation style that considers biculturalism/multiculturalism and individualism. Weinreich (1986) suggests that migrants who make up communities introduce ethnic identities and lifestyles that differ from the majority 'superordinate' community. Those who lack positive identity and self worth – possibly because of unemployment or non-achievement – may perceive this as a threat. Their threatened identities may lead them to challenge the ethnic minority group or 'immigrants'. Nevertheless, members of the majority community who have 'robust' positive identities and are integrated may not feel their identities threatened and are likely to accommodate the ethnic minority group. For the ethnic minority group amalgamating and identification with others cannot occur without some conflicts in identification with others and with those of the same ethnic group.

Focusing on the Chinese in Hong Kong, South African blacks in South Africa and young Muslim youths in Britain, using the ISA conceptual framework, Weinreich (1999) proposed that ethnic groups tend not to acculturate towards the dominant group. They maintain their differentiation albeit in modified form (Weinreich, 1999, p. 136). According to Weinreich the enculturation of cultural elements of salient groups into one's identity frequently occurs in people's elaboration of their own ethnic identity (p. 132). In contrast to Berry's 'acculturation model' he maintains that these groups cannot be said to have acculturated though partial identification with other groups enculturate aspects of these. Partial identification depends on biographical experiences in socio-historical contexts of relationships between ethnic groups. They identify with powerful role models and identify to varying degrees with elements of the other cultures without losing their distinct sense of ethnicity. Their identification and enculturation is partial and a varying process.

Individuals' ethnic identity is redefined for contemporary times through adoption of certain elements of the alternative culture. They grapple with existing values, beliefs and give them new meaning. Based on his findings Weinreich argues that in-group, out-group notions are limited because they do not take into account social relations of varying degrees, cross-ethnic identification, situational and historical contexts and differences in cultural orientation within an ethnicity. Enculturation varies due to socio-historical context within which benign, hostile or ambivalent relationships between ethnic groups ensue. Their biographical experience is unique and emerges within context of socio-cultural era (1999, p. 136).

A contemporary view (one that the current government is particularly keen on) is that assimilation can be achieved through a common national identity and shared values and citizenship. However, as Modood has pointed out, even within this 'national identity' groups such as Asians are marginalised. Also what are shared values and citizenship and who determines them? Furthermore, is assimilation through a common national identity realistic given that research indicates that most children may have a preference for people of their own group? Tajfel and Jahoda's (1966, in Tajfel, 1978) study of 6 to 12 year olds illustrated that younger children demonstrated a distinct preference for people from their own national and ethnic identity. They also found that this preference did not disappear, although it may diminish, as they became older. Similarly, Rutland (1999) found that children of ten years disliked other ethnic groups and preferred their own groups.

In terms of interethnic relationships, Bonnett (2000) challenges the notion that interethnic relationships and children can lead to racial harmony and suggests that such 'mixing' can both challenge and affirm racism. For example, Latin America's 'mestizo' (interethnic) population is often cited as a route to racial utopia. However, upon close examination the notion that when 'whiteness' and 'blackness' are blended together these concepts of fixed 'races' would disappear and lead to racial utopia itself affirms racism. The Latin America example, whereby pale characteristics are favoured, illustrates that it can reinforce the idea that some 'racial elements were more desirable than others'. 'The process does not promise the destruction but the final victory of white racism' (Bonnett, 2000, p. 30).

Acculturation/assimilation is, therefore, an ongoing and complex process that is likely to change with time. For a multi-ethnic society the concept of 'assimilation' needs to be closely examined in the social context. The notion of 'integration' however is somewhat different to assimilation, it refers to an individual both maintaining their culture and adapting to the majority culture. Nevertheless, this still does not encompass those who may not wish to integrate into the majority culture.

Conclusion

There is very little literature available; and no empirical study, on the ethnic identities of children or adolescents from an *Asian* and white/black family. This is despite the rapidly increasing number of such individuals. Current studies of interethnic identity (Tizard and Phoenix, 1993, 2001, Katz, 1996, Wilson, 1987 as discussed in the previous sections of the literature) may be inadequate to address the experiences of Asian-white/black children because they focus on black and white interethnic people. Asian and white interethnic children may have different social and cultural representations. It can be argued that for an accurate and contextual understanding of these children it is important to explore the daily life experience of Asian interethnic children. This maybe different to black and white interethnic individuals: there are differences of religion, clothes, culture, customs, traditions, ideologies etc and these differences will contribute directly to identity. One thing is agreed that although there maybe *different* issues to negotiate, the identity processes remained the same across groups.

The literature suggests that peer and the family have an important role in influencing the child's social and ethnic development. The peers' and parents' attitudes are internalised by the child, which affects the way the child negotiates his/her identity. Marginal theorists predict that interethnic children will be rejected by society and will have an identity crisis. However, research (Wilson, 1987, Tizard and Phoenix, 1993, and Katz, 1996) shows that interethnic-parentage children experience little psychological disturbance or identity conflicts. Community factors were important and will be discussed in this book.

PART 2
The Research

Chapter 4
How the Research was Carried Out

This chapter discusses the methods and techniques used in the book. The first study was a large scale qualitative one based on semi structured interviews, using the techniques of grounded theory. The primary aim of this work was to explore the factors that influence interethnic identity, in particular those with an Asian and white background. The aim also of this initial study was to see what common themes emerged. The second study was based on both biographical diaries and semi structured interviews. These were analysed using the approaches of discourse analysis.

This work sought to explore further the themes that emerged from the first study and to get an insight into the discourses and discourse functions of the themes. Finally, the last study was quantitative in the form of a questionnaire administered to new interethnic participants. The aim behind this was to explore the findings from the first two studies using quantitative measures and also to examine the experiences of interethnic individuals with backgrounds other than Asian and white. The research is presented in the order that it was conducted.

The Approach Taken

This book adopts the overarching approach of social psychology. The developmental psychology approach was employed to look at the subjective experiences of adolescents and their identity. The researcher felt that to get a full understanding of identity of participants it was important to explore this from a range of perspectives and research methods. Hence the use of grounded theory, discourse analysis and quantitative based approaches. This combination of perspectives and methods is expected to provide an insight into the identity construction and experiences of participants that may otherwise have not been possible. Also, it is generally agreed that qualitative approaches are useful for theory building and quantitative for testing these theories.

The children and adolescents (as well as the adults studied) in this study were seen as 'active social actors'. When children and young people are studied they should be seen as 'creators' and social actors who are active in creating themselves in a different context. This approach to understanding young people also requires a methodology that puts the young person at the centre of focus. According to Mayall (1996), for example this approach should have three major components: 1) it has to conceptualise and accept children as competent reporters of their own experiences; 2) give children and adolescents a voice, taking them seriously and putting their views at the centre of analysis and; 3) the aim should be to work *for* children rather than *on* them to describe their social worlds. The research presented in this book mainly focused on children and adolescents and thus attempted to follow these components at all stages from fieldwork, analysis to verifying findings.

Recruitment of Participants

Attempts to locate participants through schools were unsuccessful as many of the schools had no official way of identifying Asian interethnic pupils. A few stated that the topic was too sensitive and did not wish to participate. Participants were recruited from secondary schools and colleges. It was difficult to recruit by liaising with the Head teachers and Principals because they were hard to contact. The researcher, therefore, decided to contact personal tutors and have them identify interethnic students who could take part in the study. These tutors were more successful in obtaining permission from the Heads and Principals and also helped with the arrangements.

Other recruiting methods included approaching community centres and voluntary agencies, personal contact and placing the questionnaire on the researcher's work email/internet system. Couples were recruited on the street and in other public places (including IKEA) and through friends and personal contact, as well as through the researcher's work internet site. The bulk of the sample came from London, although, a few came from Luton (four non-interethnic, three Bangladeshis and one Pakistani), Bradford (two interethnic) and Watford (one interethnic).

Generally, it was difficult to locate interethnic participants. This may be because although the number of South Asians in relationships with white people is steadily increasing, there appeared to be fewer children between the ages of four to 18. The interethnic people were either adults, whose parents had married in the 1960s and 1970s, or very young babies from recent relationships. The Asian partner from the families with young children tended to be second or third generation British Asian. This supports the patterns of South Asians and white relationships as discussed by researchers such as Anwar (1998) and Visram (2002).

Reflexivity

There is an increased awareness of relationships and representations of the research participants in the social science. The researcher has an impact on the relations with participants and the way that data is presented (Silverstone, 1997, Holliday, 2002) and this needs to be acknowledged. According to qualitative research theorists, researchers are entangled in the social world they study (Holliday, 2002, Hammersley and Atkinson, 1983). The researcher must not escape subjectivity but must acknowledge it 'rather than engaging in futile attempts to eliminate the effects of the researcher, we should set about understanding them' (Hammersley and Atkinson, 1983, p. 17). Although some argue that the researcher's reflexivity, particularly when writing up, should be handled carefully as it 'has the potential to silence participants' *(*Denzin and Lincoln, 2000).

Howarth (2002) also believes that researcher reflexivity is important. She explored researcher representations and dealing with 'difference' in research. She argued that researcher relationship needs to be examined closely and cites an experience of being accused of racism as a middle class white conducting research of black youth in Brixton, South London: 'the youth worker slammed his hand down on the desk and accused me of racism and exploitation' (2002, p. 25). She suggests that this experience has taught her about the relationships and interpersonal dynamics in research and between the researcher and participant: 'the power of the researcher to construct the identities of the researched, the destructiveness nature of the gaze and the consequences of difference in research relationships' (2002, p. 26).

The researcher, and author of this book, was aware of this throughout the entire research process and that the results were her interpretations. She attempted to explore the issue of identity construction through the representations of the participants and her own. She was consistently reflexive through data collection, how the theories were framed and the write up. The researcher built a relationship with the participants and respected their stories and representations. She attempted to reflect the realities of the participants in her writing by keeping to the language used, and expressing ideas in a simple language, thus making it easily accessible and identifiable for them. It was after all their constructions that she was sharing.

FIRST STUDY – THEORY BUILDING

Aim of Study

The aim of this first study was to describe and develop an understanding of the experiences of Asian and white interethnic young people and the processes of identity construction and negotiation. To fully understand the factors and spheres that influenced participants it was important to interview not just the interethnic participants but also their parents. A second aim was to explore the experiences of non-interethnic Asian and white adolescents to understand the factors that influenced them in comparison to the interethnic. The research approach in this work was explorative, not aimed at theory testing since Asian interethnic adolescents have not been studied before in this country.

Design and Method

This study used grounded theory as developed by Charmaz (1990, 2000), but underpinned by Glaser and Strauss (1967). Glaser and Strauss, who spearheaded this theory, take the position of positivism that assumes that there is an objective and external reality. Strauss and Corbin (1998) have developed it into discovering how individuals view their reality. Charmaz (1990, 2000) has built on all of these works to produce a more constructivist approach. Given that this book takes the view of individuals constructing their realities Charmaz's approach of grounded theory appeared to be the most suitable method. The perspective that individuals locate themselves as social actors within a societal context underpins this approach. The constructionist approach emphasises the social world and devices used, such as language. It views individual's identities as being situated in social contexts but they are also influenced through biographical history and future aspirations as also outlined by Weinreich (2003).

The grounded theory approach has been challenged for a number of reasons, briefly summarised these are that: it limits understanding of the participants and their word, it relies on the researcher's representations and the analysis is based on a set of objective procedures. Much of this criticism can be challenged by adopting the constructivist grounded theory approach. The techniques have been moved into the realm of interpretative approach where there is an emphasis on the construction of social reality both by the participants but also by the researcher.

Grounded theory methods have evolved since Glaser and Strauss. Their objectivist approach assumes that the systematic method of grounded theory will lead researchers to discover an objective reality. In contrast, a constructivist approach takes the view that the researcher has interpreted a reality based on their and the participants subjective experiences. It does not seek to find the truth but *a reality* which may have multiple realities and viewpoints (Charmaz, 2000). Charmaz for example explored the chronically ill by viewing pain as a subjective feeling. Her version of grounded theory means the researcher explores the subjective meanings of the participants as well as the researcher themselves, and reviews this throughout the research process.

The grounded theory approach has a number of strengths; it guides the researcher step by step through the process of research, it is 'self-correcting' and involves re-visiting the theories and, the emerging theories are constantly refined as a result of its techniques, e.g. memoing, and comparative methods. As a method grounded theory is recognised to be, when used appropriately, a reliable research tool (Coffey and Atkinson, 1996, Bryman and Burgess, 1994, Hammersley and Atkinson, 1983, Charmaz, 2000).

With regard to the practical process, grounded theory focuses first on examining the descriptions and accounts and then identifying the process involved. The main characteristics of its methods are:

- collecting and analysing the data simultaneously
- writing memos to explain/explore the data before writing up findings
- setting aside preconceived ideas and creating analytical codes and categories that fit in with the data
- theoretical sampling, i.e. constructing theory to refine the themes and categories that have emerged, the theory applies to the sample only and is not representative in any way

Participants

There was a degree of randomness in the sample but it is not representative of the population. For reasons of confidentiality all the participants have been given pseudonyms. The names given reflected the ethnicity of their real names, for example, if their real name was a western name, another western pseudonym was allocated to them.

The Non-interethnic Adolescents

Twenty non-mixed white adolescents and 20 Asian adolescents were interviewed. Wherever possible their parents were also interviewed. Participants were selected if they agreed and were suitable, e.g. in terms of ethnicity and age. This resulted in 13 Asian parents and 12 white parents participating in the study. The children and adolescents were aged between eight to 17 and were from the middle and working class.

The Interethnic Adolescents and their Parents

Twenty interethnic children and adolescents were interviewed. They were aged from four to 18. All the interethnic participants had one parent who was white and the other parent was South Asian i.e. Indian, Bangladeshi or Pakistani. Fifteen parents, nine mothers and six fathers were interviewed. A parent was eligible for inclusion in this study if they were in an interethnic relationship (one partner was South Asian and the other partner was white) with a child. Of the mothers, five were Asian and four were white. Four of the fathers were Asian and two were white. Two mothers were single parents, one through divorce and the other through the death of her partner. More mothers offered to be interviewed than the fathers. Apart from one couple, all participants were interviewed separately. Class differences, with regard to the findings, are discussed throughout the book as they arose. The parents were aged from 25 to 46. They were all either in an interethnic relationship at the time of the interviews or had been in the past. All the children/adolescents had at least one parent interviewed.

The Pilot

A pilot study was conducted with ten participants. Ideally this should have been done with both interethnic and non-mixed participants. However, given the difficulty in recruiting interethnic participants for the study it was decided to conduct the pilot just with non-interethnic in order to use more interethnic participants for the actual study. Following this trial run some changes were made to the interview schedule.

Interview questions were redefined and tightened. The pilot also allowed the researcher to gauge suitable probe questions and the best form of body language to follow while conducting the final interviews. In addition, this process helped decide on the optimum length of time for the interviews.

The Interviews

Semi-structured interviews were conducted to discover themes that would emerge on discussions around identity. This method allowed freedom of expression for the participants and also lets the researcher concentrate on specific areas. The 'funnelling' technique was used whereby questions were asked in a broad fashion, followed by more probing questions. This allowed participants the ability to respond freely. Interviews were viewed as 'directed conversations'; the aim being to collect materials from which descriptive codes and concepts would be generated so that broad themes and findings might emerge from the analysis. The semi structured format was used because it is the most precise for obtaining sensitive information whilst focusing on specific areas of interest, in this case ethnic identity. To facilitate discussion a semi-structured topic guide was used. As a result no interview was the same, because of the wide range of social contexts and the individual being interviewed.

With the permission of all participants the interviews were tape-recorded and later transcribed. Most interviews lasted around two hours. A few lasted a little over three hours. Almost all interviews were conducted in the home of the participants. It was possible, therefore, to observe the home environment, the family dynamics and the neighbourhood for additional insights. There was however some problems in interviewing at home, for example, phone calls or other forms of disruptions led to some interruptions.

The interview questions were on identity, attitudes, family, parents, friends and peers, the community and culture. The aims of the interview questions were to explore:

- the issues that influenced Asian and white interethnic children and adolescents
- the factors that influenced ethnic identity. This is where interethnic identity is pertinent, to explore whether participants identified with elements of aspects of both Asian and white cultures, the degree to which they identified with parents and siblings and the reappraisals of themselves depending on the social context
- how they perceived themselves compared to other interethnic individuals such as Afro-Caribbean and white and Chinese and white interethnic.

Transcription

The interviews were recorded and transcribed in full. The transcription system used was a simplified version of the 'Jefferson style'. Pauses were included, a dot in brackets indicated the pause, and each dot represented one second. For example, [...] represented an approximate pause of three seconds.

Coding and Analysis

The data was analysed using Charmaz's grounded theory techniques. The techniques used included examining the interview transcripts for themes and coding the transcripts to see if the broad themes fit and to conceptualise the data. Glaser and Strauss argue that theory should be generated from the 'empirical world' ensuring that the theoretical model that evolves from the data 'must fit the situation being researched' (Glaser and Strauss, 1967, p. 3). Charmaz too warns about qualitative researchers not fitting data into preconceived categories but that they should, when collecting data, follow their hunches.

Using Charmaz's techniques, the data needed to be coded during the process of collecting it. According to Charmaz, coding helps the researcher to achieve the following: 1) Focus a new perspective on the data and further data collection. 2) Coding starts the process of theory development and build ideas inductively. 3) The process of line by line coding (see table [Figure?] below for example) means that the researcher was deterred from imposing her own beliefs on the data. 4) Line by line coding also 'sharpens our use of sensitising concepts' and helped to deepen perceptions of the emerging theories.

A major technique of grounded theory is in making comparisons. This means comparing accounts from different people, accounts from the same individuals at different points in time and comparing data with category and categories. All of these constant comparisons lead the emerging theories to be complex and precise (Glaser and Strauss, 1967, Charmaz, 1990, 2000).

The next phase was selective coding which involved more directed and conceptual coding. This assisted in ensuring that the categories are more precise. Diagrams were also used to integrate themes and to portray relationships between the themes. They were useful in clarifying the framework of the family members and relationships, the community and the influence on their identity.

Memos were written to capture the first impressions and to develop the process of conceptualisation. They were also useful for integrating the interviews and the emerging themes. Memo writing is an important feature of grounded theory and takes place between coding. According to Charmaz (2000) memo writing helps researchers to tackle ideas about the data, generate and refine themes but also in linking 'analytical interpretation with empirical reality'. Below is an example of a memo written by this researcher:

Line by Line Coding	Interview Transcript
Parents and culture Upbringing Others identification of them is important Made to feel 'different' by others Questioning of identity Their ethnic identity versus others identification of them Physical appearance important	My parents never told me about the Asian culture, I was raised as being the same as everybody else. I used to think that it was a good thing. But other people are always saying how I'm different and I didn't know what to do when they used to say that. I realised that the way my parents have raised me, I mean they did it because they thought it best, doesn't reflect how people really see you. The first thing they see is that you look different.

Figure 4.1 Example of line by line coding using Charmaz's (2000) approach to constructivist grounded theory

> It seems that the process of ethnic identity construction is complex. In today's interview, Asha spoke about factors that influenced her ethnic identity. Culture, knowledge of the Asian language and physical appearance were all important contributory factors …

A later memo helped to refine the above ideas:

> Choice or lack of choice appears to be an important element in the accounts. Factors such as culture and physical appearance for example, affected the ways in which other people perceived participants which in turn influenced their own self identification. More importantly, these factors had an impact on the participants' perceptions of choice. For example, Asha spoke about not having a choice over her ethnic identity because of the ways she was identified by others:

> Everyone keeps mistaking me for being Asian, so I have to just go along with it. There's not much I can do.

> But Omar appeared to be less reliant on others' identification of him and perceived having more autonomy over choosing his ethnic identity. *Revisit previous interview data, discuss agentic self/personal agency*

These two memos illustrate the ways that the process of memoing helped in refining the emerging themes and sparking off new ideas. Memos were particularly useful for writing down ideas that may have emerged straight after interviews, whilst fresh in the researcher's mind. The last memo above also illustrates the use of theoretical sampling. Charmaz believes that it is important to conduct theoretical sampling at a point in the data collection process when the researcher looks for precise information to provide more insight into an emerging theory. She recommends that this is done at a later stage of the data collection process to ensure that the 'analytic directions' are not forced to fit the data. In this study theoretical sampling was conducted, at a later stage of the data collection when the concept of 'choice' had emerged. The researcher re-visited the interviewees to further explore this concept. Charmaz believes that this ensures that researchers go back into the field to gain more insight rather than produce theories based on one set of interviews.

The sorting and ordering of memos means that the analytical work continues. The computer package NUDIST helped to sort out and integrate the codes and the memos, although much of the analytical work was also conducted manually. Over 150 research codes were generated during the first analyses stage; Charmaz, (1990) calls this a 'middle range theory'. These middle range theory codes were then organised into 30 main codes. These were then reorganised down to twelve codes.

This coding system could be endless and many of the codes were interrelated and later refined. The relationships between the codes are not definitive but indicate the thinking process of participants and the researcher's interpretation. It is important to point out that the aim of this study was simply to identify possible themes and processes at work in the identity construction and negotiation of the participants and not to quantify or generalise from the data. The analysis of the data continued with the process of writing as is recommended in grounded theory.

Reliability and Validity

The rigour and validity in qualitative research is in showing the workings of the findings, i.e. the ways that the results are obtained (Glaser and Strauss, 1967). Validity and reliability in this qualitative research are addressed by showing the workings of the findings from the preparation of data collection to writing the findings.

Another important way of ensuring the credibility of the findings is by presenting it to be examined both by the participants and other 'experts'. As a result a two page Conclusion[1] was given to participants and to adults and professionals who were either of interethnic background and/or were somehow involved with the research. They were asked how valid they thought the findings were and whether they had any comments on the ways that the research was carried out and its findings. Most of them agreed with the research findings, a few pointed out that it was important to highlight that these categories/themes may not be generally applicable to other or all interethnic individuals. The question of reliability is less applicable in this research as the focus was on theory building rather than theory testing.

---

1 Some asked for and were given the entire draft chapter of the findings.

Strengths and Limitations

This research study had four main strengths. 1) It had a relatively good number of participants, interethnic and non-interethnic and parents. 2) It was fairly gender balanced with approximately equal numbers of males and females. 3) The participants came from a range of backgrounds and areas in London, with a few outside of London and therefore had a good mixture of experiences. 4) The grounded theory approach was an appropriate method at enabling the exploration and theory building in a way which suited the accounts of the participants and the data.

A major difficulty in studying a select group of people such as those involved in this study is in locating suitable participants. One minor limitation of this study is that middle class participants slightly out numbered working class participants in the sample.[2] It may be the researcher was able to locate participants who are middle class Asian and white interethnic couples because they are more commonly from a middle class background than from other social classes.

Another difficulty encountered was that white mothers tended to be reluctant to be interviewed; many took a long time to be persuaded. Also, they were unsure about their children being interviewed. Some mothers completely denied access to them. The main reason they gave was that they did not want their children to be questioned about their identity or experiences relating to it because it might make children question their identity and 'put thoughts into their head'. None of the Asian mothers had these reservations; it is likely that the identity processes of such children would differ to those whose parents did not want to be interviewed. For example, in their attitudes towards their ethnic identity and cultures, but as the other offspring were not interviewed it was not possible to make comparisons. All of the Asian parents gave access to their children and were forthcoming. The reasons for this are unclear and need further research.

SECOND STUDY – DISCOURSE ANALYSIS

Aim of Study

The aim of this second study was to pick up where the first left off and further examine and develop those preliminary findings with the approach of discourse analysis. It was decided to have two groups, the first containing participants from the first study and the second group to be newly recruited participants. The rationale behind this was to compare findings from the first group with new participants and to explore the concept of choice in relation to ethnic identity. The earlier study in this research project had already shown that the children constructed identity

---

2 Tizard and Phoenix (1993, 2001) sample was also over weighted with participants from the middle class.

by negotiating influences as diverse as family, society, and culture and physical appearance. A key finding of the earlier work was that *some* children believed they had a choice over which ethnic identity to emphasise at any one time, this study attempted to explore and develop these findings. This was done however by bearing in mind that empirical data indicate that the degree of choice or autonomy is variable and limited according to whether individuals are 'progressive' or 'orthodox', and the nature of the differing contexts (Northover, 1988, Kelly, 1989, Weinreich, Kelly and Maja 1987).

Discourse Analysis

It was decided to use discourse analysis to further test the validity of findings from the previous studies. Discourse analysis explores the contradictions and inconsistencies that individuals employ to make sense of their experiences. It is an appropriate research technique for understanding how individuals construct their identity and the discursive constructions that emerge from their narratives (see Weinreich, 2003, Potter and Wetherell, 1987, Potter, 1997). In this form of analysis the focus is on discourse rather than attitudes or beliefs. Therefore, the ways the participants construct their talk and the functions were the concern of this approach.

Discourse analysis as used by social psychologists (Potter and Wetherell, 1987, Potter, 1997) emphasises constructionism. Also the focus is on language as a medium of interaction, for example, how people use language and what they do? Discourse analysts believe that language is constructed and is used to construct versions of the social world. Discourse analysis is inductive rather than deductive and takes the view that individuals construct their own reality and their own versions/discourse in order to respond to their experiences.

Potter and Wetherell argue that attitudes are not coherent or stable. In fact they are varied. They therefore suggest that what individuals say is intentional, designed to perform certain functions for them. This study examined the interpretative repertoires that individuals used in terms of their identity. Potter and Wetherell put forward this concept as a way of understanding the linguistic devices that people draw upon when constructing their accounts. They can be seen as a set of 'tool-kit' of resources. The possible functions that this repertoire performs can be such as justifying their versions of events, their behaviour, to ward off criticism or blame etc. Individuals are therefore seen as actively constructing their accounts.

The techniques and analytical manoeuvres for this study were underpinned by the discourse analysis approach to identity construction. According to the discourse analysis theory, identity is constructed out of the cultural discourses available and the interweaving, at times, of subtle factors and realms. Identities therefore, do not originate from inside the person alone but from the 'social realm'. Discourses are connected to the way society is organised and institutions such as marriage, the family and education. Therefore, the discourses that form identities are intimately tied to the structures and practices that an individual encounters on a day to day basis. Discourses are coherent sets of representation that help produce identities.

Criticisms of Discourse Analysis

Discourse analysis, including Potter and Wetherell's approach, has come under some criticism. Mainly, that it is not interested in the cognitive issues of individuals who are carrying out the construction of their accounts and that it does not discuss internal behaviours such as beliefs and motives (Burr, 1995). Others have questioned discourse analysis on the grounds that it looks only at the internal workings of a piece of text and ignores wider political implications (Parker and Burman, 1993); also that speakers' choices (in a particular community at that time) of words and metaphors may not have any rhetorical implications but might be the just the way they speak (Sherrard, 1991). They may not be aware of options of other words or the implications of it, for example using 'Miss' rather than 'Ms'. These criticisms were taken into consideration during the process of research.

Participants

This study was concerned with talk about interethnic Asian and white identity and, therefore, was not representative of the population as a whole. The original plan was to have ten participants from the first study and ten newly recruited participants in order to make comparisons between them. It was possible to recruit only six participants. Five participants (three siblings) were lost because their mothers declined permission for them to complete the diaries or to be interviewed, although they had initially agreed to participate.

   The actual data collection therefore is based on ten participants from the first study and six new participants. The additional six were recruited through word of mouth (from other participants and from personal contacts), or by contacting organisations such as Asian and family centres. Two siblings were recruited through meeting their mother at a conference on ethnic minority children and education. Of the 16 adolescents, aged from 12 to 19, there were nine females and seven males (see Table 9, Chapter 6). They were all of interethnic (one parent South Asian and one white). Consent was obtained from all participants and confidentiality assured.

The Diaries

A part of this study was based on a distinctive methodology; the use of retrospective diaries. The diary method was based on the 'biographical approach' (Denzin, 2000) and was concerned with obtaining stories and narratives from the participants. The appeal of the biographical approach is that it can help to understand major shifts in a person's life (Roberts, 2002). A constructionist view, that individuals create their own meanings, was employed for this. There has been little use of diaries in psychology but it is being increasingly recognised as an important research tool: 'these materials [diaries, letters etc] revive memories and stories which we can retell about ourselves, and may intimately connect with self-identity' (Roberts, 2002, p. 62). Furthermore, in ISA terms they can provide evidence of biographical experiences and the ways that these experiences are currently reappraised (Weinreich, 2003).

The dairies were well received by participants. This may be because the publication of diaries, even with the rise of oral and visual communications, has become increasingly popular in the media, for example, Adrian Mole, Bridget Jones, biographies of famous stars and celebrities etc.

In each case a diary was given to the participant prior to the interview. The diaries asked the participants to write about experiences relating to their ethnic identity. They were used to get a better insight into the participants' lives, past and present, and the factors that influenced their ethnic identity. A narrative, retrospective discourse was encouraged. This provided a way of exploring how the participants constructed events and experiences in their lives and the impact that this had on their identity. Participants' stories and narratives were used to identify themes and interpretative repertoires.

The Semi-structured Interviews

Themes that emerged from the diary were developed during the course of an in depth semi-structured interview. Although a formal interview structure was not followed in every case a list of questions was memorised by the researcher for reference. The degree to which this was followed depended on the response from the participants. The questions were posed in the colloquial language of the participants, in the way that the adolescents spoke, for example, slang or in a mixture of English and their Asian language. This was done in an attempt to build rapport and better understanding.

Interviews were conducted in the respondents' own homes and each lasted from an hour to two hours. They were tape recorded and transcribed in full. The interviews were transcribed in the same way as the data from the first study. As there were 16 lengthy interviews to be analysed fine details of intonation were not covered. This was not deemed crucial and would have made the task of transcription longer and the transcripts themselves less readable.

The Pilot

The diaries were piloted with four non-interethnic participants (reason discussed previously). Following the pilot some minor changes were made to the format of the diaries; they were shortened and illustrated with photographs to make them more visually appealing. In addition, some words used were changed, for example 'confidential', which a few of the pilot participants did not understand, was changed to 'secret'.

Pilot interviews were also carried out with the same four participants. This allowed the researcher to gauge suitable probe questions and the best form of body language to follow while conducting the final interviews. This process also helped decide on the optimum length of time for the interviews.

Method of Analysis and Report Writing

The data were analysed using the techniques of discourse analysis (Potter, 1997, Potter and Wetherell, 1987). In this form of analysis the focus is on discourse rather than attitudes or beliefs. Therefore, the ways that the participants construct their talk and the functions of their talk were the chief concern of this analysis. Potter and Wetherell emphasise the use of interpretative repertoires. By their definition 'interpretative repertoires are recurrently used systems of terms used for characterising and evaluating actions, events and phenomena' (Potter, Wetherell, 1987, p. 149).

The aim of the analysis process was to uncover interpretative repertoires used by the participants. Analysis was a lengthy process and involved being intimately familiar with one's data. The focus of the analysis was on:

- the identification of discursive constructions; and
- whether the adolescents emphasise one part of their ethnic identity rather than the other; the social context surrounding this.

Figure 4.2 describes the coding and analysis process.

The coding and analysis of the data involved the following processes:

1. The transcript contents were coded into categories (for example, parents, siblings, peers, school, community, and media/society). This task was made easier by the researcher writing memos during the data collection process. This helped the researcher clarify and construct initial patterns fresh from the fieldwork. Over 70 codes emerged.
2. Putting together all the transcripts and reading and re-reading them identified emerging patterns.
3. The codes between the transcripts were compared for similarities and variability.
4. A second analysis was carried out to ensure that the patterns fitted the data accurately.
5. The emerging codes were organised and identified as interpretative repertoires.
6. The functions of the interpretative repertoires were identified.

7. The results were written using quotations from the transcript as linguistic evidence. Extracts from the transcripts were used largely in the report because in discourse analysis extracts are not merely used to illustrate the data but '*are the topic itself*' (Potter and Wetherell, 1987, p. 173). The process of writing the report helped to clarify the interpretative repertoires and the discussions.

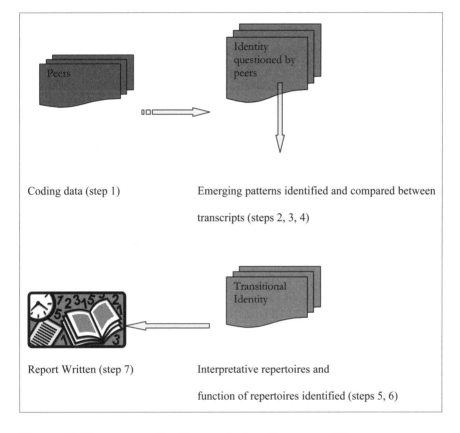

Figure 4.2 The process of coding, analysis and report writing

Reliability and Validity

Various methods were used to validate the findings. First, as Miles and Huberman (1994) point out 'findings are more dependable when they can be buttressed from several independent sources. Their validity is enhanced when they are confirmed by more than "one instrument" measuring the same thing' (p. 273). The use of two instruments, diaries as well as interviews, in one study ensured greater validity.

Second, coherence in the analysis process was used. How the discourse fitted together and the functions of the discursive constructions were examined. A discourse theme/explanation was deemed valid if it fitted the broad pattern of the data and the sequences.

Third, participant validation was used. Getting feedback from informants is an important source of testing findings. Social scientists are increasingly using this in their research. Guba (in Guba and Lincoln, 1994) used 'member checks' for confirming findings. Miles and Huberman (1994) suggest that this is not only a strong device for verifying findings but also that participants have a right to know what the researcher has found. The participants were asked for feedback after final analysis. This was so that feedback would be obtained on the researcher's final interpretative conclusions. Some of the participants were given a short Conclusion, whilst others asked for the entire chapter.

It is expected that the participants would not always agree with the findings or with each other's accounts (Miles and Huberman, 1994). It is natural for individual's interpretations to vary. The response from the participants varied though on the whole they agreed with the findings. Some were surprised but pleased by the way that it had been presented: 'I'm sure that I wouldn't have summarised that in those terms but I'm glad you did because that's what I was getting at'. A few rejected the concept of the situational identity arguing that they themselves were unable to adopt this approach to identity. It was explained to them that this was taken into consideration when writing. In addition, the researcher went through the findings again to ensure that this point had been made.

Finally, the method of triangulating was applied to validate findings. Comparisons between two groups were used to verify and confirm findings of this study. Miles and Huberman's (1994) techniques of contrasts and comparisons were followed to corroborate and validate the findings.

The two groups were analysed separately to compare similarities and differences. This was done knowing about the experiences and issues raised by the participants from the first study. The results of the comparisons showed that they fit with the prior expectations from the narratives of the first group of participants. The accounts of the new participants revealed very similar themes to those recruited from the first study. Both groups encountered similar factors and issues of negotiation. Analysing the two groups separately was useful because it corroborated the results of both sets of participants and was another method of validating the findings. Given that the interpretative repertoires of all the participants were similar it seemed more practical to write about them together.

Strengths and Limitations

Using a number of different research methods has been described as the method of 'converging operations' (Webb et al., 2000, in Sommer and Sommer, 2002). This method provides flexibility and reliability and was used for this study to provide greater validity and reliability.

The diaries enabled participants to write about their identity and dual heritage in privacy without the presence of the interviewer or parents. Although a few found it difficult to complete the diaries it was said that once they started writing they couldn't stop: 'it felt good writing down the things that had happened, it was like therapy'. Others said: 'it really made me think about my life'. In the main the diaries were very successful although two were returned with very little narrative. This is because (as the participants' comments indicated) the adolescents perceived it as 'homework'.

The diaries were useful for a number of reasons: 1) for building rapport, for example, the researcher had spoken to participants on the phone to give advice about completing the diaries and informal conversations with the participants prior to the interviews. 2) Also the diaries proved useful in opening up the discussion and allowed the interviewer to ask participants to expand on certain aspects that they had written about.

Because contact had already been made through the diaries the interviews were much less formal and having established rapport the interviewer was able to solicit more revealing information from the participants. The interviews permitted the researcher to engage the participants in a relatively informal conversation that encouraged freedom of expression.

A weakness is that the sample was slightly over weighted with offspring of Asian mothers. This is because all Asian mothers (as mothers were very often the first point of contact) consented to their children filling in diaries and being interviewed. However, as previously mentioned, some white mothers declined the interviews/diaries with their children. The main reasons given here were that they did not want their children to question their identity and did not want someone treating their children as 'different'.

Reflexive Note

Reflexivity is very important within a social constructionist framework, where it is widely taken to mean that the accounts themselves and the theories are socially constructed. As well as the participant's discourse, discourse analysis is also concerned with the researcher's discourse and interpretation of events. The researcher was reflexive and took into consideration her involvement during the research analysis process. In addition, she was aware, as recommended in discourse analysis, that the results were her interpretations only.

The interviewer did not portray herself as an expert but attempted to develop an equal power relation during the entire process; from first introducing herself on the phone, through the data collection process to final presentation of findings for feedback. Also during the process of analysis and writing, the participants' narratives were not treated as facts but as narratives that provided nothing more than personal experiences and opinions.

THIRD STUDY – QUESTIONNAIRE

Aim of Study

The first two studies of this research project focused largely on South Asian and white interethnic people. The aim of this study was twofold: to compare the findings of the two qualitative studies with a quantitative approach, for example, to understand whether the situational identity concept emerged using the methodology of a questionnaire rather than interviews or dairies. This would be achieved through administering questionnaires on newly recruited South Asian and white participants. The second aim was to explore the experiences of other interethnic people in order to gain a better understanding of these interethnic individuals and the factors that influence their ethnic identity. It was also decided that where possible social class, gender and age comparisons would be examined to get an insight into how these factors may impact on the participants' ethnic identity and experiences of being interethnic.

The specific issues explored included: how participants define their ethnic identity and the choice if any that they have over it, factors that influenced participants' ethnic identity and their experiences of being interethnic. They were asked questions on ethnic identity, religion, and experiences with grandparents and relatives, the ways they negotiate the representations of their parents' cultures and the advantages and disadvantages of being interethnic.

Method

Design

The sample is not representative of the interethnic population. As discussed it is very difficult to obtain representativeness in a sample of interethnic participants (see Tizard and Phoenix, 1993, 2002). In this case it is not representative because many of the participants selected themselves for the study. Also because some were recruited through personal contact and others were concentrated within specific areas. For the purpose of this study participants had to not have been involved in any of the other two studies. It was decided to recruit young people from the ages of 11–21. This was because, based on the previous studies in this research, it was thought that individuals below the age of 11 might not be as self-aware, articulate or may have found some questions difficult to answer. It was expected that both gender and social class would be important factors in influencing identity, therefore the aim was to interview both males and females from the middle and working classes. This would be achieved by recruiting from state funded and public schools.

Asian and white, black and white and 'Other' interethnic people were the focus of this research study. The 'Other' groups were not pre-determined but left to the type of groups that responded. The aim, therefore, was that the sample would be made up of 40 Asian and white, 40 black and white and 20–40 'Other' interethnic people. These numbers were, however, dictated by the difficulty in recruiting new participants, particularly Asian and white and because of time and budget constraints. Each group would include equal numbers of males and females.

Participants Recruited

Altogether 87 interethnic participants completed the questionnaire. There were 30 Asian and white (13 males and 17 females) and 40 black and white participants (18 males and 22 females). Individuals with parents from European backgrounds as varied as 'Danish and English' responded. They will be discussed under the category of white Other.[3] This is done for simplicity, however, it should be recognised that there were many differences within the European cultures. Ten of these participants responded, four males and six females. The next main group were of Chinese and white background (seven, three males and four females). It was difficult to recruit equal number of males and females as males tended to be reluctant to participate. However, in the main this was achieved. There were 49 females and 38 males. The age range of participants recruited was 11–21, though more of them fell within the 14 to 19 age bracket (see Table 4.1 below for a breakdown).

Table 4.1 Age range of participants

Age Category	No. in each Category
11–14	24
14–18	35
18–21	28

3 It is acknowledged that this terminology may not be perfect, however, as the participants themselves placed themselves under that category, and given their varied backgrounds this was thought to be the most appropriate term to use.

Social class comparisons were also difficult to achieve – this is because the questionnaire did not include questions on class. Therefore, social class differences will not be discussed in this report.

Questionnaire

The questions were based on findings from the first two qualitative studies in this research. There were sections on ethnic identity, religion, factors that influenced identity, experiences with grandparents and relatives and the positive and negative aspects of being interethnic. A mixture of open and closed ended questions was used. The questionnaires were self-administered and all participants were assured of confidentiality.

The Pilot

The questionnaire was piloted on ten participants and as a result shortened and a few questions were re-worded for clarity. Participants were not asked to provide their names and addresses. This was decided on after piloting because it was felt that assuring participants of complete anonymity would increase response rates. Also, it was decided to keep the questionnaire as short as possible by limiting it to two doubled sided pages to increase response rates.

Table 4.2 Response rates for questionnaire

	N sent	N received	Response rate
Schools and colleges	800	24	3%
Organisations	200	12	6%
Private contact	15	10	66.6%
Work email and Internet	1000	38	3.8%

Response Rates

Table 4.2 shows the number of participants who responded. Private contact response rate was the highest because the 15 people who were sent the questionnaires were known to be of interethnic. It was also easier to contact them to prompt for response. Recruiting through organisations was the next most successful method because people who worked there helpfully assisted in locating suitable participants within their organisations. Circulating the questionnaire on the researcher's work email and Intranet also yielded results. This was due to a number of reasons:

- individuals were able to complete an electronic version of the questionnaire without having to hand written it.
- colleagues were told that it would take no more than fifteen minutes and would make a nice break from work
- those who were ineligible emailed or sent the questionnaire to interethnic people they knew of.

It is important to point out that the sample used is based on volunteers, therefore it could be biased towards 'volunteers', who for example, may be more accepting towards the issues of ethnicity and interethnic (Sommer and Sommer, 2002). However, the likelihood of this bias in the sample may be low as feedback given to the researcher indicated that the main reason that people did not participate is because they were not of interethnic in the first place.

Analysis

The analysis used was a combination of quantitative content analysis, for example cross tabulations; counting the number of people who said they were Asian and white, black and white or who said they first thought about their identity at 'primary school'; descriptive statistics and inferential statistics. The appendix sets out charts generated from this analysis. For reasons of practicality the figures throughout this chapter will generally be referred to in terms of percentages. This is because the sample was small and increasing them to percentages made it easier to illustrate.

Inferential statistical tests were carried out to explore gender differences where appropriate. It was possible to explore gender statistically rather than other differences such as ethnicity or age because the sample size for this was larger than when split by ethnicity or age. In this case *two tailed t* tests were carried out to compare gender. ANOVAs would have been ideal tests to use however; this was not possible because of the size of the sample. The *t* test is a popular test, traditionally used for small samples, but now increasingly also used for large samples as well. The formula used was a *t* ratio for two sample, independent groups. This formula was computed and calculated using SPSS.

The null hypothesis was that there would be no significant difference between males and females. This null hypothesis was accepted (no difference) or rejected (there is significant difference) based on the probability of .05 (*p* value). For each of the questions a 0-4 scale was used to assess gender differences.

Reliability and Validity

Triangulation was used to ensure that the research was reliable and valid. Two colleagues (who are experienced researchers) of the researcher checked the data and the analysis for accuracy and reliability. Construct validity was used to assess the reliability and validity of the findings. The independent researchers agreed with the findings and were helpful in pointing out issues that the researcher had missed. Also the researcher's PhD supervisors were helpful in providing comments on the analysis and the write up.

Strength and Limitations

The sample was not representative of the population. As pointed out before other researchers have also indicated that it is difficult to recruit an interethnic representative sample (Tizard and Phoenix, 1993, 2001). Also it is slightly over-weighted with middle class participants, as more of the participants found were of that background.

The strength of this study is that it is based on a wide range of age groups from different backgrounds, from school children to professional working people. This made it possible to make generational comparisons. Also the researcher's success in recruiting relatively equal numbers of males and females meant that it was possible to make gender comparisons.[4] The data was obtained and analysed using a multi-method approach of using both qualitative and quantitative measures. In using the method of 'converging operations' it provided flexibility and reliability. It used a range of rigorous techniques to ensure that the findings were valid. The intention of the initial phase of the project was theory building given that there was no research (as far as the writer is aware) on Asian and white interethnic participants. The second and third studies tested and validated the findings.

The topic of Asian and white interethnic identity has not been academically researched in the UK. Therefore this work is original.

Also, new findings emerged here that have not been explored by other researchers on the topic of interethnic, for example, the subtle ways in which participants negotiate elements in their lives, the importance of choice, personal agency and the 'chameleon' identity

Conclusion

The first study was used to obtain a 'feel' for factors that influenced interethnic participants and to build themes and theories around it. In the second study discourse analysis proved an appropriate device for gaining a greater insight into discourses surrounding the adolescents' ethnic identity construction and deconstruction. Finally, the last study used applied quantitative method to test out the findings from the first two studies and to explore the experiences of other types of interethnic individuals.

---

4   A weakness in Tizard and Phoenix's sample was that it was heavily weighted with girls.

What are the implications of using the research procedures? The three studies used a combination of research participants, techniques and tools, in an attempt to ensure that the findings were reliable and valid. The research procedures were felt to be effective. The relatively wide range of research approaches was used to test the validity of findings. They complemented each other and helped provide an understanding of the range of factors that influence interethnic person's ethnic.

PART 3
Voices

Chapter 5
Non-interethnic Parents and Children

This chapter presents findings from interviews with Asian and white parents and non-interethnic children and adolescents – in order to understand their experiences in comparison to the Asian and white interethnic children and adolescents. The main themes include issues such as cultural identity, language, religion, education, friendships, marriage, family, bullying, racism and the community. It is important to note that the author will not be formulating theories but will be reporting on the accounts of the participants as expressed by them. Although the beliefs and narratives will vary from person to person the findings will be presented in nine grounded theoretical propositions.

The theoretical propositions presented are derived from the empirical evidence using the procedures of the grounded theory approach as outlined in the methods sections of the book.

Identity and Culture

Theoretical proposition 1: Culture is important for both white and Asians but is manifested in different ways

The research findings here can be used to argue that culture is just as important for white people as it is for Asians. The white children and parents identified themselves as white, English and Irish. They discussed culture, but in a less direct fashion to Asians. One reason for this may be that the white culture is the host culture and thus seen as being the norm. It therefore stands out less and there is less talk of it. Another reason may be that the British urban culture has seen a fusion with other cultures, as Billy Bragg, a quintessential working class English man sang: 'I had a plate of Marmite soldiers washed down with a cappuccino, and a veggie curry once a week''. Whites tended to link their culture to 'Britishness', the British flag, monarchy etc. Cultural awareness was just as important for many of the white participants, as it was for Asian. This was especially so for parents who wanted their children to learn and appreciate other cultures and to strive for a multi-cultural society, as participants frequently commented:

> I think it's important that our children appreciate other cultures because living in London you should know about other cultures. It's full of people who are from a multi-cultural background and also it broadens your mind. [Charlotte]

Apart from culture broadening their mind another common reason given by parents was multiculturalism and a wish for a society where people from all ethnic groups are treated equally. Individuals from the host population may have less of a fear than Asians of losing their cultural identity. A few white individuals spoke about their feelings of losing the British identity. Participants wanted the British identity to be reconstructed in a positive way, to take it away from negative connotations of the BNP and skinheads. They also said that their children should learn first about the British culture followed by other cultures.

> They should learn about their British culture and be proud to be British. These days its like if you carry the British flag people think you're BNP or if you're patriotic then you're seen as being racist by black or Asians and the media. I mean it's ridiculous that X [son] is always learning about this culture and the other and not his own. [Becky]

White individuals felt that in the quest for learning and appreciating other cultures their children were not doing the same with the British culture. In general there is a growing feeling and resentment amongst white people, in particular working class, that their 'voices' are not being heard, as illustrated by the Bradford riots in June 2000, between Asian and white young men.

The Asian people tended to identify more directly with their Asian culture but had the same sense of its importance to their identity as white participants. It was important to them that their children appreciate the Asian culture that they had inherited and did not become too westernised. A wide variety of social scientists have documented the importance of culture to South Asians (Ballard, 1979, Baumann, 1996, Anwar, 1998, Modood et al., 1997). Similarly in this study, most of the Asian children stressed the importance of their culture. Many of their phrases began 'in my culture we always' or 'in our culture we don't' or 'we have been brought up as... [citing culture or religion]':

> We have been brought up as a Sikh, it's been drummed into us how important that is and it affects our whole way of life, the food we eat, the things we're allowed to do, the people we can marry. [Harbinder]

Language was more of an important element in the ethnic identity of Asians than whites in particular how fluent they were in both English and their Asian language. Some Asian parents spoke fluent English, whilst others understood it but spoke little. The children spoke their mother tongue as well as English. How fluent people were in their mother tongue depended on a number of factors; 1) how much they used the language, 2) whether they were taught it formally and 3) the extent to which they had acculturated into British society. The Asian parents reported that it was important for the children to know their mother tongue and their culture:

> Researcher: What languages do you speak at home?

We speak Bengali with my parents. With my sister and my friends we speak English and Bengali, you know you mix words sometimes and speak both English and Bengali together, it's become like a joke, how we mix the words up. [Layla]

This mixing of languages was an aspect of language development that was commonly reported by Asian children and adolescents. A popular name given by Bengali speaking participants to this was 'Bengalish'. This is perhaps a natural progression of youth culture. The mixing of Patwa (Afro-Caribbean language) with English is popular within the youth subculture and Caribbean identity (Modood et al., 1997). Back (1996) in his exploration of adolescents and urban culture discussed the creative ways that language, in particular Creole, was used both by black and white adolescents to express their identity.

Theoretical proposition 2: Religion was more important to Asians than whites

Religion, like language also appeared to play an essential part in the foundation of the ethnic identities of Asians. A national survey showed that 45 per cent of South Asians are Muslim, 24 per cent described themselves as Sikh, 23 per cent as Hindus (Modood et al., 1997). However, 31 per cent of white people said they had no religion and 68 per cent said they were Christians. According to another finding, 56 per cent of young Asians pray, compared with 18 per cent of white adolescents (Anwar, 1998).

When asked about the importance of religion the findings showed it as being more important to Asians than whites (Modood et al., 1997). Baumann (1996) found religion to be one of the most frequently used marker that 'Southallians' used to define their culture and boundaries. In the East End, Alexander (2000) discussed the importance of religion to young Asian Muslim men.

Other research showed 78 per cent of Muslims to say that their religion was very important to them (GFK, 2006). Research findings presented in this book supported this and indicated a wave of adolescents who had embraced the Muslim religion wholeheartedly. This has augmented since the September 11 bombing of New York. Since then increasing numbers of Muslims appear to be turning towards their religion for comfort and to reify their Muslim identity:

Researcher: How religious would you say you are?

I am very religious now and so are most of my friends, I belong to the Muslim society at College, it helps you realise who you are, makes you strong against violence, crime, racism, war, everything. [Ashraf]

The narratives of the participants' suggested that embracing the Muslim religion provided them with a sense of identity, of togetherness in a society where they are a minority and on occasions maybe made to *feel* like a minority. This is not a new phenomenon. People have in the past turned to religion when their community was undergoing upheaval or struggle (Armstrong, 2000). A poll showed 48 per cent of Muslims thought that the general public was less sympathetic towards them than before the attacks on September 11 (ICM, 2002). Follow up interviews with participants,[1] after this and the wars against Afghanistan and Iraq indicated an overall feeling, amongst both Asian and white participants, that it was a difficult time in Britain, in terms of increased political tensions and the fear of terrorism:

> Researcher: What has been your experience following the September 11 events?

> People are scared at the moment, all this war business, and terrorism. I know friends of mine who are thinking of leaving London, even Britain, because if we get bombed that would be the target. It's a horrible time for everything, to bring up children, everywhere, and all around the world. [Sam]

Alexander (2000) has suggested that, even prior to the September 11 events and the wars, the aftermath of the Satanic Verses affair, the Gulf War and Bradford riots has led to a British/Muslim division 'with Muslims placed as the new social and cultural pariahs' (13). This has led, she argues, to a new culture conflict theory around 'fundamentalism'. In short, the debate around 'black' has become linked to 'Muslims'. 'Muslims have then, ironically, become the new "black" with all the associations of cultural alienation, deprivation and danger that comes with this position' (Alexander, 2000, p. 15).

This focus on religion also had negative impact on other ethnic minorities, particularly those who 'visibly' looked ethnic or what others perceived to have 'markers' of being Muslim (Modood, et al., 1997, Hall, 2000):

> I know of Sikhs who have been attacked because they wear a turban and people think that they are Muslims. [Parmjit]

Indians (and Asian Christian) participants also reported that religion was important to them. Some Hindus were as fervent about their religion as for example the Muslims (see quote below) although the issue of religion was brought up by Muslim participants more than by others possibly because of present climate:

> Researcher: How religious would you say you are?

---

1   These interviews were conducted with Asian, white and interethnic participants, during the last phase of this book, after the wars to gage their reactions and experiences as it was a topic that participants had raised previously. However, as the findings are outside the boundary of this book, it will be referred to briefly but not discussed in depth.

> My parents are really strict about our religion, we all practice and follow it, everyone in the community is really strict about it, about doing pujjas[2] and things and sticking to your religion, it is important to practice your religion, a lot of Hindu friends we have feel quite strong about it too. [Deepak]

Generally, religion was reported to be less important by white participants. Other researchers (Modood et al., 1998) also found this.

> I'm an atheist, but it doesn't mean that I don't have any of the values, I mean I try not to lie, would never kill, you know all the things that the bible teaches you, but that doesn't mean I'm religious. [Jane]

The reasons why religion may be more important to Asians than whites seem to be linked to a number factors such as: a) being brought up with religion as an important aspect of identity; b) embracing religion is a way of dealing with social disadvantage and internal tensions; c) religion has became more important as a symbol of identity and achieving togetherness following the September 11 events.

Attitudes to Interethnic Relationships

Theoretical proposition 3: Asians and Whites have similar attitudes to interethnic relationships. Key influencing factors were rejection by others such as the community and having a common culture/ethnicity

When participants were asked about their views on interethnic relationships many whites initially said that ethnicity did not matter as long as their children were happy. However, deeper probing revealed more than half of these participants to think it would be better for their children to marry a white partner. This echoes other research findings, which indicated that 52 per cent of white participants said they would mind if a relative married an ethnic minority (Modood et al., 1997). A poll showed 41 per cent of white people to say that they would not marry someone of another ethnicity (ICM, 2002). The reasons behind this attitude appeared to be similar to ones given by the Asian parents. They believed there was more of a chance the relationship would last with partners of the same ethnicity because of common culture and interests:

> Researcher: Why do you feel it's generally better for people to 'stick to their own race'?

---

2 A Hindu practice of worshipping their God/s.

The cultures are so different, different food, clothes and even religion … I mean I probably won't know how to relate to the person or even the kids. They wouldn't be just someone at work or a friend, they would be a member of your family … well families are supposed to be close and really understand each other. [Elizabeth]

As with Elizabeth others also reported worries of being unable to relate to their son or daughter non-white partner, as well as any children they may have. They assumed the 'other' culture would be very 'different' and thus difficult to understand or relate intimately with. It seemed easier to relate to someone of another ethnicity professionally or as a friend than as a family member. This, they suggested, was because one needed to be more intimate with family members:

Researcher: Do you have work colleagues from ethnic minority backgrounds? If you do, how do you get on with them?

Yes, we do have black and Asian people at work, it's different working with someone and having them in your family, a family's more close and all that, at work you just work with them […] you might think I'm being racist but I'm not, I'm being practical. I've seen it and it just doesn't work. [Jack]

There was a difference in normative statements and statements of intent as illustrated below:

Researcher: What are your views on a person marrying someone of a different background?

Mary: How do you mean, race and things?

Researchers: Yes, that's right.

I think people should be allowed to marry who they want and I think it's good if they do marry someone of a different colour … [Mary]

However, this changed at a later stage in the interview … for some:

Researcher: Are you saying that you're more likely marrying someone of a similar background to you?

I suppose yes I would most probably marry someone like me … it's not that I'm racist or anything but I just think that I would have more in common with them. [Mary]

Mary's statement above illustrates the tension between her general ideological belief surrounding race and ethnicity and the actual personal choices she would make for herself. With regard to the attitude of Asian participants, a previous study showed that 64 per cent of Pakistanis, 52 per cent of Indians and 34 per cent of Bangladeshis would mind very much *'if a close relative were to marry a white person'* (Modood, 1997), with adults being more negative than young people. The reactions from the Asian parents, in this study, were also generally negative. This applied to 'mixed' marriages even within the same country/culture. For example, a marriage between a Bangladeshi from the North of the country to one from the South can be problematic. These sorts of tension illustrate the importance of localised identity (Thompson et al., 1999)

> Researcher: How would you feel if your daughter married someone of a different background?
>
> I wouldn't like it for lots of reasons, they wouldn't have anything in common, the family wouldn't support it, it would bring dishonour to the whole family, you know. [Shupna]

The negative reaction from others and fear of not being accepted appeared to be a big influencing factor in participants' attitudes to interethnic relationships. It was believed that the marriage might not last because of a lack of support from the community. It was commonly said that even if the family accepted the union, relatives and community members would not. The community would make an outcast of not only the son or daughter but of the entire family. Being in a relationship with a partner of another ethnicity would mean dishonour (loss of *izzat,* honour) to the individual and their family and relatives.

Some of the Asian participants also believed that white people would not accept the interethnic couple. They cited racism that they had experienced or heard of to support this belief.

> A boy or a girl who marries a white person or a black person has lost his or her culture. No matter how westernised you get you are still an Asian, you can't forgot your roots, it's in your blood. I'm sorry but people would not support them either. And what about the white relatives? They would never accept the person or the grandchildren as one of them, the amount of racism that there is from them shows that. [Rita]

Differences in culture (including languages spoken) were also given as another reason why the union would be unsuccessful. It was assumed that even if the Asian individual was born and brought up in Britain he or she would still differ culturally from the white partner. They would not be able to understand each other's cultures as fully as someone of the same ethnicity. Understanding Asian traditions was important. It was stressed that one could not forget one's inherited culture; it was '*in your blood*'. The assumption was that the Asian individual would never lose his or her cultural identity. However, in some cases this was inconsistent with other references they made to culture, as illustrated by the quotes below:

> Researcher: Why is it important for them [her children] to learn the Indian culture?

> If you're an Indian, Asian whatever, that's what you are, you never forget it, and it's in your blood. [Madhuri]

At another time on the topic of interethnic relationships, she said:

> Madhuri: They marry them because they have forgotten their culture, they don't think they are Asian, they are too westernised.

> I think girls and boys who are too westernised, they think they're white or black and marry someone like that to make them feel even whiter or black ... They're selfish, just think of themselves and marry who they want. They lose all their Asian identity. [Madhuri]

This inconsistency maybe linked to a desire for their children not to forget the Asian culture versus the frustrations of living in an unfamiliar cultural environment. Similarly, other people said those who had interethnic relationships were selfish and not thinking of children that they may have. It was thought that this would lead to 'impure blood' and also result in identity confusion, for example:

> Researcher: What do you think about people who marry someone of a different background?

> I don't wish to talk about it. [...] These people who do these things, why don't they think of the children? Their children would not be Asian, but have mixed blood. They might be teased, they'll be confused about who they are. It's a very selfish thing to do. [Raj]

Family

Theoretical proposition 4: Family experiences are very similar for Asians and whites although the extended family is more of an important aspect of Asian family life

Family life plays an important role both in the lives of whites and South Asians as illustrated by social scientist such as Baumann, (1996), Anwar (1998) Alexander (2000). The extended family system remains a feature of Asian family life and

Asian households generally tend to be larger than white (LFS, 2001, Modood et al., 1997). Family life and being a couple appeared to be the same for Asians and whites. Both had reported similar conflicts, if any, which were linked to finance and children. The main difference reported by Asian couples, particularly the women, was with regard to living with their husband's family (if they were living with them, as many of the participants' in laws were abroad). The difficulties involved conflicts with mother in-laws over, for example, domestic issues and bringing up of children, as this account reflects:

> It was very difficult when we used to live with my husband's family, my mother in-law used to criticise my cooking and things with the kids … you know anything from when to change their nappies, what to give them for food. [Rita]

Males reported fewer difficulties with in-laws. This may be because it is traditionally the wife who stays with her husband's family. Generally, however, the Asian participants said they were supported by both their extended families. The Asian extended family tends to be very involved in the lives of the couples. Support included financial, child-care and emotional support.

> We've got lots of aunts, uncles and cousins and we meet up during family things like weddings, festivals, dinners. We're close, but there are sometimes rows but not for long. [Hithrik]

The above account was a common response among the Asian parents and children. They met with their extended families and relatives regularly and, despite some family conflicts, felt close to them. White families did not appear to rely on their extended families, although this does not mean that they were not as close and supportive as Asians when they did see them. White families also tended to be more spread out around the country:

> Researcher: How much support do you get from your family?
>
> I moved to London and my family is spread all over really, Yorkshire, Nottingham […] so that means that we don't really see them that often but we're still close. I suppose we rely on friends and the nanny and things like that. [James]

Family support had implications relating to 'social capital' (Putnam, 2000), for both the Asian and white people. At first glance it seems that more of the Asian participants received support and had a better social network because of their reliance on their family and relatives. However, white participants also had an equal social network but of a different nature. They tended to be more reliant on friends and paid help (baby sitters/nannies, cleaners). Their financial support was obtained from outside of the family network; generally from financial institutions.

Community

Theoretical proposition 5: The community is an important influencing force for Asians. There are generational and gender differences.

The word '*izzat*', (honour) is used by all South Asians and is crucial to them. It is important for individuals to safeguard the '*izzat*' of the family. A single member of the family incurring some form of dishonour and shame can taint the entire family. The notion of respect as a value is obvious to probably all South Asians and is tied with Asian social rules and the community, which is an important force in the lives of the Asian participants. Unlike the interethnic families interviewed the non-mixed Asian families reported that they had support from their community and participated in community events:

> Researcher: How involved are you in the Asian community life?

> We're always involved in community things, we go to our local community centre but it's more than that, we know that we have lots of friends in the community who will support us, if we want to borrow money, or people to talk to, turn to for anything. [Reena]

Nevertheless, there are negative aspects to being a part of such close knit communities:

> I know everyone goes on about the community but it's not all that. I mean there are lots of bad things about it. [Anisa]

> People just gossip all the time, my parents are really scared of what people will say and think, you know … its all sorts of things like … you have to wear selwar kamiz when we have guests so that they won't think that we're too westernised. You can't do anything because everyone's scared of what people will think. It feels like someone's always watching you … it's much easier for boys. [Anisa]

Accounts such as above indicated feelings of being constrained by the community and for example, pressure to dress traditionally and to conduct themselves in a way that did not bring dishonour to their family. Being under the gaze of the community meant they felt they had little sense of freedom and autonomy. Rumours were spread within the community. As a result some who had behaved outside the norm of community 'rules' had been made outcasts. The fear of this happening meant many young women felt bound by the community and its social rules. Many of these issues appeared to be linked to generational differences between the young people and their parents and older members of the community. There also appeared to be gender differences in the way the community treated its members. Young women reported that their conduct and actions were under closer scrutiny by members of the community than that of their male peers.

The narratives of the young men indicated that they too felt pressurised, but for different reasons, for example, to be the breadwinner and support the family:

> Researcher: You were saying that you thought there was a lot of pressure on men too, what kind of things did you mean by that?
>
> People ignore what the boys do more than they do with the girls. But you know the boys have other pressures, like getting a job, supporting the family, girls don't have that. I've seen boys who have taken to drugs because they can't cope with that pressure … it's the son's responsibility … but nobody knows what the best way of dealing with things is, the parents don't know, they can't cope with their kids who take drugs and the kids can't cope. [Ashraf]

There were numerous accounts from the male adolescents of being under pressure to 'support the family' which they felt was intensified by the expectation that it was the son's responsibility to remain with parents and look after them and the extended family. It appears that they were attempting to find ways of coping with the tension between these expectations and the constraints/barriers they were faced. Falling short of family and community expectations meant that some were unable to cope with the psychological pressure and turned to ways of coping such as gangs and consuming recreational drugs or even dealing in drugs to make money. There appeared to be extensive generational differences, with both the young and the old being unable to cope with these differences. Parents, for example, according to the accounts here, seemed ill equipped at dealings with some of the issues that their children were facing, for example, drugs.

Accounts from white participants indicated a lesser sense of community and this also meant they felt less pressure to conform. They were more relaxed about community reactions to their behaviour:

> Researcher: What are your feelings about community life, involvement etc?
>
> Community life? Emmm [long pause] Yes, there is a bit of community here, it's all quite amicable, there's a few people we're friendly with, but it's not so strong that we care what they think of us or anything, I mean who cares what they think of us … [Jane]
>
> Researcher: It sounds like you're not too concerned about what people in the community think?
>
> No, not really … who cares what people think; we live our lives the way we want to. Everyone pretty much keeps themselves to themselves. [Jane]

This relaxed attitude may reflect the importance attached to individuality in western culture. It may also be that they do not feel the insecurity some Asians feel with regard to loss of cultural identity. Indeed, ex-pat communities abroad, the British 'community' in India, Africa, Argentina being examples, tended to also preserve their identity as closely as some Asians, perhaps for the same reasons.

Theoretical proposition 6: Sub groups within communities led to added pressure for Asian individuals

Another facet of the Asian community which put an extra pressure on members was the communities within communities. Baumann's study of people in Southall illustrated vividly the ways the distinct communities/groups within a community and a 'mosaic of separate communities' exist (1996, p. 188). He found members of sub communities drew upon shared values and version of their history that distinguished them from other sub groups. Also, community boundaries represented post-migration cultures and segregation based on the case system. These were all illustrated in this study – by, for example, Indian participants who reported a division between castes in their community:

> There's good things and bad things, mostly bad [laughter]. [Rita]
>
> Researcher: What are the good things and bad things?
>
> Good things, emmm can't think of anything [laughter], bad things, well, like it's ridiculous but the Brahmins don't want anything to do with the lower castes, they have their own centres and things, you'd think that in this country that won't happen, but it's sometimes worse here than in India. [Rita]

Such divisions within communities meant that certain sub groups, while retaining engagement with the wider Asian community, might nevertheless keep a distance from other sub-groups within that community. This sometimes meant intense pressure to conform and maintain the unique identity of the sub group as well as the larger community. Not conforming to the social rules of either meant the individual could become the subject of gossip and depending on what they did, risk shunning. This affected their freedom and sense of autonomy. Asian communities abroad tend to be more traditional and conservative in some ways than communities in their country of origin. The reason for this may be because in foreign countries groups tend to remain static and feel a greater need to preserve an identity and culture they perceive as being under threat.

Bullying and Discrimination

Theoretical proposition 7: Asian children experience bullying based on their race and religion

There is an extensive amount of research on bullying, particularly in the school environment (a few leading to suicide) as recently seen in the media. A study found that 12.2 per cent of pupils had been bullied 'two or three times a month' (Smith and Shu, 2000). Also 2.9 per cent of pupils said they had bullied others. With many interventions and programmes to reduce bullying in schools across Europe it may be on the decrease (Smith, 2003). However, what happens outside of the school environment? Some of the bullying reported here was on the street and in public places. The accounts of the white and Asian children and adolescents were similar:

> Researcher: Have you ever been bullied?

> I've never been bullied but my brother has, there was a group of boys who were always picking on him. [Jade]

> Everyone knows it's [bullying] there, that black and white kids don't really like Asian kids, you get it from all of them, I had one who kept trying to pick fights with me and then would call me a chicken and Paki when I didn't fight. [Neelam]

The narratives indicate that almost all of the young participants, both Asian and white, had encountered racism or bullying in some way. Most had witnessed racism or bullying or heard of someone who had. Almost half had been victims themselves. In addition, many of the Asian children and adolescents spoke about having either been victims of racial bullying or had seen it happen to peers/ friends. The Asian children and adolescents indicated that they perceived racism or bullying to have increased. Much of the racism and bullying was based on racial and religious differences. The bullying took the form of racial taunts about their physical appearance, the clothes they wore and the food they ate (for example, they were told they smelt of curry).

Religion was also an issue of tension, for example, a few Asian girls spoke of having their Muslim headscarves torn off their heads. For some, the taunts developed into physical assaults and fights:

> There's some girls in the playground, some white but mostly black, who pull our scarves off, if you don't do anything you're a chicken and if you fight back, like X [female friend] did a few days ago then it turns into big fights and they'll wait for you at home time. [Anisa]

Religious discrimination generally seems to be increasing, particularly against Muslims and Sikhs (Home Office Research Series, 2000). This may be for two main reasons; first, the Muslim and Sikh religions both have visible symbols. For example, Muslim women may cover themselves from head to toe and the men have beards and Sikhs (men) may wear a bracelet and wear turbans to symbolise their faith. On the other hand, Christians and Hindus can practice relatively discreetly with few outward symbols. This may make it easier to discriminate against these 'visible' minorities.

Second, 11 September 2001 and subsequent events appear to have made matters worse. This is supported by other findings, for example, a study showed 48 per cent of Muslims thought that people living in Britain were less sympathetic towards them than before the September 11 attack (ICM, 2002). From follow up interviews conducted later many of the Asians spoke of an increase in racism, particularly in the form of religious taunts, abuse, and assaults. Tahir, for example spoke of extreme religious discrimination:

> A black girl, our neighbour, wanted us to move our car so she could get her car out. I was looking for my keys to move it and as I was coming out I saw her crashing my car in anger, I didn't say anything because she knows lots of black men but she screamed from her window, you know all sorts of swear words and.. [....] you're all like Osama Bin Laden', I have nothing to do with it, and I come from a different country. [Tahir]

Theoretical proposition 8: Racial bullying against non ethnic minority children is taken less seriously

Another important finding, not widely discussed in academic literature, was that of racism against white children and adolescents:

> A lot of the black girls have such an attitude, and they're always cussing us because of our clothes, you know saying that it's bad taste, they've even called us white trash, none of the teachers do anything. No-one thinks its racism because they do it to us, but if we were racist to them it would be worse, they just treat it like it's nothing, there have been a couple of Asian girls too who've made racist remarks. [Sarah]

Racist bullying against white children and adolescents is an area that is neglected in social science research and, according to the participants here, by professionals and practitioners. A common theme in all these accounts was the perception that their complaints were not taken seriously, even by school teachers. There were also instances of racism between ethnic minority groups and a feeling that this form of bullying was taken less seriously than interethnic bullying

> Researcher: Why do you think that nothing is done about it?

Teachers do more about it if it's a white person being racist to you than if its some one black, or Bengali, Indian whatever coz they think its not really racism then, but it is. [Asha]

Both Asha and Sarah's accounts indicate that racism, when it does not fit the widely accepted definition, is not taken as seriously or handled in a sensitive way. There may be many reasons for that such as lack of awareness and training, all of which, underpinned by the false assumption, that it is not a form of 'racism'. The accounts of the children in this study show that it can be such as serious and painful for children who experience this form of abuse and the effects as lasting and detrimental.

Theoretical proposition 9: Asian adults experience more racism than white adults and they have fewer strategies to deal with the racism they encounter

When the parents/adults were asked about racism most of the white participants did not report having experienced racism themselves or their children. However, the few that did tended to speak of 'looks' they had received or 'knowing' that they were disliked because of their race:

I'll have to be honest and say that I've had people being racist to me, you know black or Asians giving me looks and that, you just know that they don't like you. [Becky]

In contrast, more Asian parents reported having experienced overt racism, although some in less direct form than others. The accounts varied, for example; 1) shop assistants not touching their hands when taking money from them 2) people from the health profession making direct racist remarks 3) racism in public places:

I work for the Inland Revenue and sometimes you get accountants ringing the office and refusing to speak to blacks or Asians, they want to speak to someone English. [Reena]

Reena's experience of racism in her job was echoed by many of the Asian participants. Racism and discrimination in the workplace is acknowledged and the government has put measures in place to combat it (CRE, Race Amendment Act, Home Office). Nevertheless, a government study showed the general public to believe that racial prejudice has increased (Singh et al., 2003).

Some parents felt their children had internalised prejudicial attitudes and had become embarrassed by their Asian culture. For example, if their parents spoke their language in public or wore Asian traditional clothes:

You know Pakistan will always be our home, we don't belong here, we came here for our children, but even they don't feel good about being Pakistani. Even

> my little one is embarrassed if I go to pick him up from school because I wear
> a selwar kamiz. [Sim]

This was a common complaint amongst Asian adults. They felt that their children
were uncomfortable with their Asian culture and were 'embarrassed' by some
aspects of it, for example refusing to wear their traditional clothes or eat the food
or had become too westernised. A few reported their children were 'embarrassed'
by the clothes they wore. This contributed to a longing, amongst many older Asian
participants, to 'go back home'. There was, in some cases, feelings of helplessness
and self-defeatism linked to not wanting to remain in Britain and a desire to 'go
back home' (Bhatti, 1997).

When it came to dealing with racism many parents tended not to be proactive.
They often advised their children to 'take no notice'. This may be because they
were not equipped or have never been taught how to resolve these issues, with the
consequence that some of the children reported that there was no point in telling
their parents. Only one younger parent had moved her child from a school where
he had experienced racial harassment and bullying:

> A group of white children were bullying my son so badly; the worst was when
> they took him into the toilet, took off his turban and cut off all his hair. The
> headmistress didn't do anything about it. The bullying got so bad that we had to
> move him to another school. [Parmjit]

*Theoretical proposition 10: Asian and white participants had similar views with
regard to race and ethnicity*

The participants were asked if they themselves had been racist towards any
individuals or groups. The majority of them reported that they had not. A minority
of children and adolescents, both Asian and white, said that they may have made
comments that could have been perceived as being racist, but was not intended as
such:

> Researcher: We've spoken about you experiencing racism from other people
> and I just wondered whether you felt that may be you had been like that with
> anyone. You know perhaps even unintentionally, and it had been interpreted as
> being racist?
>
> I've made [unflattering] comments about being white or black whatever, you
> know but its only when they've said things to me, so I, and my friends, say it
> back, it's not meant to be racist. [Reena]

It was difficult to know for certain what the true intentions of remarks such as
above were. However, unflattering comments based on insulting a person race
can be perceived to be 'racist' and obviously hurtful to the individual that they are

directed at. There were other participants, who had more clear prejudiced views, although they had said that they have never been racist towards anyone:

> Researcher: Why would you not accept your daughter marrying someone white or black?
>
> Well, you know we're not like white or black people, we don't go running off with people, we don't leave our children and go off with another man or women. [Sunil]

This participant had obvious prejudicial and stereotypical views about white people and their lifestyles. A few white adolescent participants also said they felt black and Asian people were taking over the jobs and houses, recent immigrants were abusing the benefit system. This may have been picked up from parents and recent media handling of asylum seekers. Some adult participants' accounts also revealed negative views of immigrants in Britain:

> They [immigrants] should go to their countries because people who belong in Britain can't get jobs, housing and benefits. [Harry]

These views are not surprising and have been documented by other researchers such as Modood (1997) and Home Office survey (HORS, 2004). The HORS study found that 26 per cent of white participants had said that they had racist views. In this study, however, the majority of the white participants' reported not being racist or prejudiced and stressed that they wanted to have a harmonious and multicultural society. For example, according to Jack's account below, as with others, racism was fuelled by the media which people should ignore and live harmoniously and appreciate differences:

> This asylum business has been hyped by the media; there are people entering Britain, but how many people realise that they live on a voucher of £20 to £30 a week. Also they can't work so that means that the state has to support them. We have to ignore what's in the papers and live together in a peaceful way. [Jack]

Conclusion

For people in this study their behaviour or attitude in reference to culture occurred with striking regularity. Their heightened awareness of culture allows a shared social world and provided a common conscience collective among them that interethnic adolescents may not share. Language and clothes were aspects that helped form this collective identity. For example, unlike the interethnics the majority of the Asian children and adolescents spoke their Asian language fluently.

Those that did not speak it fluently were frowned upon and seen as being 'too westernised'.

Religion was another key difference between Asians and whites and heightened even more by the aftermath of September 11 events. Asian parents made special efforts to ensure that their children were educated in their religion, in some cases going so far as to employ private tutors for their children. Social deprivation was a factor which affected individual's sense of how important religion was to them. Participants from deprived areas such as the East End of London seemed to be more passionate about their religion. Modood et al. (1997) and Anwar (1998) have suggested that the group that suffers the worst discrimination is working class Muslims, although this has been criticised by others as denying the prejudice experienced by Jewish and Irish people, for example, in Britain (Cohen, 1989).

Discrimination may be linked with social conditions; turning to religion may be a way of dealing with poverty, deprivation and keeping away from drugs and crime. It seemed to provide individuals with a collective togetherness, at a time when they were facing upheaval and uncertainty, as we saw from the accounts of Muslims, particularly after the war against Iraq. History shows people often turn to religion for comfort and emotional support at times of uncertainty (Armstrong, 2000). Gardner and Shakur (1994) found that Bengali young people's interest in Islam emerged in a context in which they experienced persistent racism and marginalisation. Pakistani and Bangladeshis have increasingly emerged as an underclass (Alexander, 2000). And this may be one reason why these groups have increasingly turned to their Islamic religion. It provides them with security and reassurance in a world otherwise plagued by discrimination and deprivation. Religion may not be as important to white people in the UK for a variety of historical and cultural reasons. However, whilst Christianity is less popular as an organised religion its core values are still embedded in British society. Hinduism has fewer 'practising' followers than Islam or Christianity (Modood et al., 1997, HOCS, 2003).

Asians and whites had similar attitudes towards interethnic relationships. That is, they were equally as negative and positive towards interethnic relationships. Their influencing factors were also similar; many for example spoke about the importance of having a common culture and ethnicity. Being rejected by others and cultural differences were key influencing factor in attitudes towards interethnic relationships. Asians tended to emphasise community reactions more strongly. They feared negative reactions from extended families, the community and society in general. Lack of acceptance of such a relationship was a strong factor in their attitude. 'Arranged marriages' with partners of the same ethnicity are still the norm within the Asian community (Anwar, 1998). But the attitudes of the Asian adolescents appear to be changing.

Both the young men and women spoke of community pressures. Some members' understandings of 'community' can uphold the illusions of fixed modes of identity and cultural homogeneity (Archer, 2003, Alexander, 2000) where there can be little room to exercise choice of freedom to make life style decisions. The struggle for a positive identity can be difficult for ethnic minority youth even in a multicultural community context where in fact cultures can overlap and are in a process of hybridity. The young Asian men and women spoke about juggling both the communities' traditional attitudes and changing nature of the wider society and the overlapping of cultures.

There were extensive generational differences between young and old Asians. The young people in this study reported being under extreme pressure and dealing with internal psychological tensions as a result of what is expected of them as well as external family, community and societal issues. There has been a growing trend in cultural mixing within Britain's multicultural society. For example, black and white working class youth in London have come to exchange and borrow from each others cultures (Back, 1996). Other analysts such as Bhabha (1990) have gone even further to emphasise a 'third space' as a result of globalisation and cultural mixing. However, young Asians indicated that they felt that their families and community did not recognise or acknowledge these changing trends – most of whom were determined to uphold cultural homogeneity. Community and family spheres as discussed here illustrate powerful ways in which group membership is upheld and influences people's lives as outlined by the social identity theory (Tajfel, 1974, 1978a).

Aside from the family and community pressure, young Asian men are represented, by the wider society, as being troublemaking 'fundamentalists' in comparison to young Asian women who are portrayed in domesticated settings and as oppressed (Archer, 2003, Alexander, 2000). These dominant representations are important because they can be internalised by the groups themselves as well as the wider society. However, as argued in this book, ethnic minorities can and do resist images and identifications imposed on them by others. Studies of Asian young people have illustrated this, for example Dwyer (1998) found that young Muslim women resisted representations of Muslim women which they considered as derogatory and sought ways of expressing their identities in their own terms and expressed affiliations to a range of social worlds.

Older Asians appeared to be experiencing feelings of disillusionment and the fear that they were losing their cultural identity. Some spoke about returning to their country of origin. This 'myth of the return' – where migrants claim that they would not/or did not want to stay permanently in Britain was also found by Bhatti (1997). This is particularly emphasised when experiencing family, social or political instability. This was also reflected by some of children who would say that wanted to go back 'home' when they faced personal and social instability and conflict in Britain. White participants did not report pressure from their community and were much more relaxed in their attitudes towards it. This may be because westerners tend to believe more in the ideology of individual freedom and autonomy.

There are differences within ethnic minority groups based on the length of settlement, religion and class. In recent years there has been increasing work on the diversity of experiences among ethnic minority groups (Back, 1996, Baumann, 1996, Alexander, 2000, Modood et al., 1997, Anwar, 1998, Leibkind, 1992, Ali and Northover, 1999). There are also clear differences within the South Asian community. Moreover, it appears that recent events have caused, or deepened, interethnic divisions whereby increasingly there is conflict within the same ethnic groups, for example, one set of Asians against another. As indicated by some of the comments in this study, Asian Hindus, in particular had negative views of Muslims. As reported in the media, some had even joined the BNP to voice their views against Muslims. Contemporary events have also helped to bring to the fore past historical conflicts against Muslims and Hindus and succeeding in embedding present day divisions.

It was found that Asian and white children and adolescents experience similar patterns of discrimination but Asian children experience more religious discrimination. The accounts in this study illustrated both Asian and white children encountered bullying and racial prejudice. Asian children and white children also reported experiencing bullying on racial grounds from other ethnic minority peers. Connolly's study of South Asian girls found racism from white and black peers against Asians (Connolly, 2000). Smith (2003) suggested that there is increased racial tension in many European countries, However, there has been much less research on the racial prejudice experienced by white children and on interethnic children and this form of racial prejudice appears to be taken less seriously by teachers and other professionals.

Finally, it was suggested that Asians and whites have similar prejudicial views. Whilst, the Asian participants denied having been racist towards anyone, some of their comments during the interviews indicated that they may hold prejudicial views of people of other ethnicity. It can be argued that all individuals have 'racist' thoughts, indeed it may be part of our human make up (Dyer, 1997); equally most people have an innate sympathy with people of their own group. It is whether they act on these feelings that is important. The findings in this study indicate that there is plenty of scope for improving race relations in Britain. There have been improvements but many people still experience discrimination. Current Government policies in this area are backward looking, tending to revert to earlier models of assimilation into British society are not helping (see discussion on the concept of assimilation in the literature review). It is perhaps not surprising that participants reported increased racism, as also supposed by other findings (Singh et al., 2003). The adolescents reported experiencing racism from teachers, peers and the general public. Further, where there is racist bullying between ethnic minority groups or against white adolescents it was reported that less was done to tackle this than if it was a white person being racially prejudiced against an ethnic minority individual. These issues need further research.

There appeared to be some similarities in the experiences of the interethnic and the non-interethnic. Interethnic children and adolescents (discussed in-depth in the interethnic chapter) reported that they had to negotiate a number of issues such as language, religion and culture, which were important elements of their identity. It seems that the non-interethnic children also felt that they had to negotiate such issues; particularly Asian children and adolescents who reported battling with western values and traditional Asian values. Both interethnic and non-interethnic Asian adolescents appeared to have ambivalent feelings towards the Asian community. While the non-interethnic families had the community's support they also felt constrained by community rules. As interethnic couples and their interethnic children symbolise the breaking of one of the most sacrosanct of these rules it is hardly any wonder they reported feeling rejected by the community. As we shall see the Asian interethnic children and adolescents had an added dimension of having parents with two different cultures, which they had to negotiate even if it meant that they appeared not to emphasise one over another.

Chapter 6
Interethnic Couples

Whilst the focus of this book is on interethnic children it is important to understand the experiences of the couples in interethnic relationships (South Asian and white) – the parents of the interethnic children interviewed. These experiences will be presented here. The issues that will be discussed are attitude and culture, their children's identity, racism, family and the community. It is important to discuss such topics from the parents' perspective to allow a fuller understanding of their relationships and the ways that they might impact on the children and their ethnic identity. That is, a more complete picture can be obtained about the interethnic children and adolescents by exploring their families. The findings will be theorised in nine grounded theoretical propositions.

The Relationship

Theoretical proposition 1: Ethnic/cultural differences are important in terms of the experiences participants faced as a couple

The couples in this study had met and fallen in love; their reasons for choosing a partner of another ethnicity varied. The choices they faced in forming their relationships were complex. However, they emphasised one thing that – ethnicity was not an important reason behind their choice partner:

> Researcher: Did you think about his ethnic background when you first started going out?

> I fell in love with him; the fact that he was Indian didn't matter. When I am with him I forget that we're different colours. [Anne]

Social scientists have suggested a number of reasons why people form interethnic relationships (as discussed in the literature review), ranging from feeling marginalised by one's own ethnic group to economic and status advancement (by marrying a partner from the majority community (Benson, 1975, Breger and Hill, 1998). But findings presented here indicated that the reasons were similar to those of non-interethnic couples. Reasons such as love at first sight, common interests, working together led to close bond. However many of the individuals appeared to have a common factor that non-interethnic couples may not have – they, as individuals had made life choices that were different and outside of the norm from their own family or community.

> I was always doing did things differently from my sister, voting for different party, going into a profession that no one expected me to so no one was really surprised when I married X. [Jeremy]

Like Jeremy, his partner, had also spoken of making choices were not expected of her. This trait that the individuals shared, by many of the individuals, was the one common factor that they had and may explain why they were able to form interethnic relationships where others may have thought too taboo a life choice to make.

Being of the same social class was another similarity between the couples. Most of them shared the same social class as their partner, as also found by other researchers (Alibhai-Brown and Montague, 1992, Breger and Hill, 1998). This may be because many of them had similar educational achievements, had met through work or social settings.

When asked what their experience of dating as an interethnic couple was, some younger Asian individuals stated that they felt uncomfortable being seen together in public because of the negative reactions they received from other Asians, particularly the older generation:

> I used to feel really embarrassed in public, especially if someone Asian saw us, particularly the older ones, they would just stare at us. I would be too embarrassed to hold hands with him. We would also get stares from white people. [Shabbana]

Asians in particular appeared to be 'embarrassed' by the negative attention they received. Stares and comments received from other Asians tended to affect them *more* than those from whites. Other couples, however, did not feel uncomfortable and a few even said that they enjoyed the attention that being an interethnic couple brought:

> Sometimes it's nice, people really want to know about us because we're both so different and they'll say what gorgeous kids we'll have and things and how nice it is to see a mixed couple and there should be more of us. [Pamela]

The initial experience of dating and being an interethnic couple is therefore different depending on the individuals concerned, their experiences and how they viewed it. However, participants' narratives revealed that ethnicity and culture were nevertheless important influencing factors both in the ways they were treated as a couple and within the relationships. By definition, interethnic relationships involve wider cultural practices in same ethnic relationships such as gender roles, child-rearing, languages and general lifestyles. Some individuals said that they had to initially negotiate cultural differences such as food (whether to have curry or a western meal) and a fuller understanding of each other's customs. Others stated that they had not made any cultural compromises. Others made conscious decisions on which customs or religions they preferred or wanted to practice:

> Researcher: Have you made any compromises as a result of being in a relationship with someone of a different ethnic background?
>
> Yes we have had to make some choices. We made a conscious effort and a pact in the beginning that we would never let it affect us. He can't eat pork or drink because he's converted but I make an effort to buy alcohol free wines and pork free ham and he appreciates that. [Khalida]

Khalida's way of coping with cultural differences was to be creative in the aspects that she chose to accept and reject. This was echoed by other individuals. It involved each respecting the other's cultural custom and findings ways of compromising and/or accommodating. In this way most of the cultural differences were successfully negotiated, for example, being able to appreciate their partner's culture. This in turn led to a wider appreciation of both the need for cultural diversity and personal gains:

> Researcher: What are the positive and negative things about being in a relationship like this?
>
> I have gained so much from this relationship, apart from personal growth I know what it's really like to be a part of another culture and this has made me appreciate other cultures so much more. [Anne]

However, the reaction from other people was not as positive. It meant encountering and negotiating negative experiences. A few said that people's attitudes had changed towards them after forming an interethnic relationship. For example, some of the Asian women said that people criticised them for marrying outside the race. There were subtle remarks, whilst others were more openly prejudiced:

> There'd be times when X (partner) and I would walk together on the street and someone would say 'oi why don't you stick to your own kind' it hurts that people still behave like that. [Shabbana]

Negative views of interethnic relationships were not only directed at Asians but also experienced by white individuals from other white people, for example they spoke of being snubbed and accused of being 'socialists':

I've had people say, jokingly, but you knew that they meant it, that I was going too far in proving to be a socialist, that I didn't have to do that, you know jibes like that. [Jeremy]

Other people's experiences were more positive, for example their friends provided encouragement and admired them for their choices:

Most of my friends were so supportive and admired us for following our hearts and having the courage to go ahead with it even though we experienced so many problems to begin with. [Jaspal]

Nevertheless the majority of people reported some negative experiences as a result of having a partner of another ethnicity. Generally, it is assumed that many of the older barriers to interethnic relationships and marriages are eroding. The above accounts illustrate that some prejudice against interethnic couples still exists in today's society.

Attitude and Culture

Theoretical proposition 2: Couple's attitudes to ethnicity/culture differed widely depending on the individuals, their biography, history and social experiences

The participants were asked about attitude and culture in order to gain an understanding of how their attitudes may affect the development of their children's identity. Broadly speaking they can be divided into three groups according to the responses: 1) Asians who did not emphasise their Asian heritage or culture, those who felt strongly about being Asian; 2) White partners who reported to being very interested in their partner's culture and, in contrast, white partners who were not interested in their Asian partner's culture.; And 3) Asian partners who were interested in the white culture.

White individuals who said they were interested in their Asian partner's culture had made efforts to learn about it. They attempted to speak the language and learn other aspects of their partner's culture. Also some had been to their partner's country of origin:

Researcher: How much of X's [partner's] culture do you know about?

I've always been interested in other people's cultures and more recently the Asian culture because of marrying X [partner], I've been to India several times, read books by Indian authors etc. Sometimes X [partner] teases me and says that I married her only because I was so interested in Indians, she thinks she's another one of my Indian collections ... [laughter] well that's not true, but I can see why she thinks like that, I have a fondness for all things Indian [laughter]. [Toby]

Asians who felt strongly about their culture thought it should play an important part in the upbringing of their children. For most, however, there was a feeling that an appreciation of the English/white/black culture would come naturally to their children through schooling, peers and the media. Some couples made an effort to instill the Asian culture in their children. They tended to engage in cultural activities, such as attending cultural festivals, taking holidays to the Asian partner's country of origin and participating in Asian cultural music and dance. They felt that this would help their children to achieve a balanced appreciation of both their Asian and English heritage, while simultaneously better equipping them to deal with questions and prejudicial attitudes from outsiders:

> I feel very strongly about being Asian and it's important that our children know about the Asian culture and really appreciate it. If they know about their Asian culture then other Asians would respect them more and they would be able to stand up to any prejudice or discrimination that they experience. [Hamid]

There were a number of parents who said that they felt strongly about how their children viewed their ethnic identity because of having witnessed the experiences of other interethnic children:

> We would like our children to appreciate who they really are and both their cultures, especially their Asian side, I've seen other kids, mixed and Asian who think they are white and can't handle it when they experience prejudice, we don't want to make that mistake with our kids. [Khalida]

In the next group a few Asian individuals seemed to be uneasy with their own ethnic/cultural identity and experienced conflictual feelings about their identity:

> Researcher: How do you feel about the Asian culture?

> Just because I have a brown in me doesn't mean that I should act Asian. I don't feel comfortable with Asian things. I mean all my life I've been with white people, I had a public school education, where there's mostly white people, I don't have anything cultural about me. My children will be brought up as white of course, their father is. I just wish people would stop being so obsessed with skin colour. [Mariam]

The reasons for feeling uncomfortable with the Asian culture and this identity conflict may be because of a number of factors, for example, the way that it is represented in the media and the wider society and socialisation, but also the individual's past experience and psychological identification with the self and identity aspiration. Weinreich (1979, 1983, 1986) found in his study of ethnic minority adolescents that, for example, West Indian and Asian adolescents, tended to have identification conflicts with others of the same group because of dual socialisation. Ali and Northover (1999) also argued that ethnic minority (specifically Kashmiri) adolescents have higher identification conflict with their own group. According to them, this is as a result of 'dual socialisation with their own ethnic group and later identification with white majority society" (p. 35). Identification conflict, however, is not a negative state, it is an impetus for change and development and induces re-evaluations of the self (Weinreich, 2003).

Other individuals in this study felt they did not have to make an effort to learn about their partner's culture or attempt to instill it in their children for reasons of 'individuality'. For example, partners who stated that they were not very interested in their partner's Asian culture said that they saw their partner as an individual and as a result learning about their partner's culture was not as important to them:

> I love X (Asian partner) as who she is, I don't see the need to get to know about Asian things, I treat her as who she is, if anything if I was going on about her Asian roots then that would be racist. I was brought up to treat people as individuals. [Henry]

Children's Identity

Theoretical proposition 3: The ways that parents view their children's ethnic identity depends on their own attitudes and experiences. Parents, more than their children, are influenced by other people's views of a particular ethnicity

Some of the Asian parents believed that their children emphasised the Asian culture more than white culture. They said that they themselves had a strong Asian identity and wanted to pass that on to their children. Even to the extent of expressing a preference for wanting their children to marry an Asian, thereby carrying on the Asian lineage:

> Researcher: It sounds like you feel quite strongly about the Asian culture?
>
> I do feel strongly about being Asian, and I want my children to feel like that too. I'd be happy with whoever X (son) choose to marry but it would be better if he was Asian, I fear that otherwise our Asian lineage would completely disappear. [Abu]

This parent's strong identification as an Asian meant that he wanted his children to also have a strong Asian identity. Others wanted their children to emphasise the white culture, again as a result of their own experiences. They viewed their children as being primarily white because they were brought up in Britain and emphasised their white culture. A few of these individuals also said that they would prefer their children to marry a white partner:

> Researcher: What do you think is their [her children's] ethnic identity?
>
> Their identity is white as far as I can see; they just act like everyone else [other white people]. If I'm honest then I would like X [daughter] to marry someone white, like I did you know, I just think he'd treat her better than an Asian man would. [Kavita]

This mother believed, based on her experience, that white men treated women better than Asian men. Having married someone white she wanted her daughter to do the same. Similar to Kavita, some of these parents also felt that their children should be brought up as 'white'. They said that as the child is 'seen' as white by others it is 'best' to bring him/her up to fit with that description. They seemed to be influenced by the way others identify and ascribe identity to their children, as also found by Hall (2000). However, the children tended to be less influenced by other's ascribed identification of them. This is also illustrated by Weinreich's study which showed that people do not accept 'alter-ascribed' identities but prefer their own 'ego-recognised identities' (Weinreich, 2003).

There was a clear preference for some partners wanting their children to emphasise a white identity:

> We've brought him up as an individual, not to be Asian or white … X [son] looks white and other people think of him as white and I think it's best that way … it's just easier, isn't it? […] well, you know jobs, life … [Andrew]

Like Andrew, the father above, parents stressed that their children would have easier lives, in terms of jobs and progression, if they were white. Andrew pointed out that his son looked white. And both Asian and white, tended to be preoccupied with the physical appearance of their children, more so than parents of the same ethnicity. This may have been because, as indicated by the quote below, they did not know any other children of interethnic background, did not have others as a marker or to compare with, and were therefore particularly curious about physical appearance. Parents often speculated about their children's physical appearance even before birth. Perhaps because they were experiencing a sense of 'new' identity that they could not access as role models that parents of the same ethnicity could. Some of these participants worried that the child's physical appearance would impact on extended family relationships. For example, the belief that their child's appearance would affect the grandparents and extended family's views of him/her:

> If he looked more white then his family would feel closer to him … His mother has said that she wouldn't know how to relate to an Asian baby. [Shabbana]

On the other hand, there was also an expectation that the birth of their child would help to ease the sense of rejection experienced from extended families:

> Researcher: You were wondering what the baby would look like before it was born?
>
> Yes, everyone said 'have a child' and they'll [parents] come around and it's not just that ... we'd heard of so much parents who were against the marriage and then when the child was born they'd accepted it and were really happy. [Jaspal]

Mothers especially discussed other people's attitudes towards their children, in particular people's reaction to differences in physical appearance between child and parent. In such cases they said they experienced stares or/and comments from people in public places:

> Last week I was holding my daughter in a queue, and I had a woman say to X [baby daughter] 'are you crying for your mommy'. I replied 'I am the mommy' and she looked really shocked and embarrassed, they think you're the nanny. [Khalida]

This illustrates the importance that individuals and society place on physical markers to ascribe ethnic identity (Modood, 1998, Sarup, 1996, Hall, 2000) and the confusion that can follow if there are differences in a child's appearance in comparison to its parents. It can be argued that parents of non-interethnic children also experience similar reactions from people, in particular those who have adopted a child of a different race to them. But it might be that parents of interethnic children were more embarrassed and upset as they are the biological parents.

Race and Religion

Theoretical proposition 4: Being in an interethnic relationship bought issues of race to the fore

It is important to examine the issue of prejudice and tolerance of other cultures for two reasons; a) discrimination and racism were common themes in the parents' accounts; b) their attitude to racism needs to be examined to understand its bearing on the children's identities. That is, parents' ideas of ethnicity may impact on their children's identities. Both Asians and whites said that they were aware of racial discrimination and that there was still discrimination in British society. Most Asians said they had experienced some form of racism in the past. An extreme case was one Asian father who reported being beaten up by a group of white men:

Researcher: Have you ever experienced anyone being racist to you or discriminating against you?

I've experienced racism, at school, at work, you name it, the worst was probably when I was beaten up by a group of white men for no reason except that I was the wrong colour. [Rajan]

The people who had experienced discrimination said that they felt angry and helpless – as victims of racism they had to deal with very painful feelings. The above individual for example, who had experienced racism said, partly joking:

Researcher: It sounds like a really painful experience?

They can treat me however they want, but I've married one of their own. [Rajan]

Although at the beginning of the interview this man, like others, stated that the ethnicity of his wife was not a factor in his choice, from his later accounts it appeared that it might have played some part. For him at least, marrying a member of the majority group that had rejected him could have been a way of obtaining power over that group (Henriques, 1975) and membership of a group that would otherwise have not been accessible (Moscovici, 1976).

For some participants being in an interethnic relationship led to a greater appreciation of the culture of their partner and discrimination in general:

One of the best things about marrying X [partner] is having a better understanding of their culture and being able to also be a part of that culture, but you also realise the extent that racism exists. [Toby]

White partners said they had a better understanding of the impact that racism plays in the lives of ethnic minorities. It also made them realise how prejudiced Asian and white people (including their relatives) could be. Asian partners tended to focus on how their perceptions of the Asian community had changed. According to them, by marrying someone of another ethnicity, they had come to form a better understanding of racism within their own community and what it felt like to be isolated:

I've always known about racism from whites and blacks, have even experienced it, but never from my own community. It's opened my eyes to them, how insular and how narrow minded, and yes racist, they can be. [Sita]

Asians said that they felt that their white partners had developed a better understanding of racism. That, in some ways, they shared this experience that would otherwise have not been possible:

> X [partner] had no idea about racism, he's lived in a world where he's never
> experienced it, to know what it's like when the first thing someone notices is
> your skin colour but now he can. We can see people's reaction to us when they
> first see us as a mixed couple, that there's something different about us. It's
> nice because we share it, when people look at us; they're judging both of us.
> Shabbana]

This 'insider' understanding of racism is something that the white individual may
not have otherwise experienced and could perhaps be key to why the people in
these relationships seemed to emphasise understanding and appreciation of different
cultures. This also appears to have influenced their children, as many of them reported
a greater appreciation of other cultures. For this reason, it is understandable why
some social scientists have advocated more interethnic relationships and children
as a way of reducing racial tensions and encouraging harmony. Group membership
as being a positive aspect of being in a interethnic relationship was also reflected
in the accounts of both Asian and white participants who believed that one of the
benefits of marrying someone of another ethnicity was having a sense of belonging
to another group.[1] They reported the benefits of being able to have access to and
affinity with both the Asian and white (or black) groups:

But for others being in a relationship with a partner of another ethnicity did not
necessarily mean a) they were more tolerant of other ethnicities and cultures; b)
are better equipped to deal with prejudice and racism that they encounter. Although
there appeared to be greater tolerance and appreciation of other cultures for some,
for others it made little difference. When asked if they themselves had been
prejudiced towards anyone, a few said that they might have been without knowing
it. For example, calling people names in anger or stereotyping certain groups of
people. Some of these individuals argued that most people were prejudiced in
some way or another but that they would never be openly racist to anyone:

> I suppose if I'm honest then I have been prejudiced and have stereotyped people
> before but I wouldn't be intentionally racist to anyone. [Kavita]

They may not necessarily be less prejudiced or have a greater awareness of race
issues than those who have not formed relationships with a person of another
ethnicity. Nor are they more able to deal with racial discrimination that they or
their children faced. Participants were asked whether they talked about racial
discrimination with their children. A few reported that they did not believing that
if they did so they would become too sensitised to it. That is, that they would seek
out racism, losing objectivity about people and situations. These people said that
they did not think their children had experienced racism and therefore had not

---

1   The children also reported that one of the benefits of being interethnic was having a
dual identity and having membership to both the Asian and white group.

considered any strategies for dealing with it. As expressed by the participant below for example:

> Researcher: Have you brought up the issue of racial discrimination with your children at any time?
>
> No, not really. What is the point of talking about something constantly if you don't even know if it will happen to your children? It will just make the children too sensitive; I think that kind of thing is best left alone. [Henry]

Others stated that only a certain kind of person experienced discrimination, for example, people who were aggressive and 'brought it on themselves', or that individuals used 'racism' as an excuse and had 'chips on their shoulders':

> You find what you're looking for, if you look for racism you'll think that everyone will be racist, it's just silly. I think it's people who go around with chips on their shoulders who use racism as an excuse for their own inadequacies. [Phillipa]

The risk associated with this approach is that it may lead to their children believing that only bad people are discriminated against or that if it occurs to them it is their fault (Tizard and Phoenix, 1993, 2002). The parents in this group emphasised individuality: individual qualities, abilities and achievements to their children. They stressed that teaching their children to be individuals was a better way of raising them than teaching them about the possibility of encountering prejudice.

In direct contrast to those who did not wish to discuss racism with their children were other individuals who believed that racism and discrimination was widespread in Britain. These parents said that they ensured that their children were aware of racism so that they would be better prepared to combat any discrimination they may experience:

> Britain is still such a racist society, you hear about people being abused all the time or people being killed by racists. I, and other people I know have experienced racism at work, at school, on the street … We are trying to teach our child how to deal with it, it's our responsibility as parents … I do worry what kinds of treatment they'll get being mixed race and how they're going to deal with it. [Mariam]

These people tended to be Asian rather than white and had either experienced racism themselves or knew of people who had. They pointed out that their children would need to work hard to overcome discrimination and were particularly worried about the impact their interethnic background would have on them. It is difficult to say what impact this had on the children or exactly how they internalised it. Interviews suggested they did not become too sensitised to racism, appeared to have a more philosophical view of racial discrimination and were better able to deal with it if and when they had encountered it, as also illustrated by Tizard and Phoenix, (1993, 2001)

Theoretical proposition 5: Inter-religious relationships are not easy

Some of the couples, though of different ethnicities (e.g. Indian and white) were of the same religion, for example Christian. Those who are not of the same religion either had one partner who converted or chose to live with the two separate religions. For the couple where a partner had converted the issues that arose depended on the reasons for conversion:

> Well X [partner] had to convert because of my parents, they would not have let us marry otherwise and also religiously we wouldn't have been able to marry. Emm ... I'm religious myself ... X isn't so it mattered to me. As X isn't religious at the time he didn't mind converting. But as the years have passed I sometimes wish he didn't have to because in his heart his still a Christian, you know. And his family never accepted it. He was never really happy with it and for that reason I was not comfortable. You know. Our children sense that. We've talked about it and decided that he should follow his heart, don't care what my parents or community think. [Sita]

For the couple above, having a partner who converted because of pressure from their extended family or community regretted the decision as their relationship matured because it was something that both partners did not really feel comfortable with. This tension was also picked up by their children. Not surprisingly, there were fewer issues in the relationships where the partner had converted for religious reasons. Both partners shared the same belief and practices with little difficulties.

Other couples decided to live with the different religions and to bring up their children with both religions.

> I'm Christian and X [partner] is Muslim. Our children ... we teach them both and they can choose to be what they like when they grow up. It gives them a choice, you know ... it's up to them then. [Toby]

On the surface, this seemed to work well with both partners and their children. All had the freedom to choose their beliefs and practices. However, a few of these partners spoke about a sense of loneliness that their partner did not share their beliefs or practices. For one individual it brought up fears of life after death:

> It's ok, having different religion but then we practice Christmas, Eid, it's confusing for the kids. And what happens when we pass away. I mean do we go to different heavens, can we be buried at the same place. Do we see each other again? [Laughs] It scares me. [Shabbana]

Family

Theoretical proposition 6: The reactions from Asian and white extended family was similarly negative to individuals forming a relationship with someone of different ethnicity – but the white extended family were more disapproving in the long term than the Asian

A few of the families had little or no contact with their Asian and/ or white extended family. The majority of the extended families had been initially hostile about the relationship but had eventually accepted the couple:

> My father didn't want to know X [partner], I admit he was racist and had all sorts of negative stereotypes about Asians. Things are better now that he's got to know X [partner], personally I think he prefers him to his other son-in-laws. [Anne]

The above account illustrates many of the participants' experiences of hostile reaction to and rejection of the relationship, followed by a gradual acceptance as they got to know the individual that their son or daughter had formed the relationship with. This change in attitude can be understood in terms of Moscovici's (1976) suggestion that people feel threatened by the unfamiliar and attempt to make the unfamiliar more familiar. Making an individual (or representation) more familiar or getting to know this 'other' in such cases led to greater acceptance and even fondness for this individual.

It was more common for the couples to have had little or no contact with the white extended family in the long term. This was because white relatives appeared to be more disapproving of the relationship. There were instances where some relatives would ignore the different ethnicity of the partner whilst others openly made racist comments based on negative stereotypes of the Asian partner's culture, as the following person said:

> Researcher: What is your relationship like with your family?
>
> My parents and relatives have so many stereotypes about Asians and they've said some horrible things to me, I don't want to really go into it because it would bother X [partner] and anyway we're doing our best not to let it affect our relationship, but I don't really have much to do with them. [Jeremy]

Asian relatives tended to have strong initial negative reactions but, unlike the white extended families, came to accept the relationships at a later stage. As a Bangladeshi, Muslim woman stated:

> My parents went berserk when they found out. I can understand why they did, to them it was a betrayal for me to marry outside the race for a number of reasons,

they face racism from whites all the time, they had expectations of me marrying
someone Bengali from a good family and I think they also dreaded what the
community was going to say. [Khalida]

This strong reaction may have been as a result of being faced with something
outside normal values and an individual from a group who had previously been
seen as the 'other' (Moscovici, 1976, Tajfel, 1978). It is possible that the initial
reaction was stronger from Asians than whites because it was a more 'unfamiliar'
concept to them. The explanations provided by the participants tended to be
'cultural' based. For example, some said that the difficulty was with language
differences rather than prejudice or racism.

Community

*Theoretical proposition 7: A) Participants experienced more disapproval and
rejection from community members than family members. B) Being rejected by
one's own ethnic group was said to be more painful than by another ethnic group*

On the whole, community members were not as accepting of the interethnic
relationships as most family members were. Many of the participants reported
experiencing negative reactions from the Asian community. Some of these
individuals were treated as 'outcasts' and snubbed by the community. Others
experienced negative comments and isolation at social events. According to their
accounts, they experienced more rejection from the Asian community than the
white community. When an Asian member marries outside the race, there may
thus be a sense of betrayal and fear of losing their Asian identity. Certainly, it
was said that one of the main reasons why members of the Asian community had
been so opposed to the interethnic relationships was because of the fear that their
own children might imitate the individual who had married out. They may have
been concerned that this in turn would lead to their own exclusion from their
community. This was illustrated both in the interviews with the Asian parents and
the interethnic parents:

> Researcher: What has been your experience with the Asian and white
> community?
>
> People don't want me to talk to their children anymore because they're afraid
> that I would influence them and their children would end up doing what I did.
> [Khalida]

Individuals whose relationships had been met with hostility stated that they were
hurt and angered by the rejection they faced from the community. Those, Asian
individuals, who had previously been full members of the community, said that

they had more to lose than their white partner, that they had experienced feelings of pain and isolation:

> It hurts me when I hear about a wedding because I know we wouldn't be welcome and I know that so many people did not attend our wedding. I used to love weddings but know I feel sad every time I see one, even on TV. [Sita]

For Sita, having lost something that she had previously had, the acceptance of the community, led to a greater sense of loss and rejection. Although the reaction from the white community was not as strong, some of the couples had experienced racist comments and stares from people in public places as illustrated by the account below:

> We've had people give us dirty looks, or drunkards saying things like 'why don't you stick to your own kind.' It hurts but not that much […] maybe because we're used to racism anyway. [Sundip]

It is interesting to note that many Asian participants who spoke of this open discrimination from members of the public were less concerned by it than their partners, for whom racism had previously been less of a reality (as discussed above).

Racism and discrimination was also experienced by white participants, some of whom spoke of not being accepted or snubbed in public:

> It's been quite difficult, his parents are nice, but the rest of the community have been difficult, they make derogatory comments, sometimes even ignore you at weddings, if we get invited [laughter] or what's worse is that we get invited and people just stare or talk about you, say things in Indian and just look at you. [Jessica]

It would appear then that despite multiculturalism, interethnic relationships are still, to some extent, disapproved of both by the minority communities and the white community. As illustrated by other writers (Alibhai-Brown, 2001) the accounts of the participants here point towards the sense of rejection and lack of belonging that these individuals experience because of the community's disapproval of such relationships. Being rejected by one's own ethnic group appeared to be more deeply felt than by another community.

Theoretical proposition 8: Being with a black partner was seen as worse, by the Asian community, than being with a white partner

The researcher felt that the experiences of participants who were in or had been in an interethnic relationship consisting of an Asian and a black partner should be explored separately and in more depth. This is to fully justify their accounts and experiences, as some aspects appeared significantly different to those in white and Asian relationships. It was commonly said that being with a black partner was perceived to be worse, by the Asian community, than being with a white one:

> The whole Asian community looks on me as a wild tart; they gossip about me and don't want anything to do with me. They're racist; of course they are, towards blacks. They've made comments about how my kids will be and how X [partner] will leave me because they think that black men leave their women … they don't treat X [daughter] well, they just stare at her and say that she looks really dark and has curly hair, even my relatives. [Jaspal]

Even those who had formed relationships with white partners mentioned this:

> Oh god, it would have been a hundred times worse if X [partner] was black. They would not have wanted anything to do with us ever. [Shabbana]

The reasons behind the Asian extended family and the community's strong negative reaction appeared to be linked with their perceptions of black people, in particular black men. There were also negative reactions from the black community (as also documented by Alibhai-Brown, 2001), against both the couple and the children:

> Black people do give us dirty looks, like other black women have said things to my mum about sticking to her own kind and stuff … yeah I've been teased by Asians for being dark and curly hair and black kids have cussed me and said that I was a Paki and call me a Coolie. [Natasha]

As there were only two participants in an Asian and black relationship it is important to point out these are only their perspectives – interviews with other participants in such relationships may indicate different experiences. This proposition should be tested further for validity.

Would Participants Form an Interethnic Relationship Again?

Theoretical proposition 9: Participants would make the same decision again to form relationships with someone of a different ethnicity

Finally, all the participants were asked if they had any regrets about being in or having formed a relationship with someone of another ethnicity, and whether they would form such a relationship again. Most said that they had no regrets and would make the same choice again – including those who had experienced problems with their relationships. Also they reported being happy and proud of having children of dual ethnic heritage. Two of the participants' relationships had ended, and they were unsure whether they would form a relationship with someone of a different ethnicity again. A few said that given the things they had been through they were not sure whether they would have 'the courage' to do it again. They were also asked if there was anything they would like to change about their relationship and the common replies were that they did not. Some, however, stressed that they would like to change the negative response of their families, the community and society to their interethnic relationship and (for a few) their children:

> We're very happy in our marriage; I don't think I would have been as happy if I'd chosen anyone else. Fifteen years on, we're still madly in love. We have beautiful children who are doing well. The only thing I'd like to change would be the way people react to mixed marriages, not much has changed since we first got married, people still stare at us on the street, and we still get things said about it sometimes. [Phillipa]

People were also asked questions on the impact of interethnic children in society. On the whole, some felt that their interethnic children might result in a society with less racial conflict because they thought that their children appreciated other cultures better than any other individuals. They hoped that (as also argued by some assimilation theorists, see literature review), more people forming interethnic relationships would lead to greater acculturation. The account below is illustrative of the type of narratives provided by these participants:

> More people should get married to people from other races; everyone would mix more and appreciate other cultures more. I know from my children's attitudes and the things that they've said that they really appreciate and try to understand other cultures because they themselves are from two different cultures […] hopefully that will mean that when they grow up we'll have a society that's more racially tolerant. [Sita]

Conclusion

It was found that the issue of race and religion seemed to play a more important part within interethnic families than in families of the same ethnicity[2] or religion. This was also true of parents who believed that race was superficial and did not matter. They had thought more about race than families of the same ethnicity, even if this meant making a conscious decision not to discuss race or to let it affect them. It may be that having formed a relationship with a partner of another race, they were forced to face issues of race and religion linked both to their partner and children. This may have occurred as a result of internal issues of the 'self', within the relationship, or in relation to friends, relatives and society at large. Inter-

---

2   This is based on interviews with both interethnic couples and couples of the same ethnicity.

religious relationships brought with it difficulties in terms of religious practices but also a sense of loneliness for some partners and fear of being separated after death i.e. that a partner may 'end up in a different heaven or hell'.

The attitudes towards ethnicity, race and religion differed widely, depending on the individual, their biography and history and life experiences. Some of the people had very strong ethnic identities of their own. It appeared that in the case of such individuals their attitudes to ethnic awareness, although strong prior to marriage, had strengthened further after it. It may be that marrying someone of another ethnicity had increased his or her race awareness. These individuals seemed to have a need to compensate for marrying outside their race, having been portrayed as a 'social deviant' (Goffman, 1963, Moscovici, 1976) they were attempting to make amends, and perhaps even seeking to be accepted back into the fold of the community. This was true for some Asian and, to a lesser degree, white participants. Other attitudes towards both the Asian and white culture were more diffused. For example, their practices and lifestyles choices were intermingled between the two cultures.

Parents who were very racially aware and emphasised this awareness to their children tended to define their identity as Asian or dual Asian and white. The message to their child that ethnicity and culture is important was internalised leading to a greater cultural awareness. Parents who denied the existence of discrimination, in some cases contradicted the child's own experiences. The narratives of the children and adolescents in this study indicated that those who received conflicting messages tended to reject their parent's explanations and adopted the view that better reflected their own experiences both at school and in peer groups.

Parental influence lessened as the children matured, at which point they were more influenced by peers and social contexts outside of the family environment (see chapters on interethnic children). The family dynamic, was however, an important influencing force for the children. The experiences of the parents, as a result of having formed an interethnic relationship, appeared to have an impact on their children. For example, those who had good relationships with their extended families found their children having greater contact with them and subsequently felt a greater sense of acceptance from grandparents and relatives.

There is no denying, therefore, the importance of the family unit to interethnic individuals in this study. It formed a basis for their ethnic identity as, social psychologists acknowledge, it does with most people. There was a sense that most of the parents here, compared to those who had not formed interethnic relationships (see last chapter), made greater efforts to provide a family environment that attempted to insulate the children from external social forces and experiences they may encounter later on.

The reactions from Asian and white extended family was similarly negative to the individuals forming a relationship with someone of a different ethnicity – the white extended family were more disapproving in the long term than the Asian. They tended to reject the interethnic couple and their children more than the Asian extended family appeared to. This may be because they found it more difficult to accept someone of another race, particularly of a 'different skin colour' as well as biological grandchildren of another race. The Asian grandparents' acceptance of the interethnic family might be because they generally tend to be close knit and believe in the ethos of 'you stick together no matter what'; although in some cases this acceptance was superficial, as with some white families. That is, it was more 'tolerance' than 'acceptance'.

However, the Asian community was not as 'tolerant' as the Asian extended family. The couples reported that the Asian community in general had rejected them and their children. Paradoxically the reason for this may be the same reason which led the family to tolerate the family, that is the community is also very close knit and they strive for unity amongst themselves (Hiro, 1991, Anwar, 1998). For them it is important to achieve the rejection of individuals who behave outside the group norm. The closeness is based on a shared Asian identity that may have been threatened by marriage to a non-Asian individual – shattering and betraying the collective identity (Tajfel, 1974, 1978a).

Those who experienced rejection from their own community e.g. Asian community said that it was more hurtful than rejection from another community. The community was exerting social pressure on this individual but also sending a message to other possible deviants by disowning or rejecting this individual. They can be said to be engaged in a struggle for social control versus social change.

Despite some of the difficulties that participants had encountered they still viewed their relationship as being the best choice for them. They were also proud of the children's dual heritage and had aspirations for them, including the hope that their children would impress on others the importance of cultural diversity in Britain and lead to greater acculturation in British society. For the individuals presented here, there were benefits to forming an interethnic relationship. Such as an appreciation of their partner's culture. By marrying someone of another ethnicity participants spoke about having a greater understanding of issues, in particular racism. Many of the couples reported a greater awareness and appreciation of their partner's culture and also the importance of appreciating cultural differences in general.

PART 4
The Coming of the Chameleons

Chapter 7

Who am I? Identities Adopted

The focus of this chapter is on the identities that the young people presented. They drew on four main interpretative repertoires labelled as: 1) identity in transition; 2) one ethnic identity; 3) interethnic identity; and 4) situational/chameleon-like identity. They were categorised in this way because these are the representations of identities that participants' accounts revealed. These identities will be explored here using the discourse analysis approach (see chapter on how the research was done for more detail). Analysis of the transcripts revealed that the adolescents used interpretative repertoires in a range of different settings to carry out particular functions. It should be noted that the interpretative repertoires discussed in this chapter are based on the participants' cognitive language – they did not label these repertoires themselves. Also a number of subsequent contradictory constructions were employed in the narratives both in the diary and in the interviews.

Interpretative Repertoire 1: Identity in Transition

The negotiation of ethnic identity was a complex process. Some of the older participants spoke of going through a transitional phase of change in their self-identity over time. An interesting trend here is that children, at an early age, had tended to take on the identity of mothers, perhaps reflecting her role in raising them. The following 15 year old adolescent explained her transitional process:

> Researcher: What would you say your ethnic identity was? For example is one culture more important than another?
>
> My mother is white and when I was young I used to think I was white. We had English food and English everything really. My father didn't really pressure me to be Indian and my mother used to treat me as white. But after I started school and things I thought about my background more. Now I can understand Indian culture better and I am proud to be an Indian. [Nita]

Time (or development) was of particular importance in the formation of racial attitudes and ethnic identity. For many of the participants as they moved towards greater understanding of their family, friends, peers, community and society their preferences shifted. They became more aware of their dual heritage and, whereas at a younger age they might have considered themselves as wholly white or Asian (one or the other); they shifted their identity to emphasise their interethnic parentage. Or they adopted a situational identity i.e. they emphasised a certain ethnicity to suit the situation:

> When I was young I used to think I was white, probably because I used to spend a lot of my time with my mum, but gradually I realised that I didn't have to choose one, I am both and I can be one or the other or even both when I want to. [Paul]

The young people recounted experiences of negotiating ethnic identity from birth to present day in retrospect. The discourse surrounding this included references to a transitional identity, changing over time and influenced by their experiences of growing up. Many said that they began to question their identity when their self-identification was first challenged by other people's views of them. This normally occurred when they first interacted with peers at school.

> Diary question: When did you first start thinking about your identity?

> When I was at school, about 7 or 8. The kids knew that I was different to them because of my colour and because my mum would pick me up and she looked different to me. I didn't feel bad about it, I felt special, that I was not just like everyone else. I had lots of friends and all the kids loved the food I would take to school, they thought it was exotic. [Zara]

Being identified as different to other children enabled Zara to feel special. She had a culture that was different to her peers, which they interpreted as being exotic. For other individuals their first experience of realising that people perceived them as being 'different' was not so positive:

> In primary school, we had to make drawings about each other, but my friend said she couldn't find a colour to draw me, she said, you're not pink, not brown … it wasn't that she was being mean but it upset me, that's how she saw me but that's really when I started thinking about who I was, about my identity, before at home I used to think that I was just me and everyone would accept that. [Gemma]

For most children, the school context and interaction with peers provides them with an opportunity to construct their social and ethnic identity. They also tend to categorise each other by their skin colour and hair (Wilson, 1987). Peer interaction is a powerful influencing factor in children's and adolescents' life (Harris, 1999). The people in this study appeared to be constantly re-enacting their ethnic identity as result of their everyday interactions with peers. This was particularly for individuals whose previous ethnic identity was challenged, as in the case of Gemma, above. Being told by another child that she was neither pink, nor brown had Gemma question her skin colour and ethnic identity for the first time. She reported being upset that her peer could not find a colour to draw her. This made her feel different from other children and triggered feelings of insecurity, as indicated by the last sentence '*I used to think ... everyone would accept me'*. Gemma's world had changed. Having being told that she was 'different' from her peers she began to re-examine and then reconstruct her identity.

Gemma was not the only participant to find her first memory of 'differentness' occurring at school during the phase of transition into interacting with peer groups; it also applied to other young people:

> Researcher: Did your ideas about your identity change as you grew up?
>
> Yes. Over time my ideas about who I was changed. I think when I started going to primary school, I realised that people saw me as different because of the way I looked and you know having my mother who looked so different from me pick me up from school, the kids couldn't understand it, it took me a while to figure but that's when I started to really think about my identity and when it started changing. [Sanjay]

Sanjay began to evaluate his ethnic identity as a result of other people viewing him as being 'different' and against a mother who visibly looked dissimilar to him. The language of 'differentness' appeared in the accounts of a number of individuals such as Sanjay's. Away from their safe and secure family environment where they were generally not made to feel the same, they appeared to encounter their first experience of discourse conflict. But this seemed to be only a transitional phase in identity formation, and one that led to the adoption/emphasis of other forms of identity. A transitional phase was implicit in the language and discourses of most of the older participants in this study indicating that the interethnic individuals' process of identity development is similar to people of other ethnicities.

Interpretative Repertoire 2: One Ethnic Identity

The proposition presented here is that some young people emphasised one specific ethnic identity, rather than modulating/emphasising different ethnicities depending on the context. They adopted one ethnic identity over another, be it white, black or Asian rather than an interethnic identity, which involved acknowledging more than one culture/ethnicity. They did so as a consequence of several factors. They tended to be younger, and had yet to come to the understanding that they did not have to choose one or the other, but could be both (see quote from Paul, above). Out of those who identified themselves as 'more' white some said it was because they were rejected by the Asian community and felt they did not belong or could not identify with members of that community. These individuals also tended to have the physical attributes that enabled them to pass as white. That is, for example, they were fairer in colouring than the other children:

> I would say I was more white because that's how we've been brought up, we
> don't have much to do with our Asian side, or our white relatives for that matter,
> but we do have lots of white friends. Anyway, I look more white so I feel more
> white. [Anya]

Generally, they had white mothers and or their parents either had a 'colourless'
attitude towards race or considered race awareness as divisive to their children
i.e. it might make them too sensitive to race issues. Additionally, they appeared to
have received less exposure to the Asian culture than others.

What about the consequences of emphasising a white identity? According to
these individuals, taking on the white identity meant feeling more accepted by
white peers and the majority society:

> Researcher: Why do you think that you emphasise white culture rather than
> Asian?
>
> If I act white then white people treat me like I'm one of them, they don't think
> that there is anything different about me. [James]

James reported that he was accepted more by white people. Others thought that
they were more accepted by Asians. This appeared to be for a number of reasons.
1) Parents who had an awareness of the Asian culture and were fluent in it. 2) Their
mothers tended to be Asian and encouraged Asian practices; they therefore had a
better knowledge of the Asian culture. 3) They were more accepted by the Asian
community and had regular contact with them. 4) The family had regular contact
with their extended Asian family and had more exposure to Asian role models and
culture.

> I see myself as an Indian. I know the language and everything […] and do the
> same as everyone else [other Asians] and everyone, my relatives and cousins
> and other Indian people, all treat me like an Indian, and we're close as a family.
> We eat Asian food, wear selwar kamiz, everything. [Asha]

Another possible explanation may be that over time, as the children developed,
some became more racially aware and developed a stronger race ideology:

> Researcher: Have you always thought of yourself as Asian?
>
> No. I realised that everyone else just sees me as Asian. Everyone judges you by
> your skin colour, they don't see past that. So of course I have to find out more
> about my Pakistani roots because that's who I am now. [Mohammed]

Other people ascribing an identity of Asian based on Mohammed's physical
appearance appeared to have influenced his decision to emphasise his 'Asian

roots'. This was despite his earlier identification of himself as white. Mohammed's choice to emphasise an Asian identity was really therefore not agentic choice that he made freely, but one that was influenced by the ways others perceived his identity (Goffman, 1963, Weinreich, 2003).

Interpretative Repertoire 3: Interethnic Identity

Some of the young people in this study said that they were of an interethnic background, made it clear to others that they had parents of two different ethnicities and accepted this dual heritage. Interethnic identity is different to situational identity because these individuals did not change or emphasise different ethnic identity depending on the situation. In the main, individuals emphasising this identity seemed to believe that to positively accept both cultures they needed to identify themselves as having inherited two ethnicities and as having a dual identity.

> Researcher: What would you say your ethnic identity was? For example is one culture more important than another?
>
> I am mixed both Asian and white and I am proud of the cultures, both are important to me. I am proud for people to know that. [Kam]

Young people who were older may have reached a point in their lives when they could conceive of race as being multidimensional, and able to identify as being interethnic and both Asian and white/black. This awareness may occur through maturation, experience and self-evaluation. With self-acceptance these participants appeared to be less defensive, reactive and more self-expressive. They understood more clearly the confusion of others about their identity, were less dependent on others' recognition and confirmation of them. Also they relied more on an integration of a self based on heightened awareness and appreciation of their mixed heritage:

> Researcher: You sound like you're really comfortable and happy with your identity?
>
> Yes. I feel as if I've been on a journey, I've tried to be Asian, white, different things at different times and now finally I have accepted that I am both Asian and white … I suppose psychologists will say that because I have the self-esteem to accept that I am mixed and I am positive about who I am then so are other people. It's taken me a while but I'm here. [Sanjay]

Emphasising an interethnic identity, does not necessarily mean that these participants were more psychologically at ease with their self and identity. However, participants who had adopted this identity perceived it as a positive demonstration of their acceptance of both their inherited cultures. Self-acceptance and the assertion of an interethnic according to them was a final phase in the process of their ethnic identity construction.

Interpretative Repertoire 4: A Situational/Chameleon-like Identity

The participants' narratives revealed this fourth theoretical repertoire in relation to their identity. This representation is of an identity which shifts from moment to moment based on the situation that the individual is in. The next chapter (Chapter 8) discusses this interpretative repertoire in depth.

Conclusion

There is a wealth of literature in social psychology which explores people's self presentation (Goffman, 1959, 1963, Baumeister, 1982). These theorists suggest that people modify their behaviour and talk depending on the social context. It is generally accepted that there has always been some form of manipulation, and need for successful presentation or performance of one's identity. With the variety of social realms it can be argued that, today, it is even more important to manage one's self presentation. And the young people in this research appeared to be both self aware and reflective about their identity and experts at managing it.

The narratives revealed an interpretative repertoire of transitional identity. That is individuals perceived that their identity developed over time. Of course, it is likely that non-interethnic children would also go through a phase of transitional identity, but having parents with two different cultures magnified this experience. Blos (1962) believed that adolescence, for most individuals, was a time when they experienced a heightened sense of being different from others. It may be that this experience is exacerbated for individuals of interethnic background. However, Blos goes on to say that this often leads to a second individuation process, whereby they were able to work through and come to terms with their identity. It can be argued that the transitional identity experienced by the young people, was their second individuation process. It may be a way to cope with having their ethnic identity challenged and to resolve the discourse conflict that may have arisen. It also served to justify the reconstruction that follows for some participants; that of a transitional identity phase to an ethnic identity, an interethnic or a chameleon identity.

Those who adopted one ethnic identity, either Asian or white, did so because they could 'pass' as that identity. They were also influenced by how other people viewed them. The idea of positioning within discourse stipulates that we are influenced by the way others identify us; that our choice is to accept the representations of ourselves that others have hailed it as or try to resist them (Parker and Burman, 1993). If we accept or are unable to resist then we are locked into the obligations that go with that position. (Goffman, 1959) That is once we take up the position we inevitably come to experience the world from that perspective. We then have a limited set of concepts, ways of speaking etc. Our sense of who we are and what is right and wrong will be derived from that positioning. However, it is recognised that some individuals positioning may under go constant change and may be in flux (Davis and Harré, 1990).

The construction of an interethnic identity was influenced and or empowered by their experiences, ability, culture and social protocol and physical appearance. These factors will be discussed in more depth in the 'influencing factors' chapter (9). The ability to negotiate both their Asian and white cultures influenced the extent to which they were able to be autonomous with their identity. This was also extended to dress which was used as tools to aid with the ethnic identity that they wished to present. They also provided a coded meaning to the wearer and 'others'.

The ways that the young people deal with cultures also raised questions of national identity and which nationality they felt a belonging to. Some said that they felt a sense of loyalty to Britain. Others stated they had loyalty to both Britain and their other country that one of their parents had originated from. In this case, they did not wish to make a choice. Choosing a specific country, they felt, would equal to choosing one parent and betraying the other. Not wanting to make a choice was a way of keeping the peace within the family context. It may also have been a way of avoiding any ideological dilemma and resulting discourse conflict.

Some adopted an interethnic identity early on while others initially projected an Asian or white identity or a situational identity but later shifted to an interethnic identity. The findings indicate a number of possible reasons for this, as previously discussed in the book, these participants: 1) tended to be older and had come to accept both cultures rather than taking an either/or approach; 2) had found there were benefits to being of an interethnic background for example appreciating other cultures, being a part of two cultures, and the glamour associated with dual heritage and; 3) had been brought up and accepted as 'mixed' and of both cultures by parents and extended family. It was found that Asian mothers, more so than others, tended to make greater effort to incorporate both the Asian and white cultures in their lifestyle. This may be because Asian females possessed greater positive flexibility to negotiate two cultural contexts because of their experience of navigating the Asian and British culture.

The young people adopted their identity by negotiating their cultures and experiences. Some did not adopt a simple Asian, white or even interethnic identity. But passed as Mediterranean; far removed from their own ethnic inheritance. Raz (1994) spoke about individuals 'right to exit' from their parental heritage or a group. Goffman gives us a clue on how this can be done. For example, individuals can opt out of an identity by employing disidentifiers (Goffman, 1963). This can be reflected in their choice of friends or by adopting a non traditional cultural practice. The reason why individuals may wish to opt out is because there are still so many narrow markers or stereotypes associated with, for example, what it means to be South Asian. Opting out may be the individuals way of exercising greater choice and room for manoeuvre with regard to their ethnic identity.

Chapter 8
A Chameleon Identity

It was clear from the findings that some of the young people were electing not to limit themselves to a fixed white/black or Asian identity but instead adopting a situational identity to benefit their social context. These people tended to switch between facets of their identities, that is they emphasised different aspects, depending on whom they were with or the situation they were in. This chapter, following on from the last chapter, will discuss the finding of a situational identity. It will outline both the qualitative and quantitative research findings.

The qualitative method of interviews and biographical diary led to the themes reported below as illustrated by Gemma.

> Researcher: What would you say was your ethnic identity?
>
> It's not really as simple as that. [Gemma]
>
> Researcher: How do you mean?
>
> It's not just one thing … I act like an Asian when I am with Asian friends and white when I am with white friends, that way I'm accepted by both. [Gemma]

This meant they were able to emphasise different ethnic identities or aspect of one culture over another to suit the situation and place:

> Researcher: So most people see you as white?
>
> Yeah. Only my close friends know that my dad's Indian, everyone just thinks that I'm white and that's cool coz they treat me better anyway. I'm just like them, Indian, with my Indian friends. When I leave school then I'd tell my bosses that I was white because you hear about Asians not being able to get good jobs. [Paul]

This situational identity and the ability to emphasise a different aspect of oneself appears to be used as a tool to negotiate experiences and create a smoother path – a skill that may not be as easy to adopt for non-interethnic individuals. They also appeared to shift their involvement and alliances with different groups and feel a part of one group and part of another group, depending on the situation and viewed it as giving them greater choice over their identity. These people seemed to have acquired the maturity to understand the discourses surrounding identity and ways that these discourses can be negotiated for their benefit.

Individuals' sense of personal autonomy and ability to practice a situational identity depended on a number of factors such as physical appearance i.e. they needed to be able to 'pass' physically as both Asian and white. Also an intimate knowledge of both the Asian and white language and culture was an important factor. They had to have the confidence and maturity to be able to understand the skills required to practice this identity:

> Researcher: How easy is it for people to think that you're Asian, and white and so on?

> People believe what you want them to believe, I can be white or Asian because I suppose I know how to be, speak the language, what to wear, stuff like that, but also because I'm confident about it, you know what you have to do and then it becomes kinda natural really. It's all about passing as white or Asian or whatever. [Marcus]

The language relating to young people's ethnic identity, particularly older ones, as illustrated both in the diaries and interviews were framed within discussions of actively constructing their ethnic identity. This for some led to the use of the word 'chameleon' or language related to it, for example 'passing' or 'switching', indicating a changing/shifting form of identity. The 'chameleon' identity' discourse illustrates the ability for some young people to 'change' their identity to reflect their social context. The diary account below illustrates the deployment of this discourse:

> Marcus: I suppose you could say I was like a chameleon.[1] [laughter]

> Researcher: Why is that?

> Marcus: Well, I change my colour [laughter] get it? Colour! [laughter]

> I am Asian with my Asian friends and relatives and white with my white friends. It's a bit like changing my identity to suit who I'm with. [Marcus]

Marcus, and others in this study, likened his ability to emphasise different aspects of his parents' cultures to being a 'chameleon' and the ability to change 'colour' (ethnicity) based on his social environment. He emphasised different ethnicities depending on the situations and people with which he found himself. His ethnic identity was, therefore fluid and sometimes in flux.

---

1   It is from this statement that the term chameleon was born.

'Passing' was a phrase that came up again and again within the context of a situational/chameleon identity. Like Marcus above, participants spoke about their ability or inability to 'pass' as Asian, white or Mediterranean. This ability depended on their physical appearance and cultural knowledge of the ethnic identity that they wished to pass off as.

For some young people to pass as one identity over another was easily done. Most did not lie but did it with subtle linguistic devices; dropping in an Asian word whilst speaking English when with other Asians or by mere omission; not correcting someone when they identify them as being of a particular ethnic background:

> Researcher: How do you practice the different identities then? Is it the way you behave, dress, talk? …

> It's not that you have to say anything, you don't have to, people just think it, or you just use the Asian lingo that you hear other Asians use … and wear the clothes and things. [Reena]

It seems that those who practice a situational, chameleon identity go about it by using devices such as language and clothes and changing their interactions or as according to Goffman (1959), 'resources'. The interactional 'resource' was often subtle, for example; 1) proactively seeking to be perceived in a certain way and 2) 'letting' people believe that they were of a certain ethnicity.

> When you're with friends or people from school you just want to be like them, everyone does, don't they? So you just act like them. If someone thinks that I'm white, Italian, whatever, I let them think that … because you just fit in more … and if I'm with Asian friends than I tell them that I'm half Asian. [Zara]

> Researcher: Why do you feel that you have to have a different identity with different people?

> My mum's white and my dad's Indian so when I'm with my mum it's like I'm white […] because I suppose it's easier for her if I'm like that, I mean she has enough problems to deal with…you know people saying things to her. I'm more Indian with my dad and I try to be interested in the Hindu religion. [Reena]

The purpose of the chameleon identity, in this case, was to keep both parents happy. More than parents, friends and peers were presented as being the main justification for their shifting identity. The function of the chameleon repertoire with peers and friends appeared to differ from that with parents. With peers the participants emphasised wanting to belong to a group, as illustrated by Paul's quote below who spoke about passing off as Asian when with Asian friends and white with white friends:

> You want your friends or other people to think that you're the same as them because you want them to like you because you want to belong, you want to be accepted as being one of them. So you try to be Asian when you're with your Asian friends and white when you're with your white friends, you pass off as one of them. It gives you more choice. [Paul]

There were also negative references to the chameleon identity. Some commented on the responsibility of having to manage a situational identity. They wrote and spoke about how their parents, relatives and friends expected them to emphasise and learn about a particular culture. This, they conceptualised as 'pressure' on them to conform to those people's wishes and expectations. They felt they had to juggle both the cultures, the following extract exemplifies this:

> I suppose there is a bad side to all this ... you feel that there's pressure from your Asian relatives to be like them and your white relatives want you to be like them too, it's sometimes hard to keep up with that ... but you have to so that you won't upset anyone. Being mixed means that I have to be more careful ... you know I don't want my Asian relatives to think that I'm too much like my white relatives or my white relatives to think that I'm too Asian. [Asha]

For others passing off as one ethnicity meant listening to racist discourses about another group:

> The only hard thing is listening to people even friends go on about pakis or Asian friends saying something about goras, whites, doing stupid things. It hurts but what can you do ... [Paul]

> Researcher: That must be quite hurtful. How do you react when that happens?

> Most of the time say nothing. A few times I've said something when it's been really bad but then they look at you and say what's your problem, you know. Best thing is not to say anything. At least I don't join in, I've seen people who join in just to be like them, you know when they don't believe those things. [Paul]

Paul has learnt to cope with the difficult situation he finds himself in when adopting a chameleon identity by keeping quite but said that he had seen others who join in with the racist discourses as a show of solidarity and for group membership.

The chameleon identity brought with it, therefore for some, the pressures of a balancing act. And the need, as in the case for Asha, to please both sets of families and relatives. But this cannot be interpreted to mean that the young people experiencing this are 'marginalised' as theorised by traditional researchers on ethnic identity (see literature chapter). It is a normal part of identity formulation, as suggested, for example, by Berger and Luckmann (1966). And one that non-interethnics also experience:

> Don't get me wrong, it's not just me. My Asian cousins have to do the same; they wear the selwar kamiz and stuff when they go home and all that. Everyone does it. [Asha]

But where the difference may lay for the interethnic is that having two parents of a different ethnicity means that they may feel under greater pressure and with more at stake than the non-inter ethnic young people.

There were other consequences in adopting a chameleon identity. Some spoke of feelings of guilt for not telling people they were of an interethnic background. Adopting a specific ethnic identity based on their social setting was interpreted as 'deceiving' others because they presented one ethnic culture rather than making it clear they were of an interethnic background. Expressing feelings of guilt for misrepresenting themselves to other people led to a discourse conflict with their choice of identity. This was mirrored in their narratives; when some young people claimed they emphasised different ethnicity because it benefited them and that it was only a 'white lie'. However, elsewhere some of these same people's version is changed to talk of having 'deceived' and 'lied', for example:

> I let people believe that I'm Asian or white when it suits me. It's no big deal; it's kinda a white lie because I am half Asian and half white."[Marcus]

Later, during the interview:

> Researcher: You've spoken about a lot of benefits, good things about being able to change your identity, like being Asian with Asian people and white with white people, are there any negative aspects to this?
>
> I do feel a bit guilty sometimes because of deceiving them but it wouldn't bother them anyway, if I thought that, then I would tell them the truth. [Marcus]

The sense of guilt that they were 'misleading' or 'deceiving' other people provided an ideological dilemma for them. This was resolved, in same cases, by using the discourse technique of particularisation (Billig, 1987). Particularisation involves resolving a discourse conflict by treating certain circumstances or people as a special case. Some individuals employed this technique by saying, like Marcus, that they would not adopt a chameleon identity with someone if they thought it would hurt them in any way. Or they would only 'deceive' misrepresent themselves to people who they were not close to emotionally or did not know very well:

> My friends know about my background, I wouldn't deceive them but strangers, well they can think what they like […] I mean I act like whatever they think I am […] I would never lie to my friends. [James]

Finally, having adopted a chameleon identity, to what degree, if at all, do individuals get taken in by their own 'act'? Some had come to believe they were Asian, white or black either by choice or because it was a role they always played. Others, despite the identity they projected, never forgot they were of dual heritage and clearly expressed this:

> I may *let* people believe that I'm white but I know that I'm not, I'm both white and Asian. [Gemma]

So whilst they adopted a chameleon identity to suit the social situation they were in it did not affect their core internal identity, which remained interethnic. The chameleon identity was merely a device used to benefit the circumstances they were in.

Children with an Asian and Black Parentage

The qualitative research studies included participants of an Asian and black interethnic background so it is worth pointing out some of the similarities and differences that these young people faced. Like the Asian and white interethnic participants, these individuals also emphasised a situational identity. For example, passing as Asian or black culture depending on the people and situation they were in:

> I do act more black if I'm with black people and talk about Asian things more if I'm with Asians. [Natasha]

The reasons for emphasising different facets of their identities depending on the situation maybe linked to the experiences with the Asian and black extended family and community. They spoke of negative experiences from both the Asian and black community:

> Asian people say that I'm really dark but I've had lots of nice comments from black people, because I've got long straight hair and they'll touch that and because I've got light skin. [Natasha]

As Natasha's account shows fair skin tends to be admired over dark skin. This is true of both the black and Asian community as illustrated by media representations and the sale of skin bleach creams. A child who is Asian and black may have a skin colour that is darker than some Asians but fairer than black people in general.

According to the accounts of the individuals in this book they experienced negative reaction from Asians but admiration from some in the black community (see Natasha's quote above).

Other individuals reported negative experiences from the black community such as being called derogatory names:

> Some of the black children in my school make fun of me, calling me coolie, you know it sort of means servant, and things like that because I'm a bit Asian. [Anita]

According to Alibhai-Brown (2001) although the black community in Britain had traditionally been more positive about interethnic relationships and their off spring than other communities this is changing. There is more pressure, both in America (for example the black movement who discourage interethnic relationships) and Britain for black people not to form relationships with people of other races. This they believe weakens black numbers and power structures.[2] However, this attitude also applies to the Asian community although it may not be as politicised as it is within the black community. In fact, more so than it does for the black community, for example a study showed that more black people reported they would marry someone of another ethnicity than Asians (ICM, 2002). For the children in this study, emphasising different cultures at different times may be a way of 'fitting in' and negotiating such racialised discourses.

Quantitative Results

In this study, participants were asked '*Do you feel that you have a choice over which ethnic identity to adopt?*' They were given response options of 'not at all, sometimes, a lot of the time and all the time'. The mean score (Figure 8.1) was the highest for Asian and whites in terms of having a choice of which ethnic identity to adopt. The black and white group was the second highest.

The Chinese interethnic were the least likely to say they had a choice. Seventy two percent (Figure 8.1) of them said they did not have a choice at all, followed by the white Other interethnic (55 per cent). However, 29 per cent of the Asians said they had a choice over their identity all the time and 52 per cent a lot of the time. The black group were the next largest group, with 14 per cent all the time and 21 per cent a lot of the time. Only 8 per cent of white Other interethnic answered all the time and 55 per cent answered not at all.

---

2   As discussed in the literature review.

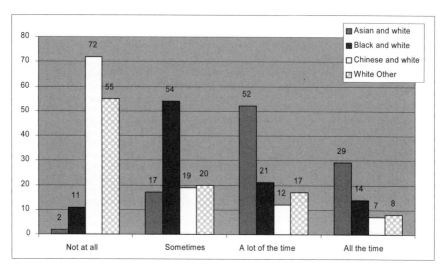

Figure 8.1 Choice of which ethnic identity to adopt
Base: The participants from each of the ethnic groups were expressed as percentage. For example, the 40 black and white participants were taken as 100%

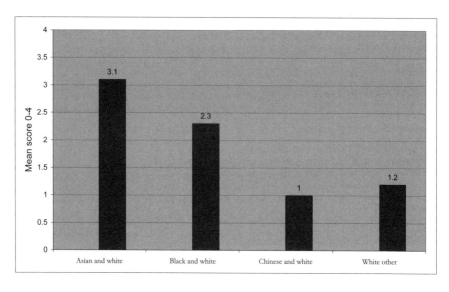

Figure 8.2 The mean score for having a choice of which ethnic identity to adopt
Base: The participants from each of the ethnic groups were expressed as percentage

Table 8.1 Percentage of participants who changed their ethnic identity depending on the situation

	With friends	With relatives	At school	When applying for college or work	With family	With the general public
Asian and White						
No never	7	29	2	0	15	0
A few times	45	47	21	28	42	11
A lot of the time	32	21	57	49	35	63
All of the time	16	3	20	23	8	26
Black and White						
No never	19	7	18	0	6	5
A few times	58	15	55	3	30	67
A lot of the time	13	59	25	67	49	20
All of the time	10	10	2	30	15	8
Chinese and White						
No never	60	71	33	8	58	19
A few times	29	36	57	20	34	59
A lot of the time	9	7	10	59	8	17
All of the time	2	0	0	13	0	5
White Other						
No never	47	29	28	2	49	23
A few times	31	37	52	70	39	61
A lot of the time	15	25	18	23	12	12
All of the time	7	9	2	5	0	4

Base: The numbers from each of the ethnic groups were expressed as a percentage. For example, the 40 black and white participants were taken as 100 per cent.

Note: There were no responses for the 'Other' category in the questionnaire therefore it was decided to leave this out of the table.

It appears therefore, that the Asian interethnic felt they had the most choice over which particular facet of their identity to emphasise. They were followed by black and white interethnic. The Chinese interethnic had the least, followed by white Other interethnic. The reasons behind this are unclear; however it may be linked with whether the individuals *wanted* to exercise choice over their ethnic identity. The qualitative interviews showed that participants changed their ethnic identity to suit the social context and in order to deal with racialised discourse. For example, when applying for jobs, it may be more of a difficulty to have an Asian or black sounding name than a white Other or Chinese name because Asians and blacks tend to experience more prejudice as documented by many social researchers (Anwar, 1998, Modood et al., 1997, 2006, , ICM, 2002, 2004).

As a follow up to the above question and qualitative findings, participants were asked '*Do you change your ethnic identity depending on whom you are with and the situation you are in?*' The response options were '*no never, a few times, a lot of the time* and *all the time*'.

Asian interethnic participants were most likely to emphasise different facets of their identity depending on the situation (Table 8.1). They commonly changed/emphasized a different identity with friends, when applying for jobs, at school, family and with the general public. The black interethnic group was the next most likely group to emphasise differing facets. They were likely to do this with relatives, with family and when applying for jobs. Participants from the white Other group were less likely to answer changing/re-emphasising their ethnic identity to suit their social context. However, when they did, it was with relatives and the general public. A relatively large percentage of Chinese interethnics ticked the 'no never' category (see Table 8.1). On the few occasions that they did, they did so when applying for jobs and with the general public.

With regard to having a choice over which ethnic identity to adopt, approximately half of participants felt they did have a choice. It is interesting to note that the 'when applying for jobs' category scored highly for participants in all interethnic groups. In particular, Asian and black scored highly in changing their ethnic identity when applying for jobs.

The statistical test on gender showed there to be no differences. In terms of the overall analysis there was a noticeable pattern of older participants saying they would change their identity when applying for jobs and younger participants saying that they would with peers. This is to be expected, as the majority of the young participants were of school age and did not need to apply for jobs. Peer influence would be a more important negotiating factor for them.

Conclusion

There has been a shift in social psychology, from the notion of identity as fixed, towards recognising that individuals are able to manipulate their identity to suit the social context (Baumeister, 1982, Harré, 1987, Gergen and Gergen,

1986, Sarbin, 1986). In addition, people use the power of language to construct their identities (Foucault, 1972, Parker and Burman, 1993, Holloway, 1989, Billig, 1987, Potter, 1997, Potter and Wetherell, 1997). It is generally now accepted that there has always been some form of manipulation, and need for successful presentation or performance of one's identity. There is an established literature that goes back a long way, James, Cooley, Mead, Goffman which can be interpreted to argue that identity is situational. Giddens (1991) argues that self identity is a modern project within which individuals can be reflexive and construct an identity to suit their lives. Nor is ethnic identity, according to some theorists, a fixed entity. It can fluctuate depending on time, situation and interests (Wallman, 1978, Nagel, 1994).

Much theory is a product of its time. Ethnic minority groups are active in constructing and recreating the cultural practices and values associated with them (Sollors, 1989, Nagel, 1994). The literature on interethnic people in America has also highlighted the concept of choice and of choosing ethnic identity. There is therefore, now more interest in the ways that people shape, choose and assert their ethnic identities. Some social psychologists use the concept of 'social creativity strategies' whereby there is recognition that ethnic identities are bounded by choices. According to Nagel, for example, since ethnicity changes situationally, the individual carries a portfolio of ethnic identities that are more or less salient in various situations and *vis-à-vis* various audiences. 'As audiences change, the socially-defined array of ethnic choices open to the individual changes' (1994, p. 154). The criticism of old paradigms has led to the emergence of new ideas that emphasise situational and changeable aspects of identity formation.

In this study the participants who had developed a situational identity were experts at self-presentation and impression management (Goffman, 1959). They were able to change or emphasise an ethnic identity depending on the social context and what suited them most. It should be stressed that it was generally the older adolescents (aged 14 onwards) who tended to construct this identity. This may be because through negotiating spheres such as family, relatives and peers they had had the opportunity to develop a chameleon identity and understand its benefit. It appeared that individuals were constantly negotiating their identities; they present one identity as more salient than another depending on their social context and personal goal. Moreover, a multitude of discourses were constantly at work for them to negotiate and manage the presentation of their identity.

The ability to 'pass' for a particular ethnic identity was an important common aspect in the adoption of a chameleon identity. Passing was influenced by a range of factors such as the visible appearance of the participants, for example, being fair enough to pass as white, and knowledge of the language and culture. The young people seemed to have a great insight into the discourses of identity construction and adoption and were able to use this to their advantage. As a result they reached a point of realisation – that they did not have to be one or the other (white/Asian) to fit a single mould but could adopt a situational depending on the social context; much more so than non-interethnic participants studied for this research.

Notions of autonomy and choice were central factors in constructing and maintaining this identity. The adolescents contextualised their identities and located a sense of self based on their setting. He/she had the ability to juxtapose different cultural behaviour according to the appropriateness of the different settings. For example, to project or emphasise an Asian identity it was not enough to know aspects of it, participants had to be able to show an intimate knowledge of the social protocols and idiosyncrasies of that culture. The successful negotiation of either or both the Asian and white culture was possible because they had intimate knowledge of the representations of both groups. This led to membership and integration within both groups and gave them greater freedom to claim both cultures as theirs. The chameleon identity, therefore, represents a sense of choice and control over the way one is recognised and may be a particularly important ability within the context of today's changing social dynamics.

The chameleon identity benefited the individuals in many ways including in dealing with racial and religious discourses. This would have been especially important in the climate that some of these interviews were conducted. There was (increased) tension between British Asians (particularly Muslims) and whites because of riots in the North of England and further exacerbated by the September 11 (2001) tragedy in America and the Afghanistan and Iraq wars. Individuals who were able to construct a chameleon identity found it easier to shift from being with whites and with Asians than a non-interethnic white or Asian person. All of this means that they have the potential to be more successful in adult life than non-interethnic individuals. Flexibility and the ability to adapt to the social context mean frequent modulations of social identities and greater benefits.

The interethnic identity, as we have seen, is a dynamic phenomenon shaped by a range of factors and realms. So how did the identity of other interethnic young people differ? Those with an Asian and black interethnic background (rather than Asian and white) shared similar experiences but also encountered different ones. For example, they too reported practising a situational/chameleon identity. However, they experienced greater prejudice from both the Asian and black community. Asian and white and black and white interethnic people were more likely to say they would change their ethnic identity depending on the situation than other interethnic groups. This may be because they have a greater need to adopt a situational identity, for example to deal with racialised discourses in the labour market. Another surprising ethnic difference was that white Other interethnic believed they were under more pressure to choose between the 'two cultures' than any of the other groups. The reasons for this are unknown.

Asian and white/black interethnic individuals were generally more adept at switching roles than those with a non-interethnic background. This may be because: (1) the parents of the interethnic children have two different cultures and therefore potentially have access to both. As well as facilitating their behaviour this may have given them the 'permission' and freedom to practice a chameleon identity. (2) Many of the young people from childhood onwards were used to emphasising different aspects of their ethnic identity to suit their relatives and situations. (3) Some had physical characteristics (such as olive skin) which others found hard to attribute to a particular ethnic background. This allowed them more scope to accentuate different ethnicities – this selection might not even be limited to simply white or Asian but be used to pass themselves off as of 'Mediterranean' origin (for those who had light skin). Finally, 4) as a result of these factors they may have a greater sense of choice over their ethnic identity and the recognition and ability to practise a chameleon identity.

Chapter 9
The Fine Art of Choosing an Identity

The relationship between an individual's identity and the ways in which wider society and social structure affect identity is a significant and intricate one. This has been illustrated by many social science theorists. According to the findings presented in this book family, peers and friends, the community, proficiency of a language and cultural knowledge and physical appearance were all important in identity construction. In particular this chapter elaborates on religion and how it influenced the young people. By presenting both the qualitative and quantitative research findings, the chapter will examine how interethnic children and adolescents negotiate these challenges and how these issues affected their identities.

Theoretical Proposition 1: The Family is an Important Influencing Factor on the Children's Identity Construction

Berger and Luckmann (1966) suggest it is within the family that a child achieves primary socialisation. Writers on interethnic identity also agree that the family context is where the child first begins to learn about racial differences and how others respond to them (Katz, 1996). Though, according to the quantitative study findings discussed later in this chapter, it is in the school environment that the young people first started to question their identity.

Early interaction and learning generally occur within the family and they are the initial source of the child's identity. Interethnic families may have varying racial attitudes, ranging from humanistic, and 'colour blind' to being racially aware and some of the children appeared to internalise their parents' attitudes to construct their identities:

> I know my mum wants me to be more white because life's easier if you are white ... she always says so ... she even said she wants me to marry someone white, she doesn't really like Indians because of the way they have made her an out-cast ... I suppose that's one of the reasons why I used to describe myself as white. [Kam]

Kam is clearly aware of his dual heritage identity and the pressures that he faces. He doesn't 'choose' his identity, but reports that he used to describe himself as white, for a particular reason, which in this case seems to be related to his mother's attitude.

The extent to which families embrace two different cultures was also important in the children's identity development. All the families generally adopted the western culture, and some, the Asian culture. Exposure to both western and Asian culture meant that the children were in a better position to appreciate both cultures. As one adolescent reflected:

> Researcher: Were you brought up with both the cultures?

> Yes. My parents have brought us up with the Asian and white culture … if they hadn't done that I wouldn't be able to appreciate and understand how important different cultures are. [Nita]

Some parents, however, did little to incorporate the Asian culture and said it would be up to their children to learn when they grew up if they chose. This meant the children had less exposure to the Asian culture and were thus less able to identify with aspects of it. Participants whose parents were comfortable in discussing and expressing their feelings on cultural and racial issues spoke about a feeling of acceptance and tended to be positive about being interethnic. Adolescents who were raised to be 'colour blind' and where culture or race was not discussed reported feeling self-conscious and a sense of isolation about their racial experiences (as also found by Tizard and Phoenix, 1993, 2001), particularly as they felt other people were constantly reminding them of their 'differentness':

> My parents never told me about the Asian culture, I was raised as being the same as everybody else. But other people are always saying how I'm different and I didn't know what to do when they used to say that. I realised that the way my parents have raised me, I mean they did it because they thought it best, doesn't reflect how people really see you. The first thing they see is that you look different. [Paul]

For Paul being raised with little knowledge of the Asian culture meant that he was unprepared for when other people identified him as being 'different'.

Being compared to parents and siblings was an important aspect of identity construction/adoption. The young people seemed to construct their identity by examining aspects of themselves in comparison to parents and siblings, for example the physical differences:

> Researcher: You said earlier on that people used to ask you how come you look different to your mum and dad.

> Yeah they did, and it used to make me feel bad at first, because I was different. I'm not like my mum or dad [at all], I am a bit Bengali and a bit white. [Zara]

Zara felt and was made to feel 'different' from her parents because physically she looked less like her parents than non-interethnic. The initial awareness of being interethnic, of being a bit of both parents yet neither, may bring with it feelings of confusion. Although this may be the case for all children and adolescents, for the interethnic, with representations of two cultures, the difference may be greater. The experience of 'differentness' to parents appeared to result in some psychological dissonance when they began to interact with peers and the community outside the family as illustrated by the account below:

> I used to think that I was white because we wear western clothes and eat white food. But when I started school people didn't think I was white. I'm different from my mum and dad, I wasn't like any of them, I'm not white or all Asian, I did feel a bit lonely because I was different. [Anya]

An underlying and difficult struggle was the question of identification with one parent *over* the other. The question of identification and loyalty with the parents and relatives resulted in constraints on choice of identity. At this stage they may experience ambivalence about their identity. Researchers agree, however, that this stage of conflict and anxiety may be resolved particularly if the parents provide support and the opportunity for the interethnic child to process feelings and experiences (Katz, 1992, Jacobs, 1992, Kich, 1992). To resolve these feelings some chose to be identified as both Asian and white (dual identity), or Asian, or white, depending on the situation (situational identity). It should be pointed out that conflict of this type is not necessarily negative but a part of the identity process.

These statements indicated that the children identified with elements of both ethnicities of their parents. This, depending on the child and the social context, may or may not be an uncomfortable state. For example, it may be perceived as being uncomfortable if the child wishes to be a full member of a particular ethnicity but be experienced as a valuable resource if perceived positively alongside a sense of being unique.

Physical similarities and differences to siblings were also important to individual identity. Some of the young people felt that they were identified or treated differently by their parents and extended family (as discussed in the next chapter) and by others outside of the family:

> Researcher: You said before that you emphasise the Indian side of you more, are there any particular reasons for that?

> Yes, I mean I look more Indian for a start, have you seen Marcus, what would you have said he was from the way he looks? [her brother who was also a participant in this study] [Nita]

Researcher: I suppose he's fairer skinned and has lighter hair.

Exactly, everyone thinks he's white, people don't think we are brother and sister. People treat him better, he doesn't get any racist comments or constantly being asked where he is from, I'm not jealous about that or anything, but people have treated us differently since we were little, even family … It is really frustrating, we don't even bother explaining anymore. My identity? Well, if I think about it, I think it makes it harder for me to act white because Marcus is more white than I am, if that makes sense'.[Nita]

For Nita, and a few other participants, having a sibling who looked physically different to her was a constant source of comparison and at times frustration because of having to explain to others that they were siblings. Their marked differences in appearance also influenced identity. Having a sibling who was identified by others as being white made it more difficult for Nita to emphasise the white culture she had inherited because, in comparison to her sibling, she was very much identified as being Indian. This seemed to be a constraining factor for Nita in terms of emphasising different identities.

Theoretical Proposition 2: Acceptance and Rejection by Peers and the Community Influenced the Identities that the Young People Adopted

When out of the parental and extended family environment, some of the young people became aware of how others see them through peer and other institutional interaction. Berger and Luckmann (1966) have termed this as the process of secondary socialisation.

Peers are increasingly recognised in psychology as being important in the shaping of ideas and perceptions (Harris, 1999). Experiences with peers (and teachers) of being 'different' to their parents and others made them feel unaccepted. Those who were accepted by a certain group often chose to assume the identity of that group:

Researcher: How did it make you feel when people kept asking you about the way you look?

Bad … People … erm … others … kids and teachers were always asking me where I come from, who my parents were because of the way I looked. My white friends accepted me for who I am, Asians did, but not as much. That's why I think I am more white than Asian. [Anya]

Anya's account above indicates identity where she experiences herself as being 'more white than Asian' but is not completely choosing white and denying Asian. She sees herself as being interethnic and as neither totally white nor Asian.

The perceived lack of acceptance by Asians may have led participants to identify more with whites. Experiences of being confronted with acceptance and rejection are powerful influencing factors of ethnic identity (Mead, 1934, Goffman, 1959, 1963). According to Erikson (1963, 1968) an individual's identity is strongly influenced by their identification with others during childhood and adolescence. When participants were asked about ethnic and racial groups they associated with most frequently the most common response was white (though a few said Asian). One of the reasons may be that they lived in predominantly white areas and went to schools where most pupils were white. This could mean they had fewer opportunities to befriend and identify with peers of other ethnicities. Some said they felt more comfortable with white friends who gave them more freedom of choice over their ethnic identity than Asian friends. The freedom to be who they wanted to be and to be accepted influenced their identity. Participants did not necessarily have 'choice' over their identity as certain facets of identities may have been blocked off/rejected by their experiences.

> Researcher: Do you feel more comfortable with one culture over the other, or is it really the same?

> I feel comfortable around white friends because they accept me more than Asian people at school. The Asians want me to be like them, they want me to cover my head and things and speak the language but I can't speak the language. My white friends accept me for who I am. [Joanna]

For James, discomfort with Asian people may have stemmed from his inability to speak any of the Asian languages fluently and being unfamiliar with the Asian culture. Those who were fluent in the Asian language and culture appeared to have better experiences with Asian people:

> I speak the language, I'm married to an Asian. I wear the hijab and I'm very religious. I see myself as a Bengali, I was brought up here [East End of London] and that's who I am. If we have children they will be nothing else but Bengali. [Shamsa]

Shamsa identified with the Asian culture rather than white and had an intimate knowledge of the culture and all its nuances. She felt accepted as Asian by others and was married to a Bangladeshi man. Feelings of acceptance by having immersed herself in the Asian culture may have led to a strong identification with that group so much so that she wanted to raise her children as Bangladeshi. Her alter-ascribed identity by Bengalis appears to have matched her ego-recognised identity, being that to which she aspired for herself and her children (Weinreich, 2003).

Unlike Shamsa many of the participants aspired to form relationships with other interethnic people. When asked about friendship they indicated that if there were more interethnic children they would choose them as friends rather than white or Asian peers:

> Only another mixed race person can know what it's really like to be mixed race, but there's not many of us around. They would accept you for who you are because they would know, don't get me wrong I have Asian and white friends, but I don't know what its like to have a mixed white and Asian person as a friend, who knows … it would be good to find out. [Sanjay]

There was a sense that they would be better understood and have more affinity and acceptance from people of the same background. But there was little chance of exploring this given they, generally, did not know others of that background. It could be argued that in seeking individuals of similar background they were seeking togetherness in a society where they felt like a minority.

Community life, as previously discussed, is a very important part of the Asian culture because it provides a sense of togetherness in a society where they are a minority. It is also a source of emotional and financial support. How does the Asian community treat children of parents who have committed one of the biggest taboos by marrying an outsider? Most participants felt that the Asian community, like Asian peers, had rejected them. This was mainly attributed to having a traditionally conservative attitude:

> Researcher: Why don't you feel like you are part of the Asian community?

> I don't feel a part of the Asian community because whenever we used to go to a community event, like to the centre for Eid [a Muslim festival], everyone would stare at me and they would whisper about me not wearing Selwar Kamiz [traditional Asian garment] or not speaking the Asian language. They just treat me differently and think that I'm not really Asian but I mean their attitude is so narrow minded, like Victorians. [Anya]

Rejection by the Asian community was internalised in different ways; for example, confusion or hurt and a sense of exclusion by members of the Asian community. The affect on ethnic identity, for some was a reluctance to adopt the Asian identity and participate in Asian community life. The people who felt comfortable with the white community attributed this to the Asian community being less accepting of them and being more culturally restrictive than the white community. Those who appeared to be less knowledgeable of the Asian culture and its nuances, for example, those who did not have an intimate knowledge of the language and the social protocol, felt particularly rejected. They appeared not to possess the social representations, e.g. cultural devices and values, of other Asian community members and thus felt less accepted into the community (Moscovici, 1976).

Cultural knowledge and religion was an important influencing factor in the young people's identity and the extent that they were accepted by the community.

Having knowledge of the Asian culture meant greater acceptance by Asians but also the tendency to identify themselves as Asian or emphasise different ethnicities depending on the social context. In short, it gave them greater choice. However, knowledge of culture may also have been the consequence of ethnic identity choice. If an individual identifies as Asian, he or she is more likely to practice the Asian customs and rituals rather than white, as in the case of Mohammed:

> You do have to know about the Asian culture to be seen as Asian, it's like any other culture, if you don't know the language, wear the clothes, eat the food then how can you expect people to believe that that's what you are? Yes, I do know all that […] as I got older because I wanted Pakistanis to believe that I was also Pakistani, you know I started learning more about the culture and the Muslim religion. [Mohammed]

Theoretical Proposition 3: Language, Religion, Knowledge of Culture and Social Protocol Influenced Identity

Being identified or recognised is an important process of identity construction and identification (Weinreich, 2003). Althusser (1971) believed that individuals' identities were placed (interpolated) on them through the mechanism of recognition. Appiah (2000) wrote about racial identification and how important it is. As he put it '*racial ascription is more socially salient unless you are morphologically atypical for your racial group, strangers, friends, officials are always aware of it in public and private contexts*' (Appiah, 2000, p. 610). The findings from this study showed that in the public sphere other people's notion of ethnicity and discourses of recognition affected individual's identity. Language proficiency was a factor that appeared to be a powerful influence on ethnic identity and on how outsiders identified and viewed individuals. Aboud (1988) also found that children were often identified as having the identity of the language they spoke. This was echoed in the research findings here; knowledge of an Asian language, for example, meant they were more likely to be identified and accepted as 'Asian' by Asian peers and the community. Those who did not speak an Asian language were labelled as being '*too westernised*' or '*they think they are as white as their father/mother*' by their Asian peers or others in the Asian community who marginalised them, for example:

> Researcher: What is it like when you go to the Asian community centre?

> I don't speak Gujurati like my dad and you get all the Asian people, especially the older ones, who come up to you and speak in Gujurati and they don't like it if I can't reply back to them and they'll say things like 'you're think you're English like your mother' and things like that. [Joanna]

Furthermore, ideas of how a person of a particular ethnicity should behave, in the case of Joanna, an Asian ethnicity, provided loose norms. Individuals who did not meet those norms were marginalised. Anderson (1999) illustrated the ways that 'bicultural' children, English and Greek, contextualise identity by the fluid way they use cultural tools such as language to signify their associations: 'By doing this he not only shows an ability to juxtapose different cultural beliefs, but judges them according to their appropriateness to himself in different contexts' (Anderson, 1999, p. 17). Individuals who were unable to speak the language could not use this cultural tool to signify their association and were unlikely to be accepted as a member of that group, like Joanna above.

Throughout this book, issues of culture and religion have risen. These spheres influenced the young people's sense of identity. There are many different South Asian groups each with its own distinct culture, as a report stated 'South Asians vary significantly not only in terms of nationality and religion but also in terms of language, caste and class, and of whether they have come to Britain from urban or rural backgrounds' (Runnymede Trust, 2001, p. 30). Of course there are also different white cultures and religions in Britain, the differences may be as pronounced as the various Asian cultures (the Welsh have their own language and culture; the Jews have their own religion, language and culture). This means the interethnic adolescents had to negotiate cultures that were often very different to each other.

The Asian culture is generally portrayed, in society, as being very different from the western culture. It also has negative connotations and representations, many sari[1] wearing Asian women and turbaned[2] men for example have experienced being laughed at or ridiculed. Indeed, there are stories of females' headscarves being ripped off by their black and white peers (findings from another project conducted by the researcher, the RELACS Study, 2001, and from the first study of this project). These experiences would explain the embarrassment and, sometimes, fear that young mixed and non-interethnic children and adolescents report in regard to the wearing of traditional Asian clothing. It is important, for most young people, to belong and be seen to be wearing the right 'gear'. Clothes and consumer products are one of the most important markers of our identity (Sarup, 1996).

Both interethnics and Asian young people spoke of enjoying wearing Asian clothes and jewellery but feeling uncomfortable being seen on the street:

Researcher: You're quite into Asian clothes and things then?

Yeah. I really enjoy wearing Indian suits and stuff, its so glamorous, western stuff just isn't like that at all, but it is embarrassing on the street, you know when

---

1   Traditional attire worn by Indian women consisting of a long piece of cloth wrapped around their body.

2   A turban is traditionally worn by Sikh men.

you go in public, on the street, people really stare at you. Mind you it's a bit easier now that Asian things are becoming more fashionable. [Zara]

The discourse of culture also provided a coded significance and meaning for participants. It operated as a medium by which individuals were able to construct their social world. The young people treated cultural aspects such as clothes and religion as a way of making sense of their identity:

Researcher: How do you feel when you wear Asian things?

I suppose when I wear a Selwar Kamiz then I automatically feel more Pakistani and when I wear like jeans and tops then I feel English … yes what you wear really affects how you feel. Like if I'm in a dressy mood then I'll wear Selwar Kamiz and I feel like a proper Muslim girl, but if I'm just going out to the cinema or something I will wear jeans and things because I feel more comfortable. [Hafida]

Those who spoke about a chameleon identity and perceived having greater choice in relation to their ethnic identity said they felt comfortable wearing clothes from both the Asian and white culture and did so to suit the social situation and ethnic identity.

The narratives also revealed the importance of cultural and social protocol. Individuals who practised a chameleon identity said they understood the idiosyncrasies, etiquette and the social protocols of Asian and white cultures:

Researcher: Do you think your behaviour changes when you are with your Asian relatives and your white relatives?

Well when I'm with my Asian relatives I do behave differently, you know you have to be respectful and everything and when I'm with my white relatives I can be different, like I call them by their names […] or I can be more westernised … well like sing pop songs, wear tight jeans you know things like that, sometimes even the jokes are different. [Omar]

Omar had accomplished this intimate understanding of both the cultures. He knew the social protocols of each and was able to emphasise his Asian or white ethnicity. Speech and linguistic devices also provided individuals with the tools to flag their identities. Sometimes these were very subtle and involved modulations. For example, uttering English words but using an Asian accent[3] to indicate that she/he was with fellow Asians or at times it was more overt; adding in Asian words even if speaking predominantly in English:

---

3   For example, V is pronounced as B; therefore, television, in the company of Asians would be pronounced as 'Telebishion'.

> I suppose if we're with our Asian friends then even if we speak in English then
> we would add Punjabi to that ... and they would too. [Safia]

The linguistic interchanging made explicit the extent to which they wished to 'belong' and the powerful way that language, even though at times very subtle could be used (Goffman, 1959, Mead, 1934). Those who understood and were able to speak both the Asian and English language represented themselves as having more choice over their ethnic identity. A participant who was unable to speak the Asian language or understand its nuances, for example, was thought to be less able to adopt an Asian identity:

> If you speak the language then of course people will accept you as Asian and if
> you don't then it's more difficult. [Omar]

Although representations of cultures, Asian and white, brought a series of choices (i.e. they had greater choice with regard to food and clothes) language used by some of the participants indicated that the two cultures were also at times potentially conflicting:

> When we had my family [Asian] around last time everyone was talking about
> India and Britain and how bad things were, and one of my uncles was making
> digs at my mum, you know saying white people treated Indians badly. [Paul]
>
> Researcher: How did that make you feel?
>
> Not nice. It seems strange that Britain colonised India and treated India like that.
> I know that some of my relatives remember that and they've said things about
> it, you know how dad could marry someone white. But when I look at my mum
> [who is English] I don't think of that, my mum was not responsible for that.
> [Paul]

For Paul, Britain's colonisation of India was a source of discourse conflict. At times the past was brought to the fore by relatives wishing to make their own personal points. Paul appeared to be torn between this conflicting past he had been told of and his sense of loyalty to his 'white' mother. He wrestled with the guilt and the need to re-assure relatives, and perhaps himself, that his mother was not responsible for the past. His way of attempting to resolve this discourse conflict was by trying to disassociate himself from the historical conflict.

Awareness of such a conflicting past for some of the respondents meant they had to tread carefully, particularly with relatives. It was important, in this instance, *not* to make a choice but to remain neutral:

> Researcher: What do you do when they talk about things like that? Do you say
> anything?

> If they talk about things like colonialism I leave the room, because I know there might be arguments ... I never take sides, like if I feel more loyalty to India or Britain or whatever. [Paul]

This also raised questions of national loyalty, for example, India or Britain. The individuals, in this case, spoke about the importance of staying neutral, of not siding with the Indians or the British. A discourse function of this is that it aided them in their quest to 'fit in' and belong with the people they were with. It also helped to keep harmony within their family environment and society.

Religion seemed to influence the young people, even for those who said that they did not believe in it. For some they emphasised and practiced the religion of the parent or relatives that they were with as illustrated by the quote below:

> Mum's a Hindu and I go to the temple and things with her and my relatives. And my dad's a Catholic and that's what I practice then ... you know we go to church at Christmas and that sort of thing ... erm ... sometimes it does get stressful, when there's a clash. I mean in their own way they are both quite religious and they try not to [pressure him] but I know they want me to be the same as them. And Hinduism and Catholics are so different, I don't know if I'm coming or going sometimes. To be honest I think it's better if the children aren't given a choice but are brought up with one or the other. It's less of a mindfxxx then coz they say different things. I don't know maybe I don't understand it. Yeah, that's the other thing I don't understand either one enough. [Paul]

Paul illustrates, what some of the other young people also expressed, the clash of religions, as well as cultures, and the pressure that parents and extended relatives, even unconsciously, placed on their children to practice a particular religion. In addition, similarly to Paul's parents many of the couples in the interethnic relationships make the decision to raise their children with both religions. But the children did not feel that this was the right choice. Like Paul, for example, they felt that being brought up with two religions meant confusing, sometimes contradictory messages or that they did not understand enough of any of the two religions to be in a position to practice fully.

However, another important finding was that, as with their identities, some of the young people were in a better position to choose their religions depending on who they were with. This was illustrated by Paul but also by other individuals:

> My dad's Muslim and mum's Christian and this sounds bad but it's only when I'm with Muslim friends then I tell them that I'm Muslim, I mean I was brought up as Muslim, not eat pork that kinda of thing. But when I'm with white friends I take on my mum's side of things more, you know Christian. It's bad I know but when everyone hates Muslims coz of 9/11 you have to do that. When I go to work and stuff I'm not gonna tell them I'm Muslim. I pass as Christian. I feel

sorry for people who are just Muslims or whatever or can't do that so I'm lucky
I've got both. [Anya]

Unlike Paul, Anya looked on the inheritance of two religions in a positive way
and was something that she used and changed to suit her situation. The general
negative attitude towards Muslims meant that she was able to emphasise her
Christian inheritance when she felt the need to.

Theoretical Proposition 4: The Embodied Self – The Importance of Physical Appearance

As well as language, physical appearance was another important element that
influenced the manner in which interethnic individuals were perceived and
identified by others. This is illustrated by Sarup (1996) who stated that physical
appearance is important in how we 'read' people when we first meet them. Often
a key criterion for group membership is physical appearance. This was important
when identifying others and describing themselves (Modood et al., 1997). It
appears to be not only important in identification, but in some societies it affected
an individual's life chances. For example, in Brazil, there is a caste system in
which there is social hierarchy based partly on skin colour. This was established
during the slave trade and still exists today (Davis, 1991). Indeed, until recently,
interethnic relationships were encouraged there in an attempt to ensure that the
population would consist of more ''white' people (Dyer, 1997).

The skin colour of the interethnic people varied from light brown to very fair.
Hair colour ranged from black to very light brown (almost blonde). The question
of 'what it is to look Asian or white' was influenced by stereotypes held by whites
and Asian; an individual who is very fair-skinned, fair haired and blue eyed may be
misperceived as white. Others considered participants who had darker colouring
as 'Asian'. Statements such as below were common:

Researcher: Sounds like how you look physically is really important?

Yes. I look Asian and everyone thinks I'm Asian so I consider myself as more
Asian, but my sister is really fair and people think that she is white, they don't
think we are related. [Asha]

Many said that appearance was one of the most important markers of how they are
treated. Researchers have also suggested an individual's ethnicity and skin colour
can influence how other people behave towards them (Appiah, 2000). According
to the young people here a fair skin colour facilitated better treatment by white
people:

I bet you thought I was white when I opened the door. [giggles] [Anya]

Researcher: I have to confess, I wasn't sure. [smile]

Don't worry, it's always like that, you're not the only one. It's because ... I am really fair and I have light eyes so people think I'm white, I think that white people more than Asian people are treated better. Sometimes people have made racist remarks to me thinking that I am white [...] feel bad about that. [Anya]

The ways that other people identify an individual based on his or her physical appearance can be powerful, as stated by Appiah 'The effects of labelling are powerful. Racial identification is hard to resist in part because racial ascription by others is so insistent, and its effects ... are so hard to escape' (Appiah, 2000, p. 611). Anya identified herself as being white. She preferred being identified as white because, in her experience, white people were treated better than Asians. There may also have been a sense of guilt about this and being told negative things about Asians (as they themselves were part Asian). Also some participants appeared to use others' identification of them as 'Asian' or 'white' to justify their own ethnic identification. There may have been a sense of being unable to escape from the ethnic identity that others had labelled them with:

Everyone keeps mistaking me for being Asian, so I have to just go along with it. There's not much I can do. [Asha]

For Asha, as with some other individuals, it appeared to be difficult to assume an identity that she did not physically resemble because of others' views of what Asians and whites should look like. What was interesting was the ways that these young people internalised others identification of them. Anya appeared to be happy and relieved by being identified as 'white' by other people. Asha, however, viewed it as a 'burden' and one that she could not change though she wanted to. This gives an insight into the ways that white culture (the majority culture) and Asian culture (the minority) is perceived by participants.

Another group of interethnic was those who were less easily ascribed an ethnic identity based on their physical appearance, for example:

Researcher: How do other people see you, you know, in terms of your ethnic identity?

Asians say 'nah she's not one of us', they think I look white. White's know I'm not one of them. Nobody wants me in their group. The only place people considered me as one of them was when I was in Egypt [laughter] but sadly I couldn't speak the language [laughter] I stopped trying to belong a long time ago. [James]

Not being ascribed an identity meant feelings of not belonging. According to the above individual, white people assumed that he was Asian but Asians did not identify him in that way. This resulted in feelings of not being a part of a group; he was made to feel different by both Asians and whites. This is potentially alienating and did not provide him with a sense of belonging in any particular ethnic group.

Other young people seemed to have a different perception of not having their ethnicity easily identified by people. They spoke about having a sense of choice because of not being constrained by other people's identification of them. As Appiah put it 'It is possible that if "ascription" is not clear, as in the case of some interethnics, then these individuals may have a sense of identity choice' (2000, p. 611). This is illustrated by the quote below:

> When I first meet people they don't know what my background is and I like that because I can choose whatever background I want. [Omar]

The body is an important aspect of identity (Mead, 1934). For the young people the ability to emphasise one aspect of their culture or even take on a new ethnic identity was said to be dependent on how they looked. The young people indicated that this made it difficult for them to negotiate an identity other than that with which they had been labelled. That is, they were limited in choosing an ethnic identity by their physical appearance. For example, having 'Asian' racial characteristics meant that they were unable to adopt a white identity even if they wanted to and hence there was a talk of 'helplessness', as in the extract below:

> Researcher: What would you say your ethnic identity was?
>
> I look Asian; everyone thinks I'm Asian so there's no point in me trying to be white. My identity is more Asian than white. [Shayla]

Shayla had little sense of choice with regard to ethnic identity. A function of believing they do not have the choice to challenge other people's identification of them may have been to shift both choice and responsibility for their ethnic identity onto others. Thus, her statement that *'everyone thinks I'm Asian, there's no point in me trying to be anything else'* may have enabled or forced her to shift the responsibility of choice away from herself and on to others.

Choice was synonymous, for some individuals, with the rhetoric of control. For Shayla, she had no choice and thus no control over her ethnic identity. Having choice over their ethnic identity was constructed as giving them a greater sense of control; allowing them to project the ethnic identity they wanted. Some of those whose ethnicity was not as easily identifiable by others expressed difficulties:

> Researcher: How do you think other people see you, you know in terms of your ethnic identity?

> People just don't know what I am; my colouring means that I could be a really fair Asian, Mediterranean, Arabic, and a dark English. I sometimes feel like an 'inbetweeny'. I'm not one or the other. But I used to feel like that more before, but now it doesn't really bother me because I know that I can be different with different people. Now I think it's quite good ... emmm ... actually thinking about it I prefer it like this now. [Safia]

Safia used the interpretative metaphor of being an 'inbetweeny' in her accounts. However, participants who used this term stressed that they had overcome this feeling. Like, Safia, they said they had grown to like the fact that others found it hard to identify their ethnicity. For them, not having their ethnic identity easily recognised and labelled by others gave them a sense of choice and greater control and autonomy over their identity.

A few demonstrated a strong sense of control over their identity by going against their visible ethnicity and the ethnic identity that others identified them as (ascribed identity, Weinreich, 2003) based on their visible ethnic characteristics and adopting an identity that they felt more comfortable with:

> People mistake me for being Indian but I'm not [...] I would say that I'm more white because that's how I feel inside [...] when people get to know me, that's how they see me, white. [Reena]

Reena's physical appearance did not match her self-identification, ego-recognised identity (Weinreich, 2003) or discourse of the self. With a clear physical resemblance to a particular ethnicity, she felt able to challenge people's identification of her, adopting an identity she felt more at ease with and one that matched her own discourses.

An aspect of physical appearance that was a popular source of discussion amongst the participants was skin colour. As discussed previously, authors have indicated that not only is other people's identification important but so was the individual's self-identification (Appiah, 2000). This is a significant issue, both for interethnic individuals and for blacks and Asians and whites. Blacks and Asians very often use skin colour to describe themselves to others (Modood et al., 1997).

For some skin colour mattered not only in the way that other people identified them but the way they were subsequently treated. Almost all the narratives showed an element of admiration for interethnic individuals who were fairer in colouring. It was reported that people in the wider community preferred 'fair' individuals. Many of them, particularly females, spoke of the prominence of 'fair' Asian, black and mixed figures and lack of 'darker' role models in the media. They cited examples from the magazines, the press, Internet, cinema and the television. Such role models in the media were constructed as influencing their discourse of skin colour:

Researcher: Who do you admire?

I wish I was fair like Melanie Sykes [an Asian and white model/TV presenter]. Asians like people who are fair and everyone you see on TV are fair, not just the English ones but also like the blacks and Asians, there are more of them than dark ones. Me and my friends think it's unfair. [Alison]

Family members and friends were also presented as having influenced discourse on skin colour. For example, the participant below indicated that she felt her mother was more comfortable with her brother, especially in public, because he had lighter skin colour:

Researcher: How do your parents see [view] your ethnic identity?

I know my mum prefers X [brother] because he can pass for an English person and it's a bit like she feels sorry for me because I can't … I don't blame her in a way because it's easier for her. When we're together people are always asking who we are, they don't think she's my mum, we don't look alike. [Reena]

The accounts of parents in the first study revealed that some were mistaken for being nannies when they were out in public with their child/children because of differences in physical appearance. It may be that this is why some parents found it easier to be in public with the child/children who resembled them more closely, it did not reflect a preference for a particular skin colour. White relatives, it was said, preferred the fairer sibling, perhaps because of the same reason; at least, on the surface they were able to relate more to this sibling who resembled them closely.

Researcher: How much of your relatives do you see?

Quite a bit, their favourite is X [brother] though. [Jade]

Researcher: Why do you think that is?

My aunt and uncle like X [brother] because he's like them, looks and everything, looks English. [Jade]

However, it also worked the other way. Some of the young people's language indicated that they felt their Asian relatives had a preference for them or their sibling because they were darker, some such as Shayla openly stated this:

I think my Asian relatives prefer me to my sister because I'm darker and look more Asian but I know that they admire my sister because she's fairer, it's really complicated … I suppose it's because I'm more like them. [Shayla]

There appeared to be a dichotomous element to Asian relatives preferring darker sibling. They admired the more 'fair' siblings but 'preferred' the darker individual. This seemed to be because the darker sibling was more 'Asian' looking. The fairer children and adolescents, whilst admired, may also have been more visibly interethnic. Of course, this analysis can also apply to non-mixed individuals. It should be stressed that these are interpretations offered by the participants of one element of their self. Other more complex factors may have greater impact, for example, personality and attitudes.

Quantitative Results

The quantitative results presented in this section supported much of the qualitative findings; however there were some areas where it was contradictory. To begin with in order to obtain an understanding of the participants' developmental process of their ethnic identity they were asked a set of questions in which they had to be retrospective. The first was '*when did you think about your ethnic identity?*' The categories for their answer were '*at home, at nursery, at primary school, at secondary school, at college, never* and *other.*'

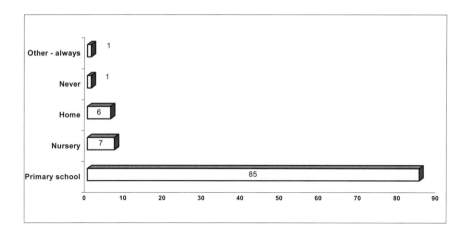

Figure 9.1 When participants first thought about their ethnic identity
Base: All participants

The majority of participants, 85 per cent, said they first thought about their ethnic identity at primary school, as also found in the qualitative research studies. The reason for this is that the primary school was the first social context in which peers (and teachers to a lesser degree) questioned the interethnic child's identity (this is discussed in greater depth in the previous chapters). There were no ethnic differences, most participants from all four of the different interethnic ethnic groups said they first thought about their ethnic identity at primary school. Also there were no age or gender differences in this section.

As an addition to the above question the participants were also asked '*what was the context that first made you think of your ethnic identity*?' The categories were *friends, peers, teachers, family, relatives, the media and the general public.*

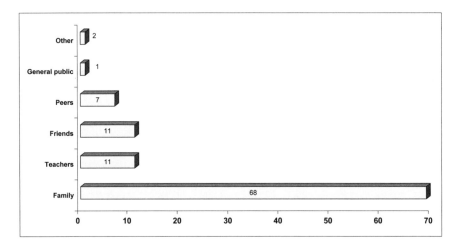

**Figure 9.2 The context in which participants first thought about their
             ethnic identity**

Surprisigly, in this section family, rather than primary school, was the most common answer with 68 per cent. The reason for this inconsistency may be explained by the qualitative findings, whereby participants indicated they first thought about their identity when their peers at school made comments or asked questions on it. However, it was at home and at times during discussions with parents that they processed this reconstruction. For example, participants said they spoke about it with their parents, siblings and relatives who helped them to internalise and think about their ethnic identity. This illustrates the importance of identification with family members followed by other identification.

Friends and teachers were equally as likely to be the first context (both 11 per cent), followed by peers. It seems spheres such as family, friends, teachers and peers provided greater opportunities for participants to reconstruct their ethnic identities than the general public, with family being essential social context factors.

Two percent ticked 'other' and wrote '*people's reactions in different countries*' and '*always*'. The first suggests that these individuals were more influenced by experiences of being interethnic through their travels in different countries than any other factors. However, it is not clear what these experiences might have been because it was not possible to probe further as it would have been in an interview. The second comment '*always*' indicated that this participants' ethnic identity was consistently at the forefront of his or her mind. Unable to further prompt in a questionnaire it can only be assumed that it is something that affected him or her all the time.

There were no noticeable ethnic or significant gender differences.

To get a further insight into participants' ethnic identities and affiliations they were asked '*which ethnic group do you identify with the most?*' The choice of answers given was 'White, Black, Asian, Mixed, Chinese and Other'.

Table 9.1 Ethnic groups that participants identified with the most

	White and Asian	Black and White	Chinese and White	White Other
White	36	18	47	73
Mixed/Interethnic	40	51	31	2
Chinese			18	
Other	5	2	4	25

Base: The numbers from each of the ethnic groups were expressed as a percentage.
Note: This was done for reasons of practicality although it is acknowledged that this is not the best way of making group comparisons as for example, there were only seven participants in the Chinese group compared to 40 in the black and white group.

Forty percent (Table 9.1) of the Asian and white participants identified with other mixed people, the rest, identified with white people and a few with Asians. A tiny minority ticked Other and wrote that they identified with different people depending on the situation. A greater identification with white people over Asians may be explained by the findings in the qualitative research studies where participants expressed feelings of rejection from the Asian community. Also it could be argued that participants might find it easier to identify with the host culture.

Results from the Chinese interethnic group were broadly similar to those in the Asian group, although slightly more of them identified themselves with white people. Black and white interethnic participants mainly identified with other interethnic people with fewer of them identifying with white people.

A very high proportion of white Other participants identified with white people. There maybe a range of factors behind this, for example, white Other interethnic participants' outward physical appearance was more identifiable as 'white'. The black interethnic were the least likely to identify with the white group. They affiliated more with other interethnic groups. Both the Asian and black interethnic participants were more likely to identify with other interethnic people than any of the other participants. Unlike the Asian and white interethnic, however, more of the black interethnic identified with their minority inheritance culture, black, than they did with the white. Findings from the qualitative studies and comments from the question, '*Please add any other things that you have experienced with regards to you being of interethnic background*' indicated that there may be a number of factors behind this. First, black and white individuals may identify with the 'mixed' group because they cannot identify fully with the white group or the black group. Second, there appeared to be a perception that other interethnic individuals understood them more than individuals of other ethnicity. Third, some also reported emotionally painful experiences with members of other ethnicities. Consequently, they felt more comfortable with those of a similar mixed heritage. This is best illustrated by one participant who wrote at the end of her questionnaire:

'I think that as a young person, a lot of men (both white and black) liked the idea of having a mixed race girlfriend and I sometimes felt that this was more important to them than other parts of my character/personality. This was very annoying and frustrating. I have always preferred my relationships with mixed race men because there was none of that possible agenda. I like the fact that my husband has a similar mixed race heritage as I do and that our future children are likely to look just like us.' [21, black and white parentage]

Many participants wrote 'It depends on who I am with' while a few wrote 'I identify as an individual', or 'don't think about it'.

Individuals who wrote that they identified with whoever they were with indicated that their identification and affiliations with people and groups changed according to their social context. For some this may extend to changing or emphasising a different ethnic identity to suit the social context. In short, 'adopting a chameleon identity.'

Younger people were more likely to say they were 'White' or 'British'. Of the 15 participants that answered 'White or British' 12 were in the 11–16 age range. This may reflect changing cultural and political views or that their attitudes changed with time. They were also more likely to identify with white people than their older counterparts. There were no significant differences between males and females.

Religion

Religion, as already discussed was an important influencing factor to the interethnic young people's lives and identity. The participants were asked '*what is your religion*' and were given nine choices.[4]

---

4   The coding scheme for this category came from the Home Office Citizenship Survey (HORS, 2001).

Table 9.2 Participants' religion

	Asian and White	Black and White	Chinese and White	White Other
No religion	15	23	28	20
Atheist/Agnostic	35	42	43	34
Christian	5	33	14	23
Buddhist	3	3	29	7
Hindu	23	0	0	0
Sikh	5	0	0	0
Muslim	13	2	0	6
Other	3	0	1	0

Base: The numbers from each of the ethnic groups were expressed as a percentage. For example, the 40 black and white participants were taken as 100 per cent.
Note: This was done for reasons of comparability although it is acknowledged that this is not the best way of making group comparisons as for example, there were only seven participants in the Chinese group compared to 40 in the black and white group.

A large number of participants from all interethnic backgrounds described themselves as being atheist/agnostic. This echoes findings from the interviews from both qualitative studies where participants spoke about their difficulty in choosing a religion as well as other sources on religion (HORS, 2001). The interview findings indicated that they were cautious about choosing a religion because they did not wish to upset parents or relatives. Hence they chose to be atheist, agnostic or to have no religion at all. More black interethnic participants said they were atheist and agnostics (45 per cent, table 9.4), followed by Chinese, white Other and Asians. Again, this is reflected in other research findings (Modood et al., 1997, HORS survey, 2001).

Chinese and black interethnic groups were most likely to say that they had no religion. The Asian interethnic group was the least likely to do so. The third biggest group was Christianity, with more black and white Other interethnic saying they were Christians. A larger proportion of participants identifying themselves as 'Christian' may be because of a range of factors. First, there were more black and white participants in the sample, many of whom said they were Christian. Second, many white Other and some Asians and Chinese also defined themselves as Christians. Hinduism was the next most popular answer because there were more Indians than others Asians in the Asian sample overall. Also more Indians tend to be in interethnic relationships than other Asians (the reasons for this are discussed in the chapter on interethnic relationships).

The Muslim religion came out the strongest in proportion to the number of Asian and white participants. Out of the 8 per cent of Bangladeshis and Pakistanis all said they were Muslim. Two per cent of Indians were also Muslim. This indicates that interethnic people whose parents were Muslim tended to have stronger affiliations with their religion. This had a direct effect on their identity in that those who affiliated with Islam chose to identify themselves as Asian.

A *t* test[5] showed a significant gender difference; t (2) =3.75, p<.05. More males than females said they had no religious affiliations or that they were atheists/ agnostics. Of the 42 per cent who said they were atheist/agnostic 24 per cent were males and 18 per cent were females, 9 per cent of males said they had no religion compared to 6 per cent of females. There were also age differences, with a trend of younger participants having less religious affiliation; this generational contrast has been echoed by other findings (Modood et al., 1997).

Factors Important in Describing Identity

Next, participants were asked about factors that were important in *describing* their identity; '*suppose you were describing yourself, which of the following would say something important about you? For each of the items choose a number according to how important you think it would be.* They were given a 4-point scale of not important to very important (Appendix, Figure A.1).

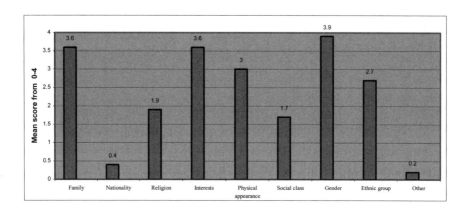

Figure 9.3 The mean score for factors that were affecting their identity

---

    5   As explained in the methods chapter a *t* test was conducted to understand gender differences on each area; the findings of this will be discussed at the end of each section.

Figure 9.3, illustrates the mean score for factors important in describing ethnic identity. Apart from gender, 'interests'[6] was 'very important' in the way they described their identity. Family and physical appearance were the next popular items to be ticked. Ethnic group was also fairly high. Nationality scored the lowest. This contradicts the findings of a study conducted by Modood et al. (1997) that found that nationality was a strong element of self description. However, their findings of family, religion and physical appearance as being important elements were supported here. More specifically, 76 per cent (appendix, figure A.1) of participants placed 'interests' as being 'very important' to the way they would describe themselves, and 68 per cent thought family was 'very important', 47 per cent of participants placed physical appearance as being 'very important'.

Participants commonly ticked nationality and social class as 'not important' descriptors of their ethnic identity. Eighty three per cent said that nationality was 'not important' and 21 per cent said class was also 'not important'. However, participants clearly think that class is of some relevance, as 71 per cent ticked it as being 'a little important'. The answers may be linked to their ideological stance. It could be that the ideology of individual interests and personalities are seen to be more significant than class and nationality. But it also suggests that social class may still be of some importance. Religion was also another factor that was seen by 29 per cent of participants as 'not important' in describing their ethnic identity, although others considered it as being 'very important' to them (27 per cent). Religion seemed to be 'very important' to some participants and not at all to others.

Four per cent of participants ticked 'other', under which they all wrote 'occupation' as being important in describing their identity. With regard to ethnic differences, black and Asian interethnic participants were more likely to say that ethnic group was important in describing their identity. The other main ethnic difference was that family was the most commonly mentioned descriptor amongst Asian and white interethnic. Ninety per cent identified it as being very important compared to 62 per cent of blacks and 59 per cent of white Other and Chinese.

There were no significant gender differences. In terms of age, younger participants tended to place interests and physical appearance as being more important in describing identity than older participants, whereas older participants said social class and family were important.

---

6   'Interests' included past time activities such as reading, music, sports, hobbies etc.

Factors that Influenced Ethnic Identity

In order to gain a better understanding of the factors that influenced participants' definition of ethnic identity, they were asked a direct question on it; '*which of the following would you say influences your ethnic identity?*' This was asked because findings from the two previous studies indicated that factors participants thought were important in their self description differed, in some cases, from factors that really influenced their identity. They were given nine categories.

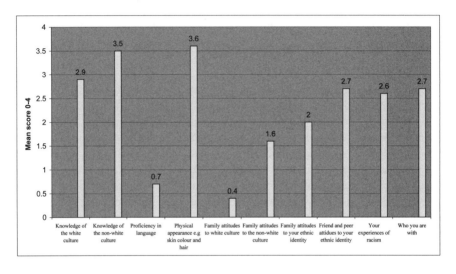

Figure 9.4 The mean score for factors that influenced participants' ethnic identity

Based on a 1–4 point scale, physical appearance and knowledge of the non white culture scored the highest (Figure 9.4). Family attitudes to the white culture and proficiency in language scored the least.

Sixty five percent of all participants ticked physical appearance as being very important in influencing their ethnic identity (appendix, figure A.2). This was also found in the qualitative research where participants indicated that other people's ethnic identification of them was based on their physical appearance, i.e. skin colour, hair and face features. This, for many affected the ethnic identity that they adopted.

Knowledge of the non-white culture and the white culture (although to a lesser degree) was the next most influencing factor. Once again, the identity that they adopted was influenced for example, by their ability to understand the customs of both the cultures that they had inherited. The importance of knowing the white culture is a surprising finding and is one that participants from the first study referred to as 'not important'. Knowledge of the white culture was 'important' to many participants (61 per cent) here. However, 27 per cent placed it as being 'a little important' compared to only 2 per cent placing knowledge of the non white culture as being 'a little important'.

'Who you are with' was 'very important' to 10 per cent of participants and 'important' to 59 per cent of them. This supports the findings in the previous two qualitative studies and the theory of a chameleon identity. Experiences of racism also influenced their ethnic identity. Although it is difficult to say why this is, it could be assumed that the experience of racial prejudice from one ethnic group might have put them off adopting this identity on the ground that this group might be less accepting of them. Friends and peers' attitudes to ethnic identity were also strong influencing factors and ranked slightly higher than family attitudes to ethnic identity. Family attitudes to white culture and language proficiency seemed to be the least influencing factors. In contrast, the findings from the qualitative studies indicated language proficiency to be an essential factor.

There were two main ethnic differences brought to light by these questionnaire findings. First, slightly more black participants placed experiences of racism as being relevant than the other ethnic groups. Second, proficiency in language was said to be less significant by black interethnic than other groups. This may be because generally both parents share the same language, unlike for example, Asian and white interethnic.

Statistically there was a significant gender difference; t (2) =2.76, p<.05. Overall, more females tended to be sensitive to physical appearance and family as they were factors that were placed as having a greater impact on their identity than on males. Younger participants tended to say that interests and physical appearance would say something important about their ethnic identity than older participants. Also physical appearance, peers and friends influenced the ethnic identity of the younger more than older participants.

Conclusion

For many children, home and school environments were when they first thought about their identities. At this stage they appeared to have little sense of choice and tended to adopt either the Asian or white identity. This is supported by other research findings. For example, Aboud (1988) has argued that the identification of ethnic groups occurs around the age of five and that ethnic identity as a group member takes places around the age of ten. Although others have indicated that it could be even younger than that (Jacobs, 1992). Wilson's (1987) study of the interethnic also showed that ethnic identification might happen even earlier.

The younger participants generally assumed they had to be 'one or the other'. According to Goffman's (1959) concept of the everyday world, children soon learn the strategies and rules of the social environment through peer interaction. The relationship between how we see ourselves and how others see us also becomes important. Mead's (1934) categorisation of the 'I' (unique individuality) 'Me' (attitudes of significant others that have been internalised) shows that what people think about us is no less significant to what we think about ourselves.

As the individuals matured, their physical appearance and increasing knowledge of both the white and Asian culture influenced them. For example, adolescents with the physical attributes of an Asian ethnicity, an intimate knowledge of their Asian religion and the ability to speak the language were identified and accepted as Asian. Physical appearance was presented as a key influencing/constraining factor in participants' abilities to emphasise different ethnicities. As Mead (1934) would argue, the self is embodied; selves without bodies do not make sense. We reach out with our selves, and others reach out to us. This begins from the body (Mead, 1934). The mind and the self coexist. The young people here signaled their ethnicity to people through their physical appearance and internalised the ways that other people received this. Based on the message from other people, some individuals believed, for example, that those with predominantly 'Asian' characteristics could not adopt the white identity as easily as those with characteristics that were less easily pigeonholed. Problems related to recognition by others are integrally related to issues of personal self definition. The young people faced difficulties because of socially defined discourses about who it is possible to be. This inevitably shaped the ways they perceived their identity and their sense of personal agency.

Other researchers have also found that individuals constructed their ethnic identity in terms of their skin colour and features. Clark and Clark (1947) were one of the first to do so when they examined black children's identity in terms of dolls and skin colour. Aboud (1998) and Wilson (1987) found that children tended to identify each other through physical appearance. Those who had siblings with more western characteristics said they were treated worse/differently than their siblings by relatives and outsiders. However, the treatment of individuals based on skin colour was a complex matter. It was said that Asian relatives tended to treat darker skinned siblings better whilst white relatives preferred the fairer sibling. This maybe because each of the sets of relatives was able to relate better to the sibling whose physical appearance represented/resembled their own ethnicity. An important aspect of physical appearance is that it can be used as a marker for making an individual feel accepted or 'different. The discourse of 'difference' is important to the understanding of ethnic identity. It involves including and excluding and for the individual a sense of acceptance or rejection.

Many studies have put forward the importance of parental influence on a child's identity. Wilson (1987) found, for example, that the mother's view on racism related to the child's identity. Mothers particularly brought into the relationship beliefs and feelings from their past which influenced the way they treated their children. In most of the families issues of race, ethnicity and culture were a central part of the family. Although Katz stressed that peer relationships and environmental factors may later affect the children's identity, it should be noted that the children might encounter and negotiate these factors as well as influence from relatives and siblings at an early time in their lives. That is, it is not just the mother's influence that they would come under.

In the US, social scientists have also found that for children to negotiate a positive identity the role of the family is an important one. If the child does not receive a sense of integrated self, of racial consciousness, from the family he/she may not be adequately prepared to deal with racism in society and may subsequently have low self-esteem (Bradshaw 1992). However, for some interethnic individuals society may fail to confirm the sense of self-esteem and integration that the family had offered.

Another key element to influence the young people's identity was religion. Parents often chose to bring up their children with both partner's religions. However, some of those children who were brought up with the choice of two religions reported feeling confused; not knowing either of the religions fully; under pressure from parents and relatives to practice their religion; and unable to make up their minds about which religion to adopt. On the contrary, a few individuals valued being brought up with two religions in that they were able to pass as being of a particular religious background when it suited them. This was especially important for those with one parent who was Muslim in that they were able to emphasise the other inheritance when faced with today's climate of Islamophobia.

Language was a powerful device in identity construction, whether a particular ethnicity, interethnic or chameleon like identity, as illustrated by Goffman (1959). The young people spoke about the importance of language and the ability to speak it fluently, manipulate their accents and intonations, all determining the ability to practice the chameleon identity. Speech accommodation in social psychology is concerned with how individuals modify their accent, dialect or intonation in accordance with different social contexts. It is recognised by psychologists that this can be used for impression management (Potter and Wetherell, 1987, Burr, 1995, Sarbin, 1986, Gergen, 1987, Harré, 1987). In addition, Sarup (1996) has argued that much of our identity depends on the linguistic (vocabulary, accent, the medium use) resources available to us.

The process of being *identified* by others based on their physical appearance and knowledge of an Asian language were predominant factors of ethnic identification. Being identified and labelled by others may have constrained participants in choosing a separate identity. They may feel unable to choose an identity that did not match outsider's identification of them, and felt compelled to go with the alter-ascribed identity rather than their ego-recognised identity (Weinreich, 2003). Nonetheless, the participants in this study did not only rely solely on other people's identification of them; their negotiation of experiences such as culture, family, friends and community also influenced the identities they emphasised.

Another factor that influenced identity was the young people's own perception of acceptance and rejection. Both appeared to be powerful indicators of which ethnicity they would identify with. They tended to adopt the identity of the ethnic group they received the most acceptance from. They generally reported more acceptance from white peers than from Asians. However, this is complicated by the fact that they perceived more acceptance from Asian grandparents and extended relatives than their white counterparts. Acceptance alone did not influence participant's choice of ethnic identity. Some reported not being accepted by the white extended families but still adopted the white identity. This may have been the result of other forms of acceptance and belonging which bonded them to that ethnicity. Alternatively rejection might itself have prompted a greater psychological need to belong to that ethnic group. It should be noted that a positive self concept and identity may be related to the acceptance of one's ethnicity, but negative evaluations do not necessarily mean lowered self-esteem.

The social identity theory explains identity as being rooted in generic human processes, with group identification being a powerful influence. Individuals usually do not identify in an all or nothing fashion but form partial-identifications with individuals and groups although of course some identifications may be more important to them than others. However, some did not rely on others ascribing of their identity but created self-definitions. As many matured and encountered greater societal experience they appeared to move away from being reliant on other people and had a better awareness of identity processes of ethnic identity. In short, they appeared to have achieved a greater sense of choice and autonomy over their ethnic identity.

Chapter 10
The Impact of being Interethnic

This chapter, in presenting some qualitative but more quantitative findings, will discuss the impact of being of an interethnic background. It has been somewhat covered throughout the book, however, because of the nature of the topic it is worth summarising in a section of its own.

The qualitative studies showed that children must create a sense of self based on their experiences and influencing factors. This includes parents, siblings and extended family. A self that emerges from parents and relatives may also then be challenged after encountering peers, teachers, the media and other societal factors.

In this research parents in general viewed their children's interethnic identity in a positive light, though some were concerned about the negative experiences such as racism and inability to fit in with either of the two cultures that the children may face. As a parent stated:

> We do worry about things erm … you know if people will be racist towards them, if they'll not fit in, already my ones are treated differently from other children. They're not quiet Asian or white. That is our biggest worry. [Khalida]

There was also concern about how grandparents and extended relatives treated the children. As discussed in other chapters both parents and children felt that the children were under pressure from grandparents and relatives to share their culture, religion, skin colour and ultimately ethnic identity.

Interviews and informal conversations with the Asian grandparents of the interethnic families indicated that they felt a sense of embarrassment about not being able to speak fluent English. This particularly affected the fathers who were seen as heads of the family. They may have felt helpless faced with a son or daughter married to a partner who spoke a 'foreign' language and had a 'foreign' culture that they did not have a full understanding of:

> It's more difficult with the father, you know, because he is the head of the family and if he can't communicate with his son in-law or daughter in-law then he feels like a failure, I mean he knows what English to use when he goes to the doctor, shopping but it's more difficult when you have to have long conversations about family, religion you know. [Abu]

Physical appearance, the ability to speak the ethnic minority language, religion and class all influenced the young people. In turn, the impact of being of an interethnic background was that the young people felt under pressure to conform to expectations of parents, relatives, and other external elements they encountered such as peers, teachers and the media.

Quantitative Results

The qualitative findings fed into questions asked in the quantitative questionnaire. When asked about the experiences of being interethnic. 'Having the best of two inherited cultures' was something that all participants placed as being one of the biggest benefits. The mean score was the highest for that item (Figure 1). Seventy one per cent said it was a benefit all the time and 22 per cent a lot of the time. Not being racially prejudiced also scored highly, 68 per cent said it was a benefit all the time, 25 per cent a lot of the time. Having relatives from different ethnic backgrounds, being able to fit in with white and non-whites and understanding of racial prejudice were other benefits, as was having a choice over which ethnic identity to adopt and being admired because of their 'exotic' physical appearance.

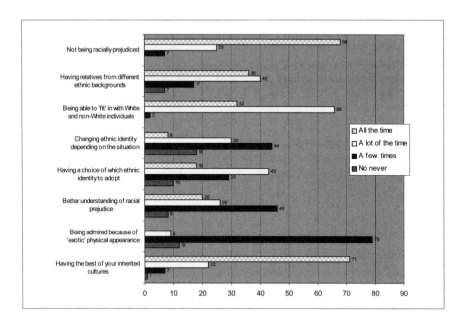

Figure 10.1 Do you think being of interethnic/mixed parentage has any benefits?

Base: The participants from each of the ethnic groups were expressed as percentage.

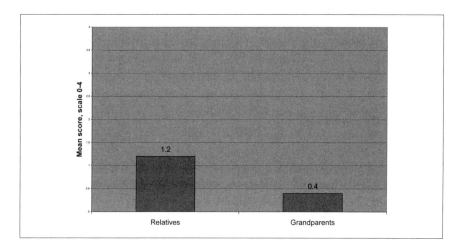

Figure 10.2 The mean score of difficulties with grandparents and relatives
Base: All participants.

Difficulties with Grandparents and Relatives

To gauge the participants' experiences with their extended families they were asked two questions '*did you experience any difficulties with your grandparents because of being interethnic/ mixed parentage?*'[1] and '*did you experience any difficulties with other relatives because of being inter-ethnic/ mixed parentage?*' They were given choices of '*Not at all, A few times, Several times* and *All the time* and *Don't Know*'.

Figure 10.2 illustrates the mean score for participants who said they had difficulties with relatives and grandparents. The scores were generally low, although relatives scored higher than grandparents.

The majority, 80 per cent (Appendix, Figure A.3), said they did not have any difficulties with their grandparents by ticking 'not at all'. However, the qualitative research findings indicated difficulties with both grandparents and relatives. It could be that participants were more expressive in their interview accounts than they were able to be on the questionnaire and also better able to ask questions to the interviewer and think of specific situations or incitements.

In terms of the findings here, 46 per cent answered 'not at all' to having difficulties with relatives, however 16 per cent answered several times and 27 per cent a few times. The reasons for greater difficulties with relatives than with grandparents are explained by interview accounts where the interethnic children (and their parents) had said their grandparents (and parents) had made greater

---

1   The term 'mixed parentage' was used for the questionnaire rather than 'interethnic' to make it easier for participants to understand.

effort in accepting them. Their relatives were less accepting. This applied to both the Asian and white extended family and, according to the findings from this questionnaire, also for participants of other interethnic backgrounds.

There were no significant gender differences or noticeable ethnic or age differences.

Literature on people with a 'mixed' heritage background discusses the risk of them being stuck between two cultures. Park's (1928) and Stonequist's (1937) concept of the marginal man is perhaps the most well known. Consequently, this questionnaire would have been incomplete without exploring this issue. It asked, '*Do you feel that you are "in between" [representations of] the two cultures?*' The response categories were: '*not at all, sometimes, a lot of the time, all the time*'.

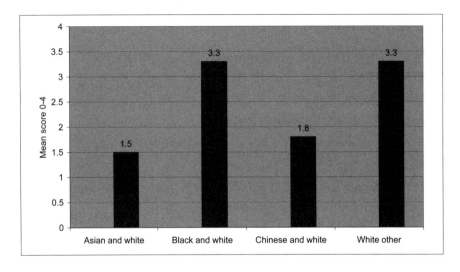

Figure 10.3 The mean score of participants who thought that they were in between two cultures

Base: All participants.

A large number of participants overall said they felt that they were 'in between the two cultures'. The black and white and white Other groups both scored highly with a mean score of 3.3 (Figure 10.3). The Asian and white group scored the lowest. It was found that 65 per cent of white Other interethnic participants answered 'all the time' more than any other group. They are followed by black and white participants who scored 48 per cent.

In terms of ethnic differences, surprisingly, white Other participants (65 per cent) were more likely to say they were 'in between the two cultures' than the other ethnic groups. The black group (48 per cent) followed them. Both these groups also ticked 'a lot of the time' more often than other groups. Also surprising was that Asians were the least likely to answer being 'in between the two cultures'. Only 13 per cent of them ticked all the time and 47 per cent 'not at all'. The Chinese and white group followed with 35 per cent answering 'not at all' and 17 per cent all the time. Many participants said they were 'in between the two cultures', particularly the white Other and black and white groups. The reasons why it is these two groups, in particular, are unclear.

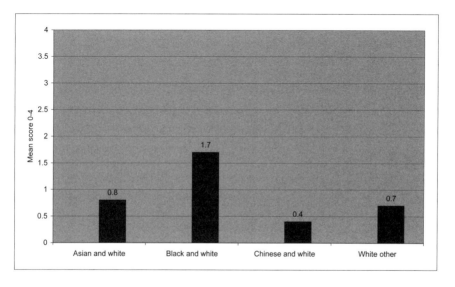

Figure 10.4 The mean score for participants who thought that they were under pressure to choose between two cultures
Base: All participants.

A follow up question asked '*how much do you feel that you are under pressure to choose between the two cultures?*' The response categories were the same as the above question.

An overwhelming number of participants answered 'not at all' (Appendix, Figure 10.4). It could be assumed from this response that whilst participants perceived that they have representations of their parents' two cultures to negotiate they did not view this in a negative way and did not feel pressurised. The other explanation, of course, may be that the questions were not fully understood, but this is unlikely given the large numbers who ticked this item and that few contacted the researcher for clarification with these two sets of questions.

According to the mean scores (Figure 10.4) more black and white interethnic participants said they thought they were under pressure to choose 'between the two cultures' than the other groups. The Chinese and white scored the lowest. They were the least likely to feel under pressure to choose between the two groups. None of them answered 'all the time' and 82 per cent answered 'not at all'. The white Other group was the next least likely to feel under pressure, followed by the Asian and whites. Overall, more black and white participants, when cross referenced by ethnic groups answered that they were under pressure to 'choose between the two cultures', with a relatively high number ticking 'a lot of the time' (9 per cent) and 'sometimes' (17 per cent).

When the answers for both these two questions were analysed together it appeared that overall black and white interethnic people felt more under pressure from their parents' cultures. Whilst the Chinese interethnic viewed themselves to be less pressured.

There were no significant gender differences. The non statistical analysis showed there to be a trend towards younger participants saying that they were under pressure to choose between their parents' cultures than older participants. The reason for this may be that older participants, because of greater experience, had negotiated the cultures and thus felt less under pressure to do so. The younger participants may have yet to reach that stage.

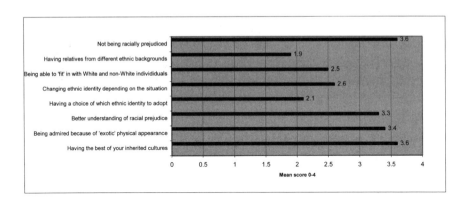

Figure 10.5 The mean score for the benefits of being interethnic
Base: All participants.

The Positive and Negative Aspects of being Interethnic

Participants were asked *'Do you think that being of mixed parentage/inter-ethnic background has any benefits?'* They were given nine response items and a scale of *'no never, a few times, a lot of the time* and *all the time.*

Having the best of their inherited cultures was something that all placed as being one of the biggest benefits of being interethnic. The mean score was the highest for that item (Figure 10.5). Seventy one per cent placed it as a benefit all the time and 22 per cent a lot of the time. Not being racially prejudiced also scored highly, 68 per cent said it was a benefit all the time, 25 per cent a lot of the time. Having relatives from different ethnic backgrounds, being able to fit in with white and non-whites and understanding of racial prejudice were other benefits, as was having a choice on which ethnic identity to adopt and being admired because of their 'exotic' physical appearance.

Changing ethnic identity depending on the situation (18 per cent), being admired because of physical appearance (12 per cent) and having a choice of which ethnic identity to adopt (10 per cent) were the most common items not to be ticked as being of benefit for some participants. But they were benefits for others; for example, being admired because of physical appearance was a benefit 'a few times' for 79 per cent of participants.

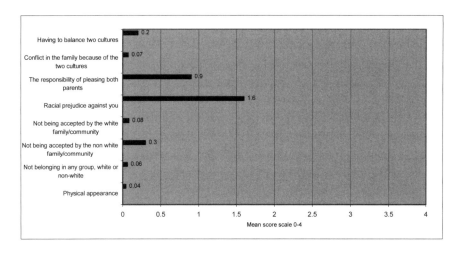

Figure 10.6 The mean score for negative aspects of being interethnic
Base: All participants.

There was only one main ethnic difference. For the Asians and Chinese interethnic group 'having the best of inherited cultures' was less of a benefit than for blacks and Europeans. Eleven per cent of Asians and 14 per cent of Chinese placed it as 'never' being a benefit. They were the only groups to tick the 'never' box.

Next, participants were also asked '*Do you think that there are any negative aspects to being of mixed parentage/inter-ethnic background?*' Once again they were given nine response items and a scale of 'no never, a few times, a lot of the time and all the time.'

Many ticked 'no never' for all items in this section. For the 'Other (please specify)' category some participants wrote '*on the whole a positive experience*' '*feel unique*' '*two world perspectives*' as their additional comments.

Experiencing racial prejudice because of their interethnic background rated the highest negative factor (Figure 10.6). The responsibility of pleasing both parents was the next highest. Physical appearance was the least negative aspect. There were no ethnic differences with the first item, however, there was with the latter. Black interethnic participants most commonly answered that they had experienced racial prejudice against them. There was no noticeable age difference, or statistical difference in relation to gender.

Discussion and Conclusion

There were many positives associated with being of an interethnic background. But there were also some negatives. Both the qualitative and quantitative findings indicated that racial prejudice was the main negative aspect. This was in the form of direct negative comments or indirect, such as comments targeted at the particular group that, unknown to the perpetrators; the interethnic individual was also a member of. Those who had multiple identities or a situational identity too spoke of feeling 'uncomfortable' 'angry' or 'sad' when one of their inherited ethnic groups came under negative comments or criticism. This was normally the minority group which was then an undesirable ethnicity to adopt by these young people. More than that, the young people disliked being made to feel 'different'. According to Goffman (1963) undesired 'differentness' can lead to stigma and that is an '*attribute that is deeply discrediting*' to an individual's identity. Goffman believed that the stigmatised person may have a variety of ways of dealing with it for example by attempting to repair the stigma or by dividing his or her world into the people that the stigma could be revealed to. This was reflected here, whereby the young people indicated that they were selective in what identity they emphasised and to whom. They managed the tension created by one of their inheritances being criticised by ignoring the behaviour or making contradictory positive comments. However, they still reported feeling hurt that their ethnic heritage was not accepted.

Overall, however, despite some of the negative consequences, the positives of being interethnic, for most of the young people, far out weighted the negatives.

And there were many positives. As already discussed being able to speak several languages, practice two cultures, having relatives from two cultures, physical beauty, and being able to adopt a fluid situational identity or having multiple identities were some of the main benefits to being of an interethnic background. But also of benefit was the appreciation for other cultures and empathy for people of all cultural and racial backgrounds that the participants reported feeling as a result of either being in an interethnic marriage/relationship or having inherited two races and cultures.

The question 'where do I fit?' may be one that is asked by all. According to the marginal theorists it is one that may be especially important for those with a 'mixed' background. They believe that interethnic people will experience social isolation and be rejected by both inherited groups. However, this challenge appeared to have been overcome by their understanding of the cultures and ability to fit in and appreciate a range of cultural nuances and requirements. The young people's empathy with diversity, ability to negotiate cultures very different to each other and move smoothly between ethnic groups is an art of to be admired in modern society.

Chapter 11
Conclusion: The Future is Interethnics

The book explored the identity of South Asian and white interethnic adolescents – a group yet to be studied in Britain. This final chapter will discuss some of the main findings and the future for the interethnic, including the impact of having Obama as the US president.

Interethnic Relationships

The research presented in this book provided an insight into the interethnic relationships between Asian and white individuals. Interethnic relationships are important to the understanding of race and ethnicity and cultural values. The findings illustrated how even today such relationships can be controversial. The literature review illustrated how relationships between Asians and whites have existed for centuries. Studies on inter ethnic relationships have attempted to understand why individuals entered into such relationships. They have suggested a range of theories, these include economic benefits, being unable to find someone from their own ethnicity and seeking a vehicle by which to prove themselves 'colour blind'. There is an implied assumption that people who form interethnic relationships do so for different reasons to non-interethnic relationships. However, people in this research indicated consistently that their reasons for entering into such relationships did not differ widely from those who enter same ethnic relationships – for example, attraction, love and shared interests.

Individuals who were in, or had been in, interethnic relationships spoke of having experienced negative reactions from their extended friends, family and – in the case of Asians from their community. Accounts indicated the Asian extended family tended to be initially hostile to the relationship but came to accept it gradually. This might be because the Asian community is close knit and strives for a collective identity; which can be threatened when an individual forms a relationship with someone of another ethnicity. According to Moscovici (1976) social interaction can be understood in terms of minority and majority, with the majority attempting to impose social 'norms' and the minority trying to makes its point of view heard. He believed that society as a whole is made up of the establishment of 'norm' and is divided into the four categories of what is permitted, what is forbidden, what is included and what is excluded. Social control is valued by the majority; however, social change is important for the minority and marginal subgroups and can manifest itself as a struggle against the 'establishment'. Therefore, change from the 'norm' often leads to conflict as found in the research presented in this book.

Negative reactions and lack of acceptance from the extended family sometimes meant a loss of contact. This loss appeared to result in the children identifiying less with that ethnicity. For example, in the case of the Asian extended family the child appeared to have greater negative thoughts towards them and less affinity with Asians. Another influencing factor on the children's identity was the parents' views of their own ethnic identities and attitudes to interethnic relationships. For example, Asians who had lived a western way of life tended to also view their children as being more white than Asian, or as 'individuals' without a particular ethnicity. The attitudes and experiences of the parents were internalised by some children. This in turn influenced the children's ethnic identity process, at least when they were young. This is borne out by other research studies on the interethnic (Wilson, 1987, Katz, 1998) which suggest that young children's perception of ethnic identity was influenced, to some extent, by parents' attitudes.

Non-interethnic Asian and White

This research shows that Asian families appear to identify strongly with their Asian culture, language and family. Religion was also an important element particularly for Muslims who are increasingly turning to religion, possibly as a way of consolidating their sense of identity and coping with recent upheaval. Accounts from follow up interviews conducted after September 11 (supported by other research findings, ICM, 2002) indicated that Muslims believe they have experienced negative reactions from the general population following the attacks.

   Some social scientists believe that there can be little room to exercise freedom of choice to make life style decisions when cultures overlap and are in a process of hybridity (Bhabha, 1990). In this study, young Asian men and women spoke about juggling both the communities' traditional attitudes and the changing nature of the wider society. There were also generational differences and tensions which some of the young and old were unable to cope with. However, there is little social science research exploring these issues. While there has been a range of work focusing on Asian females (Brah, 1996, others) Asian males have been largely ignored with the few exceptions of work such as Alexander's (2000) focusing on Asian youth, culture and masculinity and Baumann (1996). It is important to understand and take a fresh look at the experiences of young Asian men and women given some of the issues they have raised here in relation to religion, racism, community, family and identity.

   In terms of the attitudes and lifestyle choices of Asian and white young people, it was found that they tended to identify with peers of the same ethnicity; as also demonstrated by other researchers (Tajfel, 1978, Rutland, 1999), whose findings indicated that children preferred friends/peers of their own ethnicity. This was also reflected in terms of attitudes towards interethnic relationships. Both Asian and whites believed it was better to marry someone of the same ethnicity. There was, however, a trend amongst children and adolescents to be more positive about interethnic relationships than adults. Although with some of these children there appeared to be a gap between normative statements and statements of intent. That is, whilst they were positive about people in general forming interethnic relationships, they themselves would not consider marrying someone of another ethnicity. They appeared to be battling with an ideological belief (in freedom of choice) and their perception of society's disapproval of interethnic relationships. The findings here suggest that the issue of interethnic relationships was surrounded by representations of racism, discrimination and idealism.

Another key finding was the extent of bullying and racism. Most of the children and adolescents had either been victims of bullying themselves or knew victims. They also reported experiencing racist bullying. Many social writers have documented the racial prejudice that ethnic minority children and adolescents have experienced. It was found here that this also applied to white children and adolescents, though to a lesser degree. However, little was done by teachers and parents to combat this type of racism. This may be because teachers are not equipped to deal with such issues because of a lack of training.

Racism may be linked to a threatened identity. According to social identity theory, threats to identity can lead to hostility towards the out-group (Tajfel, 1974). Breakwell et al. (1984) applied this theory to the study of young people's attitudes towards unemployed workers. They found that unemployed young people upgraded the status of 'unemployment' to deal with their threatened identity. According to them, this method of dealing with devalued identity is one of the many ways we cope with threatened identities. Weinreich (1986) also argued that racism can increase when groups are faced with threatened identity.

To fully understand racism and to gain a complete picture of multicultural society in Britain we need to study white culture and identity. Indeed, when the white people in this study were asked about their identity, most were surprised. Some of the reactions found in this research supported Dyer's theory of the white identity being perceived to be the norm and not 'problematic'. Back (1996) has noted that 'while an enormous amount of attention has been paid to the study of ethnic minority young people, there is little known about the ethnicity of white youth and the way racism features in their lives' (1993, p. 217). There has however been more work on white identity, which balances this, including Back's own work (1996, as discussed previously). Also, for example, Thompson et al. (1999), who argue that ideas of white national identity take place on a local level as people draw boundaries. Nayak (1999) focuses on the cultural identities of young white males and the processes and techniques they use to enact 'whiteness'. For these men, being born British was not enough to be 'English' if you were black. Their identity was confirmed through a discourse of 'whiteness'.

A focus on white identities serves to help de-racialise ethnic minority groups and challenges the framework of constructed ethnic minorities as a social problem (Bonnett, 1996, Dyer, 1997). There needs to be more work on the experiences of white people, in particular for example the working class in Britain, amongst whom there is a feeling that their voices are not being heard, their needs not being met, both by academia and the government. Many of these individuals are sharing tight resources and living in poverty, alongside ethnic minority groups. This can create powerful feelings of resentment, injustice and fear on both sides, as illustrated by the Bradford riots and reactions to September 11.

Like the interethnics non-interethnic individuals also adopted chameleon like practices depending on their social context. This is supported by other researchers – for example research on South Asians, in Britain, indicated that 'progressive females' were able to do this most successfully, followed by 'progressive males'. However, 'orthodox' males and females were the most rigid (Kelly, 1989, Northover, 1988). They found that females tended to have a greater ability to express a situational identity than males. This situational identity is also expressed by Waters' (1990) participants in the US: 'When I'm at school, and I sit with my black friends and, sometimes, I'm ashamed to say this, but my accent changes. I learn all the words, I switch. Well, when I'm with my friends, black friends, I say I'm black, black American. When I'm with my Haitian friends, I say I'm Haitian' (1990, p. 807). However, the ability to develop a situational or chameleon identity may be strengthened for interethnic individuals because of their dual cultural heritage and physical appearance.

One common assumption surrounding interethnic people and minority children is that they are fragmented and 'between cultures' and as such do not belong to any one group (Anwar, 1998). According to Ballard (1977) Asians being 'in between cultures' is an oversimplification of a wide range of complex personal experiences. Young Asians are not faced with an either/or situation (Ghuman, 1994). The findings in this research shows that they are able to negotiate issues in a sophisticated way and express situational identities to suit the social context. They, like some of the interethnic, worked towards a synthesis of Asian and British values and presenting an identity that suited the situation.

The Interethnic

Factors Which Influenced Identity

Human identity is the result of a complex interaction between individual and society over time. Identities are located internally and externally affected by time and space, biography and history. Having briefly discussed a number of different perspectives (in the literature review and throughout the book) what is needed is a framework that allows us to understand identity processes no matter what the situation, and one which encompasses both the individual and collective. This book goes someway to developing such a framework leaning on ideas and concepts provided by Mead, Goffman, the Social Identity Theory and Social Representation theory.

The findings indicated that a variety of factors and realms influenced the interethnic: parents and relatives, peers, the community, physical appearance and cultural knowledge. Negotiating these spheres generally led to a range of identity phases for the young people. The first was constructing identities as they encountered a new social context: for example with peers and teachers. For many, home and school environments were when they first thought about their identities. At this stage they appeared to have little sense of choice and tended to adopt either the Asian or white identity. They generally assumed that they had to be 'one or the other'. According to Goffman's (1959) concept of the everyday world, children soon learn the strategies and rules of the social environment through peer interaction. The relationship between how we see ourselves and how others see us also becomes important. Mead's (1934) categorisation of the 'I' (unique individuality) 'Me' (attitudes of significant others that have been internalised) shows that what people think about us is no less significant to what we think about ourselves.

As participants matured, their physical appearance and increasing knowledge of both the white and Asian culture influenced them. For example, adolescents with the physical attributes of an Asian ethnicity, an intimate knowledge of their Asian religion and the ability to speak the language were identified and accepted as Asian. Culture was an important influencing factor perhaps because some facets of Asian and white cultures were very different, for example, food, clothes, language and religion. Cultural aspects such as language and religion allowed individuals to participate in the collective domain, the community. Physical appearance and cultural knowledge also tended to be used as markers for other people's identification of the young people.

Physical appearance, more than any other aspect, was a significant influencing factor and a recurring theme in this book. How the young people looked determined the identity that they were able to pass as. Research on African Americans has indicated the importance of the ways physical appearance such as skin colour differences affect the ways people are treated and their life chances (Keith and Herring, 1991). Darker coloured black people are more likely to experience discrimination and lower incomes than their lighter skinned counterparts (Keith and Herring, 1991). A number of social scientists in the UK have also written about the importance of physical appearance to ethnic minorities (Modood et al., 1997, Hall, 2000). Mead (1934) acknowledged the body as being an integral aspect of the self. However, there are many constraints in embodiment for example, gender, ethnicity or race, physical appearance (Mead, 1934). These factors all influence the resources available for 'impression management' (Goffman, 1959) and presentation of the self'.

Goffman (1963) suggests that visibility is very important to a stigmatised person and their identity "That which can be told about an individual's social identity at all times during his daily round and by all persons he encounters therein will be of great importance to him" (1963, p. 65). The individual's presentation of the self will be greatly influenced by whether their 'differentness' is immediately visible to others or not. For many of the interethnic people in this research their visible appearance and in particular skin colour was crucially important. It influenced their sense of ethnic identity, the ways that others viewed them and their sense of autonomy and choice. It also impacted on the sense of acceptance or rejection that they felt. Goffman argues that for a stigmatised person, acceptance is central. Stigma may have the effect of 'spoiling' ones social identity. When faced with a discredited social identity the individual needs to select a personal identity and whether 'to display or not to display; to tell or not tell; to let on or not to let on; to lie or not to lie ... to whom, how when, and where' (p. 57). This Goffman called the 'management of discrediting information' and personal identity. The research presented here found evidence of individuals managing their identity in a number of ways to reflect their social context.

The processes of identification and self-identification discussed above are also captured by discourse analysis, for example, by the concept of positioning; the notion that individuals are influenced by the ways other people 'position' them (Burr, 1995). However, some individuals may undergo constant change and resist these 'positions'. In this book it was found that the young people were influenced by others' 'positioning' of them and negotiated their own positions with regard to identity. It seemed that a decision on whether to accept or reject others 'positioning' depended on the social context and associated social and personal gains and losses. The person offering the 'positioning' was also an important factor, for example, if it was someone they did not wish to upset or offend they were more likely to accept the 'positioning'. On the other hand, if it was a person who had relatively little importance in their life they were more likely to dismiss this 'positioning'.

Another factor that influenced identity was an individual's own perception of acceptance and rejection. Both appeared to be powerful indicators of which ethnicity they would identify with. They tended to adopt the identity of the ethnic group they received the most acceptance from, and generally reported more acceptance from white peers than from Asians. However, this is complicated by the fact that they perceived more support and acceptance from Asian grandparents and extended relatives than their white counterparts. Acceptance alone did not influence participant's choice of ethnic identity. Some reported not being accepted by the white extended families but still adopted the white identity. This may have been the result of other forms of acceptance and belonging which bonded them to that ethnicity but also because a white identity is perhaps more socially acceptable than an Asian or interethnic identity. Alternatively rejection might itself have prompted a greater psychological need to belong to that ethnic group. It should be noted that a positive self concept and identity may be related to the acceptance of one's ethnicity, but negative evaluations do not necessarily mean lowered self-esteem (Weinreich, 2003).

Moscovici (1976) illustrates the importance of acceptance on 'the handicap of being different'. This was an issue that consistently emerged in this research – participants frequently referenced being seen as 'different' by others. Predominantly this was perceived to be a handicapped (though on occasion it was seen as a positive) leading to rejection. Moscovici argues that there is a basic need in humans, for acceptance and social approval. However, this may not be possible where there is too wide a gap between the 'self' and 'others'. 'Therefore it is only between persons who are close to one another, belonging to the same group, sharing a common background and a similar view of reality that interpersonal bonds happen to be shaped' (1976, p. 199). Hence individuals allow themselves to be influenced to avoid becoming 'estranged or different'. Likes (acceptance) and dislikes (non-acceptance) are powerful social dimensions. Cultural differences, which influence acceptance are tied to historical experiences and are embedded in language, ethnicity, religion and nationality (Appiah, 2000, Weinreich, 2003).

The social identity theory explains identity as being rooted in generic human processes, with group identification being a powerful influence. Individuals usually do not identify in an all or nothing fashion but form partial-identifications with people and groups, although of course some identifications may be more important to them than others. Ascribed identity was significant in participants' choice of ethnic identity. However, some did not rely on others identification of them but created self-definitions. As many matured and encountered greater societal experience they appeared to move away from being reliant on other people and had a better awareness of the processes of adopting an ethnic identity. In short, they appeared to have achieved a greater sense of choice and autonomy over their ethnic identity.

There are therefore, a range of factors that constrain an individual's choice of identity. For example, a major theoretical finding implied by the studies in this book is the importance of socio-historical contexts to the sense of identity. The culture and history that the interethnic have inherited from their parents and all the nuances, expectations and idiosyncrasies that go with this are essential to their sense of identity and choice. This in turn must be viewed within the context of ongoing socio-political events and a changing environment. Events such as 9/11, the London bombing (7/7), government polices and media portrayal/discussions will inevitably impact on ongoing debates on national identity, religion and issues of citizenship implicitly or explicitly impact on one's own sense of identity.

The Interethnic

Identity

The identities adopted by the interethnic young people included a particular ethnic identity such as Asian or white, interethnic or a situational/chameleon like identity. Adolescence is understood as part of a journey into adulthood in which identities are formed and influenced by situations and times. Choosing one particular identity may depend on securing power and resources. In current British society where being Asian has many negative connotations and is linked to discrimination would the interethnic with a choice of two ethnicities choose to be Asian? Similarly, would they choose to be Muslim in an atmosphere of suspicion, hostility and Islamaphobia? Would an individual choose a more acceptable identity, if they were able to do so? The answers to these questions are not straightforward. Some adopted an Asian identity, as well as the Muslim religion. The reasons are complex. Many of the participants in this research stated that they felt anxiety and conflicting feelings at the thought of rejecting an ethnicity or religion that they had inherited from their parents. Moreover, they chose to identify with a particular identity or ethnicity based on their physical appearance, peer interactions, family and societal influence even though that identity brought with it difficulties. Modood discusses how individuals deal with discrimination 'some will organise resistance, while others will stop looking like Muslims (the equivalent of "passing for white")' (Modood, 2006, p. 66). Interethnic individuals deal with discrimination in similar fashion. Some pass for white, the superior identity by some standards (for example employability, acceptance) and others will take on the more difficult ethnic identity and form resistance if they are so able.

A few individuals adopted an interethnic identity while others initially projected an Asian or white identity or a situational identity but later shifted to an interethnic identity. The findings indicate a number of possible reasons for this, as previously discussed in the book, these participants: 1) tended to be older and had come to accept both cultures rather than taking an either/or approach; 2) had found there were benefits to being interethnic for example appreciating other cultures, being a part of two cultures, and the glamour associated with dual heritage and; 3) had been brought up and accepted as 'interethnic' and of both cultures by parents and extended family. It was found that Asian mothers, more so than others, tended to make a greater effort to incorporate both the Asian and white cultures in their lifestyle. This may be because Asian females possessed greater positive flexibility to negotiate two cultural contexts (Kelly, 1989, Northover, 1988).

Adopting an interethnic identity may be a positive development. This identity could require personal acceptance, a sense of self, and the interpersonal and social recognition of the individual as having inherited two ethnicities. Certainly, participants here viewed the adoption of an interethnic identity as being empowering; it means equal apportionment and valuation of both parent's ethnic and cultural heritage. The simple assertion of being who they are, of their dual heritage, may be the final achievement of self-acceptance in the developmental stages of their ethnic identity. However, we should not make the mistake others have done in the past, in 'recommending' this as being the most psychologically healthy identity. Who is to say that in today's climate a situational identity may not be the most useful and empowering?

Situational Identity

There has been a shift in social psychology towards recognising that individuals are able to manipulate their identity to suit the social context (Goffman, 1959, Baumeister, 1982, Harré, 1987, Gergen and Gergen, 1986, Sarbin, 1986). In addition, people use the power of language to construct their identities (Foucault, 1972, Parker and Burman, 1993, Holloway, 1989, Billig, 1987, Potter, 1997, Potter and Wetherell, 1997). The research discussed in this book found that some young people practised a situational/chameleon like identity. An intimate knowledge of both cultures and knowing what the 'right' mode of behaviour was in specific situations were important factors in an individual's ability to practice such a situational identity. This is illustrated by Mead's (1934) work, which suggests that a person presents different selves to different people. For Mead, language and behaviour were some of the key factors that affected individual's ability to present a self. According to Moscovici (1976) behavioural styles can be both symbolic and instrumental, convey meanings and bring about reactions, as a function of these meanings. 'Inappropriate' or 'normal' behaviour is defined by a common social code. It is not enough to claim an ethnicity; it must be satisfactorily performed, as outlined by Goffman (1959). This requires resources such as language. We saw in this research how only those adept at understanding the common social code and using resources such as language and culture were able to adopt a situational identity.

The young people seemed to have a great insight into the discourses of identity construction and adoption and were able to use this to their advantage. As a result they reached a point of realisation – that they did not have to be one or the other (white/Asian) to fit a single mould but could adopt a situational identity depending on the social context. Notions of autonomy and choice were central factors in constructing and maintaining this identity. The adolescents contextualised their identities and located a sense of self based on their setting. He/she had the ability to juxtapose different cultural behaviour according to the appropriateness of the different settings. For example, to project or emphasise an Asian identity it was not enough to know aspects of it, participants had to be able to show an intimate knowledge of the social protocols and idiosyncrasies of that culture. The successful negotiation of either or both the Asian and white culture was possible because they had intimate knowledge of the representations of both groups. This led to membership and integration within both groups and gave them greater freedom to claim both cultures as theirs. The situational identity, therefore, represents a sense of choice and control over the way one is recognised and may be a particularly important ability within the context of today's changing social dynamics.

As well as more choice, a situational identity was perceived as empowering participants. For example, it could be used as a way of dealing with racialised discourse with peers, or in representing themselves as white when applying for jobs. The adoption of this type of identity may have provided participants with an identity 'passport', giving them access to both Asian and white groups, and hence dual culture and dual nationality. This meant they were looked upon by both sets of groups as being 'one of them' in a way that may be more difficult for a non-interethnic person to achieve.

Some individuals justified the situational/chameleon identity repertoire as benefiting other people, for example, peers, parents and relatives. However, it also benefited the individuals. This would have been especially important in the climate that some of these interviews were conducted. There was (increased) tension between British Asians (particularly Muslims) and whites because of riots in the North of England, further exacerbated by the September 11 tragedy in America and the Afghanistan and Iraq wars. Individuals who were able to construct a chameleon identity found it easier to shift from being with whites and with Asians than a non-interethnic white or Asian person.

However, the transition to the situational/chameleon identity was not always an easy one. The concepts of personal agency and choice were important. Participants who perceived themselves as having little choice over their identity reported feeling constrained and helpless. This at times led to discourse conflict. For example, the belief that they could only legitimately adopt one identity meant for some denying one parent's culture and thus a sense of disloyalty to that parent. The chameleon identity also provoked an ideological dilemma for some participants and a sense of guilt that they were 'misleading' and 'deceiving' people. They resolved this conflict by using the discourse technique of 'particularisation' (Billig, 1987), that is, resolving a discourse conflict by treating certain circumstances or people as a special case. For the interethnic children and adolescents, finding themselves caught between two cultural allegiances does not necessarily lead to negative consequences. Flexibility and the ability to adapt to the social context means frequent modulations of social identities and greater benefits.

The Identity of Interethnics of Other Backgrounds

Those with an Asian and black interethnic background (rather than Asian and white) shared similar experiences but also encountered different ones. For example, they too reported practising a situational/chameleon identity. However, they experienced greater prejudice from both the Asian and black community. The findings in the quantitative study of other interethnic groups, for example, white Other, Chinese and white, black and white – showed that they shared similar as well as different experiences. For example they: 1) identified with interethnic individuals more than with individuals from other groups; 2) at times had to choose between representations of their parents' two different cultures. Though this was not viewed negatively but as something, which had benefits; 3) viewed their interethnic background as being positive and; 4) adopted situational/chameleon identities.

Asian and white and black and white interethnics were more likely to say they would change their ethnic identity depending on the situation than other interethnic groups. It is argued that this is because they have a greater need to adopt a situational identity, for example to deal with racialised discourses in the labour market. Another surprising ethnic difference was that white 'Other' interethnic believed they were under more pressure to choose between the 'two cultures' than any of the other groups. The reasons for this are unknown.

The overall message seems to be that interethnic individuals of all backgrounds face experiences that are as similar and as diverse as those faced by people in general. Theirs really was a 'masala mosaic[1] of experiences'. The findings suggest that it is important not to categorise interethnic people as one group but to explore their experiences in the context of their diverse backgrounds.

To What Extent are Identities Chosen?

The post-modern perspective, stemming from interpretive and social constructionist approaches has much to say about the theory of identity. It is not easy to provide a critique of this approach as it is difficult to identify one overarching postmodernist view. However, generally, it is fashionable for post modernists to talk about identity in terms of a reflexive identity, one that is multiplicitous and in flux. It is true, as postmodernists say, that there have been advances in technology, media and mass communication and that discourses about identity have reached new levels. However, reflections about identity are not new. There is an established literature that goes back a long way, James, Cooley, Mead, Goffman (as outlined in the literature review chapter). Postmodernists have neglected much of these writings.

Giddens (1991) argues that self identity is a modern project within which individuals can be reflexive and construct an identity to suit their lives. 'Reflexive self identity' as discussed by post modernists and social constructionists appears to be overstated. They argue that individuals can reflexively construct a personal and social identity for themselves to control their lives and situations. For them identities can be chosen to suit an individual's life and aspirations. This argument is based on reflexivity, but is flawed. For example, what about people who are not reflexive and choose an identity; what about other cultures where 'postmodernist reflexivity' has not reached? Also, reflexivity is not a modern phenomenon but has been a part of human experience as far back as we can trace. For example, the same themes discussed today were discussed six hundred years ago by Indian philosophers. Shakespeare anticipated much of Goffman's arguments centuries before. Buddhism focuses on 'selfhood' and bettering the self and many of Freud's theories are named after Greek myths.

Whether ethnic identity is situational or essentialist is also linked to the social science debate about whether ethnicity is primordial or situational. The primordial perspective (Geertz, 1963, Glazer, N. and Moynihan, 1975) argues that ethnicity is unchanging and is passed down from generations. Situationists (Glazer, N. and Moynihan 1975) view ethnic identity as being changeable depending on the social context and gains.

This book has demonstrated that people can exercise some degree of choice and control in their assertion or expression of ethnic identity. But there were significant constraints and factors affecting these choices, such as: physical appearance and knowledge of a language. These factors meant they were at times

---

1   An Indian/Hindi word meaning 'mixture of spices'.

compelled to emphasise one identity over another, influencing their ability to have personal agency over their identity and thus an agentic self. The findings illustrate that ethnic identities are situational – there are some choices but there are also constraints. Ethnic distinctions are likely to be based on everyday common rules (Goffman, 1959) making it difficult for an individual to practice a multiplicitous identity that is completely in flux.

Harré's concept of the 'Self' is important to the debate of agency and choice. He suggested that through Self 1 – the agent intentionally interacts with others by linguistic discourses and conversations. The reflexive self, which has an awareness of beliefs and self conception, is labelled as Self 2. Self 3 is the presentation of self in everyday life, the public self. Weinreich (2003), using Harré's definition of the Self suggests that only self conceptions (Self 2) and public self (Self 3) are really available for evaluation/appraisal. But the agentic self (Self 1) is not. The agentic Self 1's intentions are defined from preconscious cerebral thinking and cannot be reflexive schemata (Weinreich, 2003). Nevertheless, Self 2 and Self 3 mean that people will experience various degrees of personal agency and autonomy, depending on the situation and the individuals involved. Adopting a situational identity, for example, means participants discussed in this book were activating Self 2 and Self 3. This autonomy varied over time and the social context.

The situational/chameleon like identity was presented by the young people as giving them greater choice and a sense of empowerment, however the choices they really had were limited. It could be argued that what the situational identity meant was that they had some tools that enabled them to 'fit in' to an already existing notion of a 'positive' ethnic identity established by society. Participants would have had little control over this notion of a positive identity. It is therefore questionable how much personal agency and empowerment individuals really had. At the most it gave them greater autonomy to manoeuvre/modulate between a few ethnic identities to suit existing notions of positive identities and expectations. Nevertheless, these are skills that maybe invaluable in today's climate.

Identity Conflict: The Marginal Men

Marginal theorists predict that interethnic children will be rejected by society and suffer an identity crisis. However, research (Wilson, 1987, Tizard and Phoenix, 1993 and Katz, 1996) shows that interethnic children experience little psychological disturbance or identity conflict. It is now generally recognised that being interethnic need not be correlated with being marginalised and having a 'negative identity'. Indeed, researchers have found that interethnic children were in some ways, more sophisticated and aware of racial categorisation and had a capacity to evaluate both negatively and positively their identities (Jacobs, 1992, Wilson, 1987).

The findings in this research did not indicate any clear evidence of the interethnic experiencing identity conflict, though they were faced with negotiating a range of influencing factors and constraints. What appeared to take place instead, for some people, was an identity in flux, that changed depending on their influences and the people they were with; something that dual socialisation contributes towards (Weinreich, 2003). These people were also clearly able to evaluate their social/ethnic identities. Most offered very sophisticated analysis and explanations of their ethnic identities and accounts. It may be that having parents with two different cultures means they were more aware than non-interethnic children of the importance that race plays in society. This awareness, was not, and need not, be negative. Indeed, they repeatedly argued that they had a greater understanding and appreciation of other cultures and races because of their interethnic inheritance. They felt enriched.

Other researchers (Tizard and Phoenix, 1993, 2001) support this. The people discussed in this book were not 'stuck' in between representations of their parents' two different cultures, nor does the concept of the 'marginal man' apply, although there were at times constraints and pressures as discussed.

While there was no clear evidence of identity conflict amongst the young people, there were some who spoke of the pressure involved in negotiating different cultures and identifying with the cultures, parents and extended family. For one or two this led to some internal conflict with regard to their identity. This may not be just because they are interethnic. It can be argued that most individuals, at different moments in time experience internal conflicts with regard to identity. Most psychological discussions on identity offer an insight into the internal conflicts that individuals experience, irrespective of if they are interethnic or not (Erikson, 1963, Blos, 1962, Kohlberg, 1969, Loevinger, 1976, Kegan, 1982).

Identity conflict, where it occurs can be a part of identity transition. It can be overcome by evaluating and synthesising identifications and by dispersing identification conflict with others. Adolescence is a transitional phase whereby as the adolescent grows into adulthood there are different rules, alliances and aspirations they apply as they encounter new people and experiences. Indeed, it may be healthy for one to question one's identity at times rather than 'live with' a single fixed identity that we might not be happy with. A reformulated identity if negotiated successfully can mean more acceptance from peers and community as one moves into adulthood.

Race, Class and Gender

The issue of race has been discussed throughout this book. It was an important element in the lives of the young people, whether consciously or not. It seemed to play a greater role in their lives than it did for non-interethnic individuals and families. This also applied to the few parents who had made the decision not to discuss race with their children or within the family environment. Parents' views on race, even if not made explicit, influenced the way they brought up their children. Overall though, it is argued that whilst the parents set the scene and influenced their children's ethnic identity and experiences of being interethnic, they did not decide their future adolescent and post adolescent identity. This was dependent on the children's later experiences with peers and society at large.

There were slightly more middle class participants than working class participants in the research studies presented here. This maybe because more middle class Asians and white individuals form interethnic relationships. The findings supported that of Katz (1996) and Wilson (1987) who suggested that in middle class families the children were given more freedom to choose their identities and children from the middle class families tended to adopt a situational identity more than children from the working class, more of whom took the view that they had to be one or the other. It has been suggested anecdotally and in biographies of 'mixed race' people that middle class interethnic people tended to veer towards adopting a white identity over their minority inheritance. Research indicates that there maybe some truth in this. Certainly, the young people emphasised their white heritage more when applying for jobs, university placements in the belief that this would make their applications more successful.

There were a number of gender differences found in this research, for example, the ways in which the community perceived and treated young Asian men and women differed. Young Asian women felt they were being constrained by the Asian community and, for example, experienced pressure to dress traditionally and to conduct themselves in a way that did not bring dishonour to their family. Being under the gaze of the community meant they felt they had little sense of freedom and autonomy. Some of these issues appeared to be linked to generational differences between the young people, their parents and older members of the community. Young Asian men were under pressure from family and community expectations that they would be high achievers and support the extended family. However, unable to meet many of these expectations because of personal and societal barriers/constraints they increasingly attempted to find ways of coping, some resorting to drugs. Baumann (1996) and Alexander (2000) illustrate the pressures, from the community and external others, which young Asian men can be under and the ways that they attempt to cope, for example by asserting masculinity through gang membership.

There were also gender differences in the relationships between interethnic partners. It was often women, in the interethnic relationships who became more involved in their partner's culture and were expected (both by the male partner and his extended family) to incorporate the 'other' culture in the raising of children. Many of the Asian women remarked on how much more gender equality they had being in a relationship with a white man than they would have had with an Asian man. Paradoxically, the white women (particularly the younger ones) also said that they had gender equality in their relationship with Asian men. This maybe because Asian men who marry outside of their ethnicity are less traditional and more 'unconventional' than those who marry within. The results from the questionnaire findings revealed a few social/content based gender differences, for example, that more men had no religion or were atheist/agnostic and more women placed physical difference as being an important influencing factor in their ethnic identity.

It is claimed by some social scientists that women's identity formation/ processes are different from men's (Josselson, 1996). However, within scientific psychological literature there appears to be agreement that there are few gender differences in the processes by which psychological identities are developed/ formulated, although there may be content specific differences. That is, at the ego level there are no gender differences although there maybe at the level of social identity (Coote, 2000). The findings in this book support this. There appear to be no meaningful gender differences in the psychological *processes* of identity formation. All of the gender issues that emerged were related to social and content issues rather than psychological processes.

The Future for the Interethnic

What are the implications for the future identities of the adolescents in this study when they reach adulthood? Most psychologists recognise that identity can change throughout an individual's life. The findings from the research studies conducted here suggested a very clear trend of identity being fluid and multifaceted. It was found that older children/adolescents tended to adopt a situational/chameleon identity to suit their social context and deal with racialised discourses. They perceived this as a beneficial tool and one that they were more adept at using than most. Those who had entered university or employment tended to adopt a situational/chameleon identity much more than younger participants. They did this partly as a response to racial attitudes already encountered. For example, many believed they had a better chance of being successful in achieving good employment if they emphasised their white culture. Some spoke from experience, having applied both as an Asian and as a white, they said they were inevitably more successful when adopting a white identity. Racism exists, for example a study found that fewer black candidates were selected when their biographical details e.g. ethnic groups were included (CRE, 2002).

Whether these individuals will continue to adopt a situational identity in the future is unclear. It is more than likely they will reconstruct their identities with time. They may emphasise a different part of their ethnic identity as they grow older depending on their experiences and social context. From the findings in this research it could be argued that as some of the individuals become more confident in their interethnic identity they will abandon the chameleon like status. This identity by its very nature suggests it is a device used to 'fit in' to groups, and to dovetail with society's current attitude towards the interethnic. It may be that as interethnic individuals grow in numbers and if the media and society takes a more positive view towards them they will no longer feel the need to be a chameleon. However, it is important that social scientists should not advocate a particular ethnic identity on the grounds of psychological suitability.

Ultimately, the most suitable identity should be the one that the individual feels is the best for them. What should be recognised is the importance of freedom of choice. Individuals, whether they be interethnic or not, should have the freedom to adopt any culture they wish. Whether they are able to carry this off is of course another issue.

Social scientists have argued for the transcending of race and for the 'deliberate renunciation of 'race' (Gilroy, 2000, p. 12). Whilst others have gone so far as to suggest that the increase in numbers of the interethnic might bring about racial harmony. However, in truth they are only individuals – adrift in the wider sea of society.

END PIECE

Barack Obama – What Does having an Interethnic President Mean for the Future?

As Obama, the president of the USA, is the most famous and influential interethnic person in modern day, and as his identity is debated widely, this book on interethnic identity would not be complete without referring to him and his ethnicity. There follows a brief discussion based on analysis of Obama's biographies, speeches and information accessible to the general public.

There has been much debate about Obama's identity, whether he is black, not black at all or 'mixed race'. American journalist Jonathan Weisman commented that Obama 'is much more white than black.' African Americans – Reverend Al Sharpton said that Obama was not 'authentically black' and Debra Dickerson wrote, '"Obama isn't black". "Black," in our political and social reality, means those descended from West African slaves' (Dickerson, 2007).

And yet this denial of Obama's 'blackness' contrasts with the reaction afforded Tiger Woods, the famous American golfer, when he claimed that he is not just an African American but Cablinasian, a mixture of Caucasian, African American, Native American, and Asian. The statement provoked much criticism, even from other interethnic figures such as American Secretary of State Colin Powell. In America the one drop rule means that Woods is viewed as black. Many saw Woods actions as a rejection of his black heritage rather than acknowledgement of his interethnic heritage.

This denial of Obama, for claiming that he is black and the criticism of Woods for labeling himself as something more than black, help to illustrate the complex and often emotional issues that still surround the identity of the interethnic, particularly black/white in America today. And illustrate the pressures placed by elements of society on those interethnic individuals who wish to choose their own identity.

In fact it was not entirely clear from Obama's presidential campaign whether he identified as black, interethnic or white. This could be because he was looking to secure the votes of a nation of diverse ethnicities and the opposition party had attempted to negatively use his race and his father's Muslim religion. There is little doubt, however, that Obama adopted a black identity when he became President. Symbolically the inauguration took place on the eve of Martin Luther King's birthday. There was a benediction from civil rights icon Pastor Joseph Lowry who opened his speech with lines from 'Lift Every Voice and Sing' a song referred to as the 'Negro National Anthem'.

Obama's speeches are riddled with representations of race, though he does not mention the word itself, and seem to position him as both black and white with references to his white mother, white grandmother, wider family and multi-ethnic background; being brought up in Hawaii and Indonesia. Similarly he appeared to wish to straddle both parts of his heritage in his biography (Obama, 2004) where he talks both about his relationships with black leaders and with his white grandmother and grandfather.

Like some of the people presented in this book, Obama uses a situational identity. Thus his consistent use of his identity to appeal to black, white and all multi-ethnic people during his campaign. In 'A more perfect union' speech (Obama, 2008) he appealed to the whites:

> I can no more disown him [Reverend Wright] than I can disown the black community. I can no more disown him than I can my white grandmother – a woman who helped raise me, a woman who sacrificed again and again for me, a woman who loves me as much as she loves anything in this world, but a woman who once confessed her fear of black men who passed by her on the street, and who on more than one occasion has uttered racial or ethnic stereotypes that made me cringe.

He then shifted and expressed empathy with the anger that blacks feel as a result of discrimination:

> That anger may not get expressed in public, in front of white co-workers or white friends. But it does find voice in the barbershop or around the kitchen table … occasionally it finds voice in the church on Sunday morning, in the pulpit and in the pews. The fact that so many people are surprised to hear that anger in some of Reverend Wright's sermons simply reminds us of the old truism that the most segregated hour in American life occurs on Sunday morning.

And back again to whites and what he called 'a similar anger' in the white community based on resentments over 'busing', the practice of attempting to integrate schools by assigning students to schools based primarily on race, and affirmative action, and the way in which fears about crime are often met with accusations of racism. Obama stated that these resentments were rooted in legitimate concerns.

In his democratic acceptance speech (August, 2008) he paid homage to his white mother and white grandparents. This led to some American media suggesting that he was appealing to the 'paler nation' to reassure white people that he understands them.

But he also called for the African-American community to '[bind] our particular grievances – for better health care, and better schools, and better jobs – to the larger aspirations of all Americans' and for the white community to acknowledge the 'legacy of discrimination ... and current incidents of discrimination.' Some media figures and academics (Elam, 2008) in analysing Obama's speeches and political decisions and its implications to race have suggested that these are contradictions. However they are not mere contradictions but a sophisticated use of Obama's interethnic heritage and his chameleon identity. The ways in which young people in this book used their situational identity were echoed by the ways in which Obama used his – but on a global stage.

Obama acknowledges race and racism rather than merely ignoring it. As he said 'Race is an issue that I believe the nation cannot afford to ignore right now.' (NPR, 2008). He accepts the challenges of race and racial divides rather than covering it. He was also careful of excluding himself as a 'mixed race'.[2] When the MAVIN foundation, a large 'mixed race' advocacy organisation went on a tour bus called 'Generation Mix' to raise awareness of 'America's mixed race baby boom' they met with Obama. The participants were enthusiastic that he too was a 'mixed race' but Obama stated:

'You know, I don't think you can consider the issue of mixed race outside the issue of race.' (Chasing daybreak, documentary by MAVIN foundation). All of this has meant that there is a tension between Americans of 'mixed race' and blacks. The 'mixed race' population suggests that the black community and the media co-adopted Obama as black. His 'mixed race' background has been "relegated into the invisible spaces' said Ivanovic, Director of Philadelphia chapter of Swirl Inc. a national multiracial organisation. Though Obama has adopted a black identity he does not deny his interethnic background. He suggested that he may have a white mother but when he is recognised as a black man in America, when others identify him as such he cannot be anything but black. Therefore, Obama identifies himself as black with white mother and grandparents. He may do so because of the one drop rule or because historically that is how black and white interethnic individuals have been labelled. Many interethnic Americans of a black and white heritage have said that they forged black identities because of their experiences of being interethnic; facing racial discrimination and being labelled as being black. The two are not mutually exclusive.

It is clear from Obama's autobiography that he chose his black identity. A view supported by an interview that was published in the *New York Times* (January 2008) given by his Indonesian and white sister Maya Soetoro-Ng:

Do you think of your brother as black?

---

2   The term commonly used in America for the interethnic.

Yes, because that is how he has named himself. Each of us has a right to name ourselves as we will.

Whereas she identifies herself as being interethnic:

Do you think of yourself as white?

No. I'm half white, half Asian. I think of myself as hybrid. People usually think I'm Latina when they meet me. That's what made me learn Spanish.

Obama very much identifies himself as an African American Christian with the image he has created with that of a stable black family with wife Michelle and two daughters. He comes from an interethnic union but he is clearly more interested and invested in black political issues. But this adoption of his identity has not been an easy journey. In his first memoir, *Dreams from My Father*, (2004) Obama said that when people discover his interethnic heritage, they make assumptions about 'the mixed blood, the divided soul, the ghostly image of the tragic mulatto trapped between two worlds.' Indeed, he acknowledged feeling tormented for much of his life by 'the constant, crippling fear that I didn't belong somehow, that unless I dodged and hid and pretended to be something I wasn't, I would forever remain an outsider, with the rest of the world, black and white, always standing in judgment.'

There is a more significant psychological reason why Obama might be adopting a black identity. An analysis of his autobiography indicated that if Obama, as a child, was given the dolls test (psychology test based on Clarks and Clarks study, 1967) it is doubtful that he would have identified with the black doll. As a child his identity was most likely white. Being brought up predominantly by a white mother and white grandparents and attending mostly white schools and colleges there would have been little choice. His biography showed that he might also have negative feelings about his black heritage for example, in the way he had told his school peers that his father was a prince – elevating his father in that way was designed to reduce his 'shame' in having a black father and the discourses of black racism. He was embarrassed when his father, during his only visit with him, came to speak at his school. And his shame that his father might have been brought up in a mud hut:

I spent that night and all of the next day trying to suppress thought of the inevitable; the faces of my classmates when they heard about mud huts, all my lies exposed, the painful jokes afterwards. Each time I remembered, my body squirmed as if it had received a jolt to the nerves. (Obama, 2004, p. 69)

He wrote about the pain of having shoved and ran away from the only other black person in his class. All these indicated the guilt that he felt about his negative feelings towards his black inheritance. As a child and adolescent he quite clearly felt uncomfortable and at odds with his interethnic background and a child's feelings of dislike towards an ethnicity and people he knew little of. But perhaps driven partly by his guilt towards the negative feelings of his black heritage he has taken on so strongly the very identity that he rejected as a child.

His biography is about the search for his black father but what it really depicted was his search for his identity and in particular his black identity. Through mixing with black peers at university, his work with the black community, visiting his relatives in Kenya and finally getting engaged to his wife, a black preacher's daughter Obama appeared to have achieved his black identity in adulthood and by the end of his book. This black identity has strengthened over the years and is the one that is portrayed to the public today.

There is no doubt that for now Obama is a role model particularly for black people and the interethnic. According to US Census estimates from July 2008, individuals who identify as more than 'two or more races' totaled 6.8 million people, an increase of 3.4 per cent from the July 2007 estimate (US Census Bureau, 2009). He alongside, other figures such as Tiger Woods, has demonstrated that a person of that background can be powerful and successful. This does not, however, mean that race has finally been transcended, as debated by the media and academics alike. Racism and disadvantages in all walks of life for blacks and other ethnic minorities still exist. Obama as president does not mean that we can now look beyond race. What it does mean is that there is now a greater capacity in society for individuals with talent to succeed whatever their race.

But not religion. Remarkably Obama's Muslim religious background is still not widely acknowledged or debated. His Muslim father, Muslim Indonesian stepfather and his being brought up in a predominantly Muslim country, Indonesia, for some of the time is largely dismissed. In fact, his links to Islam are denied and to Christianity amplified; as illustrated by his inauguration, closeness with Christian leaders, emphasis on wife Michelle being a preacher's wife and his own references to God. The interview extract below with his half sister summarises the tension surrounding Islam:

> Are you worried about mentioning Islam because it has already been evoked by negative campaigners trying to tarnish your brother?

> I'm not worried. I don't want to deny Islam. I think it's obviously very important that we have an understanding of Islam, a better understanding. At the same time, it has been erroneously attached to my brother. The man has been a Christian for 20 years.

By and large Obama's Muslim past remains the elephant in the room. Of course, as well as his own personal beliefs it can be assumed that Obama is acutely aware both of the importance of Christianity to many of his fellow Americans and of the power of Christian lobbyists in Washington. Nor should his attempts to forge better relations with Muslims be overlooked; as witnessed by his 'New

Beginnings Speech' in Cairo which amongst other things called for improved mutual understanding and relations between the Islamic world and the West (Obama, June, 2009).

To conclude, as well as being black Obama also identifies and is represented as 'mixed race', white, multi-racial. And therein is the key to Obama's success, that he is able to be all these things, in short to have a fluid situational identity. The ability to emphasise different facets of himself depending on his social context and cynically, the voters he wishes to please.

Parting Thoughts

There is no doubt that interethnic people such as Obama, are successful in comparison to other ethnic minorities, perhaps even all other people. Apart from Barack Obama there are many other successful interethnic figures in all works of life; 26 per cent of the football elite, in the UK, are interethnic (*Guardian* Newspaper, 2006). This is despite the factor that people of a 'mixed race' background are more likely to be raised in single parent families, sent to care homes and become the victims of crime than any other groups (ONS, 2004). In the face of all this, their achievements are truly to be applauded. And one of the main reasons for the achievement lies in their interethnic heritage and their multi-faceted fluid identities.

Each individual whether interethnic or not strives for a totalness, a sense of wholeness that is more than the sum of the parts of his or her heritage. The interethnic adolescents have the additional responsibility of negotiating representations of two cultures rather than one. The findings suggest that identity development of the interethnic is not only multifaceted but that their negotiation of ethnic identity is a continual, life-long process in which maintenance and transformation occur in daily interactions within the realms of family, peers and friends, culture and community. Identity formation is complex and evolving, especially for the interethnic.

As for the people presented in this book, their identities were a masala 'mixture' of ethnicities, cultures and sometimes even religion. Together they made a mosaic of young people who were, in the main, sophisticated in their attitude to adopting a multifaceted and fluid identity. And in spite of all the detours and decision making processes they appeared to be adjusted in their interethnic heritage. In fact, most found their interethnicity to be an asset, as reflected in the following comments: 'I've got the best of both worlds'; 'It makes me more sensitive and appreciative of other cultures and people'. These interethnic individuals may, indeed, be the 'cosmopolitan people' predicted by Park in the thirties (1937). But this need not be a warning, as intended by him, but something to welcome. The interethnic people's abilities to deal with complexity, subtlety and nuance are qualities we want for all our children. Being interethnic is part of our future.

Recommendations

It is hoped that future work will develop the findings presented here. Also the following suggestions should be taken into consideration:

- The recognition that those with interethnic background are not 'marginalised' or stuck 'between two cultures'. In fact they may have a greater choice and autonomy over their ethnic identities than those of non-interethnic.
- The importance of adopting a research approach that is sensitive to the interethnic.
- To recognise the increase in interethnic relationships and interethnic children and formulate policies which reflect this. A starting point would be to change the census categorisation from its current 'mixed race' status.
- Academics to understand the rapid increase of this group and conduct more research to reflect this.
- The media to take into consideration the changing nature of British demographic and the roles that the interethnic has in our society.
- Parents to recognise and assist with the issues that their interethnic children face.

Appendix

Notes

The following charts illustrate the answers that participants gave in the quantitative questionnaire.

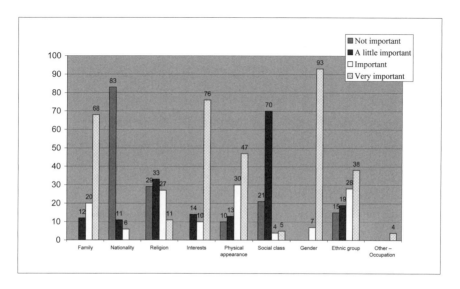

Figure A.1 Factors that were important in describing their identity
Base: All participants (numbers expressed as percentage).

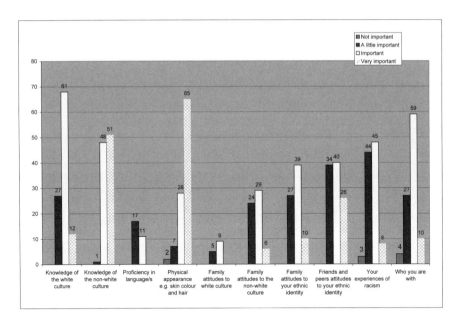

Figure A.2 Factors that influenced participants' ethnic identity
Base: All participants.

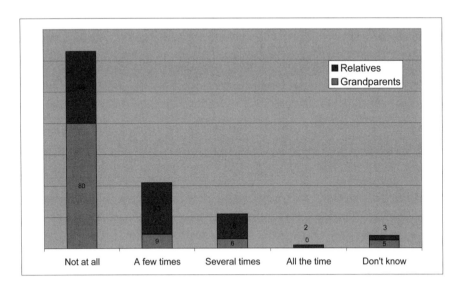

Figure A.3 Difficulties with the extended family
Base: The participants from each of the ethnic groups were expressed as percentage. For example, the 40 black and white participants were taken as 100 per cent.

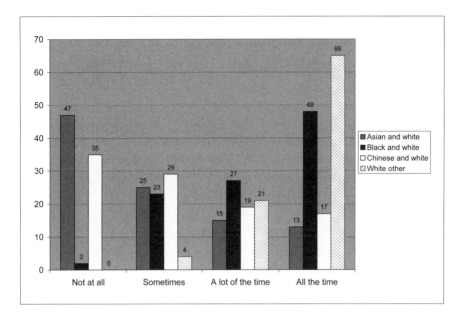

Figure A.4 Do you feel that you are in between the two cultures?
Base: The participants from each of the ethnic groups were expressed as percentage. For example, the 40 black and white participants were taken as 100 per cent.

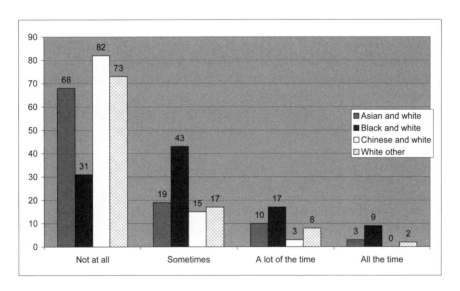

Figure A.5 How much do you feel that you are under pressure to choose between the two cultures?
Base: All participants.

Bibliography

Aboud, F.E. (1988) *Children and Prejudice*, London: Basil Blackwell.

Aboud, F.E. and Skerry, S.A. (1984) The development of ethnic attitudes, *Journal of Cross-Cultural Psychology*, 15, 1, 3–34.

Abrams, D. and Hogg M. (eds) (1990) *Social Identity Theory: Constructive and critical advances*, Hemel Hempstead: Harvester Wheatsheaf.

Adorno, T.W., Frenkel-Brunswick, E., Levinson, D. and Sanford, R.N (1950) *The Authoritarian Personality*, New York: Harper.

Ahmed, S. (1997) It's a sun tan isn't it? Autobiography as an identificatory practice, in H. Mirza, *Black British Feminism*, London: Routledge.

Alcoff, L.M. (1999) Philosophy and racial identity, in Bulmer, M. and Solomos, J., *Ethnic and Racial Studies Today*, London and New York: Routledge.

Alexander, C.E. (2000) *The Asian Gang: Ethnicity, Identity, Masculinity*, Oxford and New York: Berg.

Ali, N. and Northover, M. (1999) Distinct identities: South Asian youth in Britain, in J.W. Berry and R.C.Annis (eds), *Ethnic Psychology* (International Association for Cross-Cultural Psychology), Lisse, Netherlands: Swets and Zeitlinger.

Alibhai-Brown, Y. and Montague, A. (1992) *The Colour of Love: Mixed Race Relationships*, London Virago Press: London.

Alibhai-Brown, Y. (2001) *Mixed Feelings: The Complex Lives of Mixed Race Britons*, London: The Women's Press.

Allport, G.W. (1979) The Nature of Prejudice, in Katz, I, (1996) *The Construction of Racial Identity in Children of Mixed Parentage*, London: Cromwell Press.

Althusser, L. (1971) *Lenin and the Philosophy and Other Essays,* London: New Left Books.

Amit-Talai, V. and Knowles, C. (1998) *Re-Situating Identities; The Politics of Race an Identity*, Ontario and New York: Broadview Press.

Anderson, M. (1999) Children in Between: Constructing Identities in the Bicultural Family, *Journal of Royal Anthropological Institute* (N.S) 5, 13–26.

Anwar, M. (1998) *Between Cultures, Continuity and Change in the Lives of Young Asians*, London and New York: Routledge.

Appiah, K.A. (2000) Racial Identity and Identification, in L. Back and J. Solomos *Theories of Race and Racism*, London: Routledge.

Archer, L. (2003) *Race, Masculinity and Schooling: Muslim Boys and Education (Educating Boys, Learning Gender)*, London: Open University Press.

Armstrong, K. (2000) *The Battle for God: Fundamentalism in Judaism, Christianity and Islam*, London: HarperCollins.

Azoulay, K.G. (1997) *Black, Jewish, and Interracial: It's Not the Colour of Your Skin, but the Race of Your Kin and Other Myths of Identity*, Durham and London, Duke University Press.

Back, L. (1993) Race, Identity and Nation within an Adolescent Community in South London, *New Community*, 19 (2), 217–33.

Back, L. (1996) *New Ethnicities and Urban Culture: Racism and Multiculturalism in Young Lives*, London: UCL Press.

Bagley, C. and Young, L. (1979) The identity, adjustment and achievement of transracially adopted children, in G.K. Verma. and C. Bagley, *Race, Education and Identity*, London: Macmillan.

Ballard, C. (1979) Conflict, continuity and change, Second Generation South Asians, in Khan, V.S. (ed.), *Minority Families in Britain*, London: Macmillan.

Ballhatchet, K. (1980) *Race, Sex and Class under the Raj*, London: Weidenfeld and Nicolson.

Bandura, A. and Walters, R.H. (1963) *Social Learning and Personality Development*, New York: Holt Rinehart and Winston.

Banton, M. (1997) *Ethnic and Racial Consciousness*, London and New York: Addison Wesley Longman Ltd.

Bashi, V. (1998) Racial Categories Matter because Racial Hierarchies Matter: A Commentary, *Ethnic and Racial Studies, 21* (September) 5: 959–968.

Baumann, G. (1996) *Contesting Culture: Discourses of Identity in Multi-ethnic London*, Cambridge: Cambridge University Press.

Baumeister, R.F (1986) *Identity: Cultural Change and the Struggle for Self*, New York: Oxford University Press.

Benson, S. (1981) *Ambiguous Ethnicity: Inter-racial Families in London*, Cambridge: Cambridge University Press.

Berger, P.L. and Luckmann, T. (1966) *The Social Construction of Reality*, New York: Doubleday Anchor.

Bergman, M.M. (2000) *Would the Real Social Representation Please Stand Up?* Paper on Social Representation.

Bertaux, D. (1981) *Biography and Society, The Life Approach in the Social Sciences*, Beverly Hill, CA: Sage.

Bhabha, H. (1990) In Jonathan Rutherford, (ed.), *Identity: Community, Culture, Difference*, London: Lawrence and Wishart, 207–221.

Bhabha, H. (1994) *The Location of Culture*, London: Routledge.

Bhatti, G. (1997) *Asian Children at Home and at School: An Ethnographic Study*, London and New York: Routledge.

Billig, M. (1987) *Arguing and Thinking: A Rhetorical Approach in Social Psychology*, Cambridge: Cambridge University Press.

Billig, M., Condor, S., Edwards, D., Gane, M., Middleton, D. and Radley, A. (1988) *Ideological Dilemmas: A Social Psychology of Everyday Thinking*, London: Sage.

Blackstone, T., Parekh, B. and Sanders, P. (1998) *Race Relations in Britain*, New York: Routledge.

Bulmer, H. (1969) *Symbolic Interactionism*, Englewood Cliffs, NJ: Prentice Hall

Blos, P. (1962) *On Adolescence: A Psychoanalytic Interpretation*, New York: Free Press.

Bonnett, A. (1996) Whites Studies: The problems and prospects of a new research agenda, *Theory, Culture and Society*, 13, 145–155.

Bonnett, A. (2000) *Anti-Racism,* London and New York: Routledge.

Boudon, R. (1991) *Theories of Social Change*, Oxford: Polity Press.

Bradshaw, C. (1992) Beauty and the beasts: On racial ambiguity, in M. Root (ed.), *Racially Mixed People in America*, Newbury Park: Sage.

Brah, A. (1996) *Cartographies of Diaspora*, London: Routledge.

Brah, A., Hickman, M.J. and Ghaill, M.M. (1999) *Thinking Identities: Ethnicity, Racism and Culture*, London and New York: Macmillan and St. Martins.

Breakwell, G.M., Collie, A., Harrison, B. and Propper, C. (1984) Attitudes towards the unemployed: Effects of threatened identity, *British Journal of Social Psychology*, 23, 87–88.

Breger, R. and Hill, R. (1998) Introducing mixed marriages, in *Cross-Cultural Marriage: Identity and Choice*, edited by Rosemary Breger and Rosanna Hill, Oxford and New York: Berg. 1–32.

Brown, R. (1995) *Prejudice; Its Social Psychology*, Oxford and Cambridge: Blackwell.

Bryman, A. and Burgess, R.G. (1994) *Analysing Qualitative Data*, London: Routledge.

Bulmer, M. (1986) *Social Science and Social Policy*, London: Allen and Unwin.

Bulmer, M. and Solomos, J. (1999) *Ethnic and Racial Studies Today*, London and New York: Routledge.

Burr, V. (1995) *An Introduction to Social Constructionism*, London, New York: Routledge.

Calhoun, C. (1995) *Critical Social Theory*, Massachusetts, Oxford: Blackwell.

Callinicos, A. (1987) *Making History: Agency, Structure and Change in Social Theory*, Cambridge and Oxford, Polity Press.

Census, 2001, *Office of National Statistics*, UK.

Charmaz, K. (1990) Discovering chronic illness: Using grounded theory, *Social Science and Medicine*, 30, 1161–1172.

Charmaz, K. (2000) Grounded theory, objectivist and constructivist methods, in N.K. Denzin and Y.S. Lincoln, *Handbook of Qualitative Research*, London: Sage.

Chin, M.G. and McClintock, C.G. (1993) The effects of intergroup discrimination and social values on the level of self-esteem in the minimal group paradigm, *European Journal of Social Psychology*, 23, 63–75.

Christian, M. (2000) *Multiracial Identity, An International Perspective*, London and New York: Macmillan and St Martins.

Cicourel, A. (1964) *Method and Measurement in Sociology*, New York: Free Press.

Clark, K. and Clark, M. (1947) Racial identification and preference in Negro children, in T.M. Newcomb and E.L. Hartley (eds), *Readings in Social Psychology*, New York: Holt.

Coffey, A., Holbrook, B., and Atkinson, P. (1996) *Making Sense of Qualitative Research*, London: Sage.

Cohen, P. (1989) Reason, racism and the popular monster, in *Crisis of the Self Further Essays on Psychoanalysis and Politics*, Free Association Books: London.

Collins, S. (1957) *Coloured Minorities in Britain*, Guildford: Lutterworth.

Connolly, P. (2000) Racism and young girl's peer-group relations: The experience of South Asian girls, *Sociology*, 34, 499–519.

Cooley, C.H. (1962) *Social Organisation: A Study of the Larger Mind*, New York: Schocken (first published 1909).

Coote, A. (2000) *New Gender Agenda*, London: Institute of Public Policy Research.

Coulthard, M. (1992) *Advances in Spoken Discourse Analysis*, London and New York: Routledge.

CRE (1976) *Between Two Cultures, A Study of Relationships Between Generations in the Asian Community in Britain*, CRE.

CRE (2002) *The Guardian: Rise*, 28 September, 3.

Dalrymple, W. (2002) *White Mughals: Love and Betrayal in Eighteenth Century India*, HarperCollins: London.

Davis, D.J. (1991) *Who is Black?* University Park: Pennsylvania State University Press.

Davis, B. and Harré, R. (1990) Positioning: The discursive production of selves, *Journal for the Theory of Social Behaviour*, 20, 1, 43–63.

Denzin, N.K. (1983) *Interpretive Interactionism*, in G. Morgan, Beyond Method

Denzin, N.K. and Lincoln, Y.S. (1994) *Handbook of Qualitative Research*, Thousand Oaks, CA: Sage.

Denzin, N.K. and Lincoln, Y.S. (2000) *Handbook of Qualitative Research*, London: Sage Langenhove, London: Sage.

Denzin, N.K. and Lincoln, Y.S. (2000) *Handbook of Qualitative Research: Strategies for Social Research, 2nd ed.* London: Sage, Newbury Park, CA: Sage.

Dickerson, D. (2007) Jan. Colorblind Barack Obama would be the great black hope in the next presidential race – if he were actually black. http://www.salon.com/opinion/feature/2007/01/22/obama/.

Dijk, T.A.V. (1997) *Discourse as Social Interaction*, London, Thousand Oak and New Delhi, Sage Publications.

Dover, C. (1937) *Half Caste*, London: Secker and Warburg.

Durojaiye, M.O.A (1970) Patterns of friendship choice in an ethnically mixed junior school, *Race*, 13 (2): 189–200.

Duveen, G. and Lloyd, B. (1986) The significance of social identities, *British Journal of Social Psychology*, 25, 219–30.

Duveen, G. and Lloyd, B. (1990) *Social Representations and the Development of Knowledge*, Cambridge: Cambridge University Press.

Dwyer, C. (1998) Contested identities: challenging dominant representations of young British Muslim women, in T. Skelton and G. Valentine (eds), *Cool Places: Geographies of Youth Cultures*, London and New York: Routledge, 35–49.

Dyer, K. (1997) *White*, London and New York: Routledge.

Early, G. (1993) *Lure and Loathing: Essays on Race, Identity, and the Ambivalence of Assimilation*, New York: Allen Lane, The Penguin Press.

Eastern Eye Newspaper, July, 2002.

Elam, M. (2008) www.stanford.edu/dept/AAAS/.../Obama Mixed Race Politics.

Erikson, EH (1963) Youth: Fidelity and diversity, in E. Erikson (ed.), *Youth: Change and Challenge*, New York: Basic Books.

Erikson, E.H. (1968) *Identity, Youth and Crisis*, New York: W.W. Norton and Co inc.

Farr, R.M and Moscovici, S. (1984) *Social Representation*, Cambridge: Cambridge University Press.

Foucault, M. (1972) *The Archaeology of Knowledge*, London: Tavistock.

Foucault, M. (1977) *Discipline and Punish, the Birth of the Prison*, New York: Vintage.

Gaber, I. and Aldridge, J. (1994) *Culture, Identity and Transracial Adoption*, London: Free Association Books.

Gardner, K. and Shakur, A. (1994) I'm Bengali, I'm Asian and I'm living here', in R. Ballard et al., *Desh Pradesh: The South Asian Presence in Britain*, London: Hurst and Company.

Garfinkel, H. (1967) *Studies in Ethnomethodology*, Englewood Cliffs, NJ: Prentice Hall.

Gecas, V. and Burke, P.J. (1995) Self and identity, in K.S. Cook, G.A. Fine, and J.S. House (eds), *Sociological Perspectives on Social Psychology*. Allyn and Bacon: Needham Heights, MA, 41–67.

Geertz, C. (1963) The integrative revolution: Primordial sentiments and civil politics in the new states, *Old Societies and New States*, New York: The Free Press.

Georgakopoulou, A. and Goutsos, D. (1997) *Discourse Analysis*, Edinburgh: Edinburgh University Press.

Gergen, K.J. and Gergen, M.M. (1986) Narrative form and the construction of psychological science, in Sarbin T.R. (ed.), *Narrative Psychology: The Storied Nature of Human Conduct*, New York: Praeger.

Gergen, K.J. (1987) Towards self as relationship, in K.Yardley and T. Honess (eds), *Self and Identity: Psychosocial Perspectives*, Chichester, New York: John Wiley and Sons.

Gergen, K.J. (1989) Social accountability and the social construction of 'you', in J. Shotter and K.J. Gergen, *Texts of Identity*, London, Newbury Park and New Delhi: Sage.

Gergen, K.J. (1994) *Realities and Relationships: Soundings in Social Constructionism*, London: Harvard University Press.

GFK NOP, April 2008, NOP Social Research, GFK NOP.Com.

Ghuman, P.A.S. (1994) *Coping with Two Cultures: A Study of British Asians and Indo-Canadian Adolescents*: Clevedon: Multilingual Matters.

Giddens, A. (1991) *Modernity and Self-Identity: Self and Society in the Late Modern Age*, Stanford, CA: Stanford University Press.

Giles, N. (1995) In N. Zack, *American Mixed Race; The Culture of Microdiversity*, London and New York: Rowman and Littlefield Publishers.

Gill, O. and Jackson, B. (1993) *Adoption and Race; Black Asian and Mixed Race Children in White Families,* London: Billing and Son Ltd.

Gilroy, P. (1992) The end of antiracism, in A. Rattansi and J. Donald, *'Race' Culture and Difference*, London: Open University and Sage.

Gilroy, P. (2000) *Between Camps*, London: Penguin.

Glaser, B. and Strauss, A. (1967) *The Discovery of Grounded Theory*, New York: Aldine.

Glazer, N. and Moynihan, P. (1963) *Beyond the Melting Pot*, Massachusetts: The MIT Press.

Glazer, N. and Moynihan, D .(1975) *Ethnicity: Theory and Experience*, Cambridge, MA: Harvard University Press.

Goffman, E. (1959) *The Presentation of Self in Everyday Life*, London, New York and Toronto: Penguin Books.

Goffman, E. (1963) *Stigma: Notes on the Management of Spoiled Identity*, London, New York, Ontario, Auckland: Penguin.

Gordon, M.M. (1964) *Assimilation in American Life*, New York: Oxford University Press.

Guardian Newspaper – *The Guardian: Rise*, (2002) Race, 28 September, p. 3.

Guardian Newspaper, Oct. 2006, Colourblind, http://www.guardian.co.uk/sport/blog/2006/oct/28/colourblind.

Guba, E.G and Lincoln, Y. S. (1994) Competing paradigms in qualitative research, in N.K Denzin and Y.S Lincoln, *Handbook of Qualitative Research*, Thousand Oaks, CA: Sage.

Gunnersson, B.L., Linell, P. and Nordberg, B. (1997) *The Construction of Professional Discourse*, London and New York: Longman.

Hall, S. (1990) The whites of their eyes: Racist ideologies and the media, in M. Alverado and J. Thompson (eds), *The Media Reader*, London: BFI Publishing.

Hall, S. (1991) Old and new identities, old and new ethnicities, in A. King, *Culture, Globalisation and the World System*, London: Macmillan.

Hall, S. (1992) New ethnicities, in J.Donald and A.Rattansi (eds), *Race, Culture and Difference*, London: Sage.

Hall, S. (1996) Who needs identity? in S. Hall and P. du Gay (eds), *Questions of Cultural Identity*, London: Sage.

Hall, S. (2000) Who needs identity? in P. du Gay, J. Evans and P. Redman (eds), *Identity: A Reader*, London, Thousand Oaks, and New Delhi: Sage.

Hammersley, M. and Atkinson, P. (1983) *Ethnography: Principles in Practice*, London: Tavistock.

Harré, R. (1987) The social construction of selves, in K. Yardley and T. Honess (eds), *Self and Identity: Psychosocial Perspectives*, Chichester, New York: John Wiley and Sons.

Harré, R. (1989) Language and texts of identity, in J. Shotter and K.J. Gergen (eds), *Texts of Identity*, London: Sage.

Harris, J.R. (1999) *The Nurture Assumption: Why Children turn out the Way they do*, New York: Touchstone Book.

Harris, H.W., Blue, H.C. and Griffiths, E.H. (1992) *Race and Ethnic Identity: Psychological Developments and Creative Expression*, New York and London: Routledge.

Henriques, F. (1975) *Children of Conflict: A Study of Interracial Sex and Marriage*, New York: Dutton.

Henwood, J., Griffin, C., Phoenix, A. (1998) *Standpoint and Differences*, London: Routledge.

Henwood, K. and Phoenix, A. (1999) 'Race' in psychology: Teaching the subject, in M. Bulmer and J. Solomos, *Ethnic and Racial Studies Today*, London and New York: Routledge.

Heritage, J.C. (1984) *Garfinkel and Ethnomethodology*, Cambridge: Polity Press.

Higher Education Statistics Agency, *2000/01 ethnicity data*, www.hesa.ac.uk.

Hill, C.S. (1965) *How Colour Prejudiced is Britain?* London: Gollancz.

Hinckle, S. and Brown, R. (1990) Intergroup comparisons and social identity: Some links and lacunae, in D. Abrams and M. Hogg (eds), *Social Identity Theory: Constructive and Critical Advances*, Hemel Hempstead: Harvester Wheatsheaf.

Hiro, D. (1991) *Black British White British*, London: Grafton Books.

Hitch, P. (1988) Social Identity and the Half-Child, in J.W. Berry and R.C. Annis (eds) *Ethnic Psychology* (International Association for Cross-Cultural Psychology), Lisse, Netherlands: Swets and Zeitlinger.

Holliday, A. (2002) *Qualitative Research: Doing and Writing*, London, Thousand Oaks, New Delhi: Sage.

Holloway, W. (1989) *Subjectivity and Method in Psychology: Gender, Meaning and Science*, London: Sage.

HORS, Home Office Research Series, (2001) The Citizenship Survey, www.homeoffice.gov.uk/rds/hors.

HORS, Home Office Research Series, (2000) Religious Discrimination, www.homeoffice.gov.uk/rds/hors.

Hooks, B. (1992) *Blacks Looks; Race and Representation,* New York: Routledge.

Howarth, C. (2002) So you're from Brixton? The struggle for recognition and esteem in a multicultural community, *Ethnicities* 2 (2), 237–260.

Howarth, C. (2002) Why pick on me? School exclusion and black youth, in *Ethnic and Racial Studies* 25, no. 5.

Howarth, C. (2002) Using the theory of social representations to explore differences in research relationship, *Qualitative Research*, 2, 21–34.

Howarth, C. (2002) Identity in whose eyes? The role of representations in identity construction, *Journal of the Theory of Social Behaviour*, 32, 2.

Hoyles. A. and Hoyles, M. (1999) *Remember Me: Achievements of Mixed Race People Past and Present*, London: Hansib Publications.

ICM Research (2002) *Muslim Poll Dec* 2002, www.icm.research.co.uk. reviews/2002/bbc-today-Muslims.

ICM Research, (Dec, 2002) *BBC News Online Race Poll,* www.icm.research. reviews/2002/bbc-race.poll.

Ifekwunigue, J.O. (1999) *Scattered Belongings*, London and New York: Routledge.

Ifekwunigue, J.O, (2001) In D. Parker and M. Song (2001) *Rethinking 'Mixed Race'*, London, Virginia: Pluto Press.

Ifekwunigue, J.O. (2004) *'Mixed Race': A Reader*, London and New York: Routledge.

IPPR, (1993) *Institute of Public Policy Research,* A Report on A Survey Conducted by NOP, London: IPPR.

Interracial Voice (2002) www.webcam.com/~intvoice/williamson.html.

Jacobs, J. (1992) Identity Development in Biracial Children in M. Root (ed.), *Racially Mixed People in America*, Newbury Park: Sage.

James, W. (1890) *The Principles of Psychology*, Massachusetts and London: Harvard University Press.

James, A., Jenks, C. and Prout, A. (1998) *Theorising Childhood*, Cambridge: Polity Press.

Joly, D. (1995) *Britannia's Crescent: Making a Place for Muslims in British Society*, Aldershot: Ashgate.

Josselson, R. (1996) *The Space Between: Exploring the dimensions of human relations,* London: Sage Publications Inc.

Jovchelelovitch, S. (1996) In Defence of Representations, *Journal of the Theory of Social Behaviour*, 26 (2), 121–35.

Katz, I. (1996) *The Construction of Racial Identity in Children of Mixed Parentage*, London: Cromwell Press.

Kegan, R. (1982) *The Evolving Self: Problem and Process in Human Development*, Cambridge: Harvard University Press.

Keith, V. and Herring, C. (1991). Skin tone and stratification in the Black community. *American Journal of Sociology*, 97, 760–778.

Kelly, A.J.D. (1989) Ethnic Identification, association and redefinition: Muslim Pakistanis and Greek Cypriots in Britain, in K. Liebkind (ed.), *New Identities in Europe: Immigrant Ancestry and the Ethnic Identity of Youth*, Volume 3 of the European Science Foundation Series: *Studies in European Migration*, London: Gower.

Khair, J. (2001) *Babu Fictions: Alienation in Contemporary Indian English Novels*, Oxford, New York, New Delhi: Oxford University Press.

Kich, G.K. (1992) The developmental process of asserting a biracial, bicultural identity, in M.P.P. Root, *Racially Mixed People in America*, Newbury Park: Sage.

Kohlberg, L. (1969) in Kroger, J. (1995) *Identity in Adolescence: The Balance between Self and the Other*, London and New York: Routledge.

Labour Force Survey, 2001, *Household Structure*, www.statistics.gov.uk.

Lange, A. and Westin, C. (1981) *Etnisk diskriminering och social identitet*. Stockholm: Ceifo.

Lange, A. and Westin, C. (1985) *The Generative Mode of Explanation in Social Psychological Theories of Race and Ethnic Relations*, Stockholm: Ceifo.

Liebert, R. and Spiegler, (1990) *Personality: Strategies and Issues*, Pacific Grove, California: Brooks/Cole.

Leibkind, K. (1992) *New Identities in Europe: Immigrant Ancestry and the Ethnic Identity of Youth*, Aldershot: Gower.

Little, K. (1972) *Negros in Britain*, London: Routledge and Kegan Paul.

Loevinger, J. (1976) *Ego Development: Concepts and Theories*, San Francisco, Jossey-Bass.

Lyon, E. and Coyle, A. (2007) *Analysing Qualitative Data in Psychology*, LA, London, Delhi: Sage Publications.

Kundnani, A. (2001) The death of multiculturalism, *Race and Class*, 43 (02), Oct 2001.

Mahtani and Moreno (2001) In D.Parker and M.Song, *Rethinking 'Mixed Race'*, London, Virginia: Pluto Press.

Manning, P. (1998) *Procedure, Reflexivity and Social Constructionism*, in Velody, I. and Williams, R. (eds) *The Politics of Constructionism*, London, Thousand Oaks, New Delhi: Sage.

Mayall, B. (1996) *Children Health and the Social Order*, Open University Press: Buckingham.

McCarthy, C. and Crichlow, W. (1993) *Race, Identity and Representation in Education*, London and New York: Routledge.

Mead, G.H. (1934) *Mind, Self and Society*, Chicago: University of Chicago Press.

Mead, G.H. and Strauss, A. (1964) *George Herbert Mead on Social Psychology*, A. Strauss (ed.) Heritage of Sociology Series: University of Chicago Press.

Mengel (2001) In D. Parker and M. Song (2001) *Rethinking 'Mixed Race'*, London, Virginia: Pluto Press.

Micheal, M. (1996) *Constructing Identities: The Social, The Non-human and the Change*, London, Thousand Oaks, New Delhi: Sage.

Miles, M.B. and Huberman, A.M. (1994) *Qualitative Data Analysis*, Thousand Oaks, London and New Delhi: Sage Publications.

Milner, D. (1983) *Children and Race*, London: Alan Sutton Publishing.

Mirza, H. (1997) *Black British Feminism*, London: Routledge.

Mishler, E.G. (1997) The Interactional Construction of Narratives in Medical and Life-History Interviews in B.L. Gunnarsson, P. Linel and B. Nordberg, *The Construction of Professional Discourse*, London and New York: Longman.

Modood, T. (1988) *Black, Racial Equality and Asian Identity*, New Community, 14 (3), 397–404.

Modood, T.R (1997) In T.R. Modood, J. Berthoud, J. Lakey, P. Nazroo, S. Smith, S. Virdee and S. Beishon, (1997) *Ethnic Minorities in Britain: Diversity and Disadvantage*, London: Policy Studies Institute.

Moscovici, S. (1973) *Health and Illness: Social Psychological Analysis*, London: Academic Press.

Moscovici, S. (1976) *Social Influence and Social Change*, London and New York: Academic Press.

Moscovici, S. (1994) Three concepts: Minority, conflict and behavioural style, in S. Moscovici, A. Mucchi-Faina and A. Maass (eds), *Minority Influence*, Chicago: Nelson-Hall, 233–251.

Nagel, T. (1994) Consciousness and objective reality, in R. Warner and T. Szubka (eds), *The Mind-Body Problem*, Cambridge, USA: Basil Blackwell, 63–68.

Nayak, A. (1999) 'Pale worries': Skinhead culture and the embodiment of white masculinities, in A. Brah, M.J. Hickman and , M.M. an Ghaill (eds), *Thinking Identities: Ethnicity, Racism and Culture*, London and New York: Macmillan and St. Martins.

Nakayama, T.K and Martin, J.N. (1999) *Whiteness: The Communication of Social Identity*, Thousand Oaks, London, New Delhi: Sage.

Neal, S. (1999) Populist Configurations Race and Gender in: The Case of Hugh Grant, Liz Hurley and Divine Brown, in , A. Brah, , M.J. Hickman. and M.M. an Ghaill, *Thinking Identities: Ethnicity, Racism and Culture*, London and New York: Macmillan and St. Martins.

New York Times Magazine, Jan. 2008, 'All in the Family' Interview by D. Solomon, (http://www.nytimes.com/2008/01/20/magazine/20wwln-Q4-t.html?_r=1.

NPR, March, 2008, 'A more perfect union' speech, Transcript: Barack Obama's Speech on Race, http://www.npr.org/templates/story/story. php?storyId=88478467.

Northover, M. (1988b) Bilinguals or 'dual linguistic identities?', in J.W. Berry and R.C. Annis (eds), *Ethnic Psychology* (International Association for Cross-Cultural Psychology), Lisse, Netherlands: Swets and Zeitlinger.

Obama, B. 2004, *Barack Obama: Dreams from my Father*, Edinburgh, London, New York: Canongate.

OPCS Trends (1985) No. 40, *Ethnic Inter Marriage in Britain*.

ONS, Jan, 2004, *Population Size*, www.statistics.gov.uk.

Own, C. (2001) In D. Parker and M. Song, *Rethinking 'Mixed Race'*, London, Virginia: Pluto Press.

Parekh, B. (2003) British Muslims do not have a problem with democracy. Some of them do have a problem with multiculturalism, *Prospect Magazine*, July 2003

Park, R.E. (1928) *Race and Culture*, New York: Free Press.

Park, R.E. (1964) 2nd edn *Race and Culture*, New York: Free Press.

Parker, D. (1995) *Through Different Eyes: The Cultural Identities of Young Chinese People in Britain,* Aldershot: Avebury.

Parker, I. and Burman, E. (1993) Against discursive imperialism, empiricism and construction: Thirty two problems with discourse analysis, in E. Burman and I. Parker (eds), *Discourse Analytic Research: Repertoires and Readings of Texts in Action*, London: Routledge.

Parker, D. and Song, M. (2001) *Rethinking 'Mixed Race'*, London, Virginia: Pluto Press.

Patterson, S. (1963) *Dark Strangers*, Harmondsworth: Penguin.

Patton, M.Q. (1990) *Qualitative Evaluation and Research Methods*, London: Sage.

Phinney, J.S. (1990) Ethnic identity in adolescents and adults: Review of research, *Psychological Bulletin*, 108, 499–515.

Phoenix, A. (1997) The place of race and ethnicity in the lives of children and young people, *Educational and Child Psychology*, 14 (3), 5-24.

Phoenix, A. and Own, C. (1996) From miscegenation to hybridity: Mixed relationships and mixed parentage profile, in B. Bernstein and Brannen (eds) *Children Research and Policy*, London: Taylor and Francis.

Piaget, J. (1951) *Play, Dreams and Imitation in Childhood*, London: Routledge and Kegan Paul.

Piaget, J. (1953) *The Origin of Intelligence in the Child*, London: Routledge and Kegan Paul.

Population Trends (2001), Scott, A., Pearce, D. and Goldblatt, P., Office for National Statistics, *The sizes and characteristics of the minority ethnic populations of Great Britain-latest estimates*, 105, Autumn.

Potter, J. (1996) Discourse Analysis and Constructionist Approaches: Theoretical Background, in J.T. Richardson *Handbook of Qualitative Research Methods for Psychology and the Social Sciences,* Leicester: BPS.

Potter, J. (1997) Discourse Analysis as a way of Analysing Naturally Occurring Talk, in D. Silverman *Qualitative Research, Theory, Method and Practice*, London Thousand Oaks, New Delhi, Sage Publications.

Potter, J. and Edwards, D. (1999) Social Representations and discursive psychology: From cognition to action, *Culture and Psychology*, 5, 447–88.

Potter, J. and Wetherell, M. (1987) *Discourse and Social Psychology: Beyond Attitudes and Behaviour,* London, Thousand Oaks and New Delhi: Sage.

Putnam, R.D. (2000) *Bowling Alone: The Collapse and Revival of American Community*, New York: Simon & Schuster.

Rattansi, A. (1992) Changing the Subject? Racism, culture and education, in A. Rattansi and J. Donald, *'Race', Culture and Difference*, London: Open University and Sage.

Raz, J. (1994) *Ethics in the Public Domain*, Oxford: Oxford University Press.

RELACHS Study, 2001, *Health of young people in East London*, Department of Psychiatry, St. Bart and the London Queen Mary's School of Medicine and Dentistry.

Rex, J. (1986) *Race and Ethnicity*, Milton Keynes: Open University Press.

Richmond, A. (1961) *The Colour Problem*, Harmondsworth: Penguin.

Roberts, B. (2002) *Biographical Research*, Buckingham 7 Philadelphia, Open University Press.

Root, M. (1992). *Racially Mixed People in America*, London: Sage.

Root, M. (1992) Back to the drawing board: Methodological issues in research on multiracial people' *Racially Mixed People in America*, London: Sage.

Root, M. (1996) A bill of rights for racially mixed people, in M. Root (ed.), *The Multiracial Experience*, Newbury Park: Sage.

Runnymede Trust, (2001) *The Future of Multi-Ethnic Britain: The Parekh Report*, London: Profile.

Rutland, A. (1999) The Development of National Prejudice, in-group Favouritism and Self-stereotypes in British Children, *British Journal of Social Psychology*, 38, 55–70.

Samad, Y. (1997) Multiculturalism, Muslims and the Media: Pakistanis in Bradford, ESRC report.

Sarbin T.R (ed.) (1986) *Narrative Psychology: The Storied Nature of Human Conduct*, New York: Praeger.

Sarup, M. (1996) *Identity, Culture and the Post-modern World*, Edinburgh, Edinburgh University Press.

Sherrard, C. (1991) Developing discourse analysis, *Journal of Psychology*, 118, 2, 171–179.

Shotter, J. (1989) Social Accountability and the Social Construction of 'you', in J. Shotter, K.J. Gergen, *Texts of Identity*, London, Newbury Park and New Delhi: Sage.

Singh, G., O'Beirne M., Choudhry, S. (Sept. 2003) Perceptions of racial prejudice and discrimination in England and Wales, 2001 Home Office Citizenship Survey: People families and communities, HORS, Home Office.

Silverstone, D. (1997) *Qualitative Research Theory: Method and Practice*, London: Sage.

Smith, P.K and Shu, S. (2000) What good schools can do about bullying: Findings from a survey in English schools after a decade of research and action, *Childhood*, 7, 193–212.

Smith, P.K. (ed.) (2003) *Violence in Schools: The Response in Europe*, London, New York: Routledge Falmer.

Soller, W. (ed.) (1989) *The Invention of Ethnicity*, New York: Oxford University Press.

Sommer, R. and Sommer, B. (2002) *A Practical Guide to Behavioural Research: Tools and Techniques*, New York, Oxford: Oxford University Press.

Song, M. (2003) *Choosing Ethnic Identity*, Cambridge, Oxford, Maldan: Polity.

Spencer, J.M (1997) *The New Colored People: The Mixed Race Movement in America,* New York: New York UP.

Spickard, P. (1989) *Mixed Blood: Intermarriage and Ethnic Identity in Twentieth century America,* Madison: University of Wisconsin.

Steyn, J. (1999) *The Jew: Assumptions of Identity,* London and New York: Cassell.

Steyn, M. (1999) White identity in context: A personal narrative, in T.K Nakayamaand and J.N. Martin, *Whiteness: The Communication of Social Identity,* Thousand Oaks, London, New Delhi: Sage.

Stone, J. (1985) *Racial Conflict in Contemporary Society,* London: Fontana Press.

Stonequist, E.V. (1937) *The Marginal Man: A Study in Personality and Culture Conflict,* New York: Russel and Russel.

Strauss, A. (1987) *Qualitative Analysis for Social Scientists,* Cambridge: Cambridge University Press.

Strauss, A. and Corbin, J. (1998) *Grounded Theory Methodology,* London and New Delhi: Sage.

Swirsky, R. (1999) Migration and Dislocation: Echoes of Loss within Jewish Women's Narratives in Brah, A., Hickman, M. J. and an Ghaill, M.M. (eds) *Thinking Identities: Ethnicity, Racism and Culture,* London and New York: Macmillan and St. Martins.

Tajfel, H. (1974) Social Identity and Intergroup Behaviour, *Social Science Information,* 13, 65–93.

Tajfel, H. (1978) *Differentiation Between Social Groups,* Academic Press: London.

Tajfel, H. (1982) *Social Identity and Intergroup Relations,* Cambridge, England: Cambridge University Press.

Thompson, A., Day, G. and Adamson, D. (1999) Bringing the 'local' back in: The production of Welsh identities, in A. Brah, M.J. Hickman and M.M. an Ghaill (eds), *Thinking Identities: Ethnicity, Racism and Culture,* London and New York: Macmillan and St. Martins.

Tizard, B. and Phoenix, A. (1993) *Black, White or Mixed Race?* London and New York: Routledge.

Tizard, B. and Phoenix, A. (2001) 2nd edn, *Black, White or Mixed Race?* London and New York: Routledge.

Turner, J.C. (1978) in *Differentiation Between Social Groups,* Academic Press: London.

Turner, S. (1998) The Limits of Social Constructionism, in I. Velody and R. Williams (eds), *The Politics of Constructionism,* London, Thousand Oaks, New Delhi: Sage.

US Census Bureau, 2009, http://www.census.gov/compendia/statab/.

Van Loon, J. (1999) Whiter shades of pale: Media-Hybridities of Rodney King, in A.Brah, M.J. Hickman and M.M. an Ghaill (eds), *Thinking Identities:*

Ethnicity, Racism and Culture, London and New York: Macmillan and St. Martins.

Verkuyten, M. and de Wolfe, A. (2002) *Being, Feeling and Doing: Discourses and Ethnic Self-definitions among Minority Group Members, Culture and Psychology*, London, Thousand Oaks, CA and New Delhi, Sage.

Verma, G.K and Bagley, C. (1979) *Race, Education and Identity*, London: Macmillan Press.

Visram, R. (1986) *Ayahs, Lascars and Princes*, London: Pluto Press.

Visram, R. (2002) *Asians in Britain: 400 Years of History*, London: Pluto Press.

Walvin, J. (1973) *Black and White: The Negro and English Society, 1555–1945*, London: Allen Lane.

Waters, M.C (1990) Ethnic *Options: Choosing Identities in America*, London: University of California Press.

Weinreich, P. (1979) Ethnicity and adolescent identity conflict, in, V.S. Khan (ed.), *Minority Families in Britain*, London: Macmillan.

Weinreich, P. (1983) Emerging from threatened identities: Ethnicity and gender redefinitions of ethnic identity, in G.M. Breakwell (ed.), *Threatened Identities*, Chichester: Wiley.

Weinreich, P. (1986) The operationalisation of identity theory in racial and ethnic relations: in J. Rex and D. Mason (eds), *Theories of Race and Ethnic Relations*, Cambridge: Cambridge University Press.

Weinreich, P. (1999) Ethnic identity and enculturation/acculturation, in J.C.M. Lasrey, J.G. Adair and K.L. Dions (eds), *Latest Contributions to Cross-Cultural Psychology*, Lisse, Netherlands: Swets and Zeitlinger.

Weinreich, P., Kelly, , A.J.D. and Maja, C. (1987) Situated identities, conflicts in identification and own group preference: Rural and urban youth in South Africa, in *Growth and Progress in Cross-Cultural Psychology*, 321–335, International Association for Cross-Cultural Psychology, 321–225.

Weinreich, P., Luk, C. L. and Bond, M. (1996) Ethnic Stereotyping and identification in a multicultural context: Acculturation, self-esteem and identify diffusion in Hong Kong Chinese university students, *Psychology and Developing Societies*, 8: 107–169.

Weinreich, P. in Weinreich, P. and Saunderson, W. (eds) (2003) *Analysing Identity: Cross-Cultural, Societal and Clinical Contexts*, East Sussex and New York: Routledge.

Werbner, S. (1997) *Neither Black Nor White Yet Both, Thematic Explorations of Interracial Literature*, New York and Oxford: Oxford University Press.

Wetherell, M. (1998) Positioning and interpretative repertoires: Conversation Analysis and post structuralism in dialogue, *Discourse and Society*, 9, 387–412.

Willig, C. (1999) *Applied Discourse Analysis; Social and Psychological Interventions*, Buckingham and Philadelphia: Open University Press.

Wilson, A. (1987) *Mixed Race Children: A Study of Identity*, London: Allen and Unwin.

Young, R. (1992) Colonialism and humanism, in A. Rattansi and J. Donald, *Race' Culture and Difference*, London: Open University and Sage.

Zack, N. (1998) *Thinking about Race*, New York: Wadsworth Publishing.

Zack, N. (1995) *American Mixed Race; The Culture of Microdiversity*, London and New York: Rowman and Littlefield Publishers.

Index

Figures are indicated by **bold** page numbers, tables by *italic* numbers.